ULTIMATE
ANNUALS

ULTIMATE ANNUALS

ULTIMATE FANTASTIC FOUR
WRITER: MARK MILLAR
ARTIST: JAE LEE
COLORIST: JUNE CHUNG
COVER: GREG LAND, MATT RYAN & JUSTIN PONSOR

ULTIMATE X-MEN
WRITER: BRIAN K. VAUGHAN
PENCILER: TOM RANEY
INKER: SCOTT HANNA
COLORIST: GINA GOING-RANEY
COVER: STUART IMMONEN

ULTIMATE SPIDER-MAN
WRITER: BRIAN MICHAEL BENDIS
PENCILER: MARK BROOKS
INKER: JAIME MENDOZA
ADDITIONAL FINISHES: SCOTT HANNA
COLORIST: DAVE STEWART
COVER: MARK BAGLEY & RICHARD ISANOVE

THE ULTIMATES 2
WRITER: MARK MILLAR
ARTIST: STEVE DILLON
COLORIST: PAUL MOUNTS
COVER: BRYAN HITCH, PAUL NEARY & LAURA MARTIN

LETTERER: CHRIS ELIOPOULOS
ASSISTANT EDITORS: JOHN BARBER & NICOLE WILEY
EDITOR: RALPH MACCHIO

COLLECTION EDITOR: JENNIFER GRÜNWALD
ASSISTANT EDITOR: MICHAEL SHORT
SENIOR EDITOR, SPECIAL PROJECTS: JEFF YOUNGQUIST
DIRECTOR OF SALES: DAVID GABRIEL
PRODUCTION: LORETTA KROL
BOOK DESIGNER: JEOF VITA
CREATIVE DIRECTOR: TOM MARVELLI

EDITOR IN CHIEF: JOE QUESADA
PUBLISHER: DAN BUCKLEY

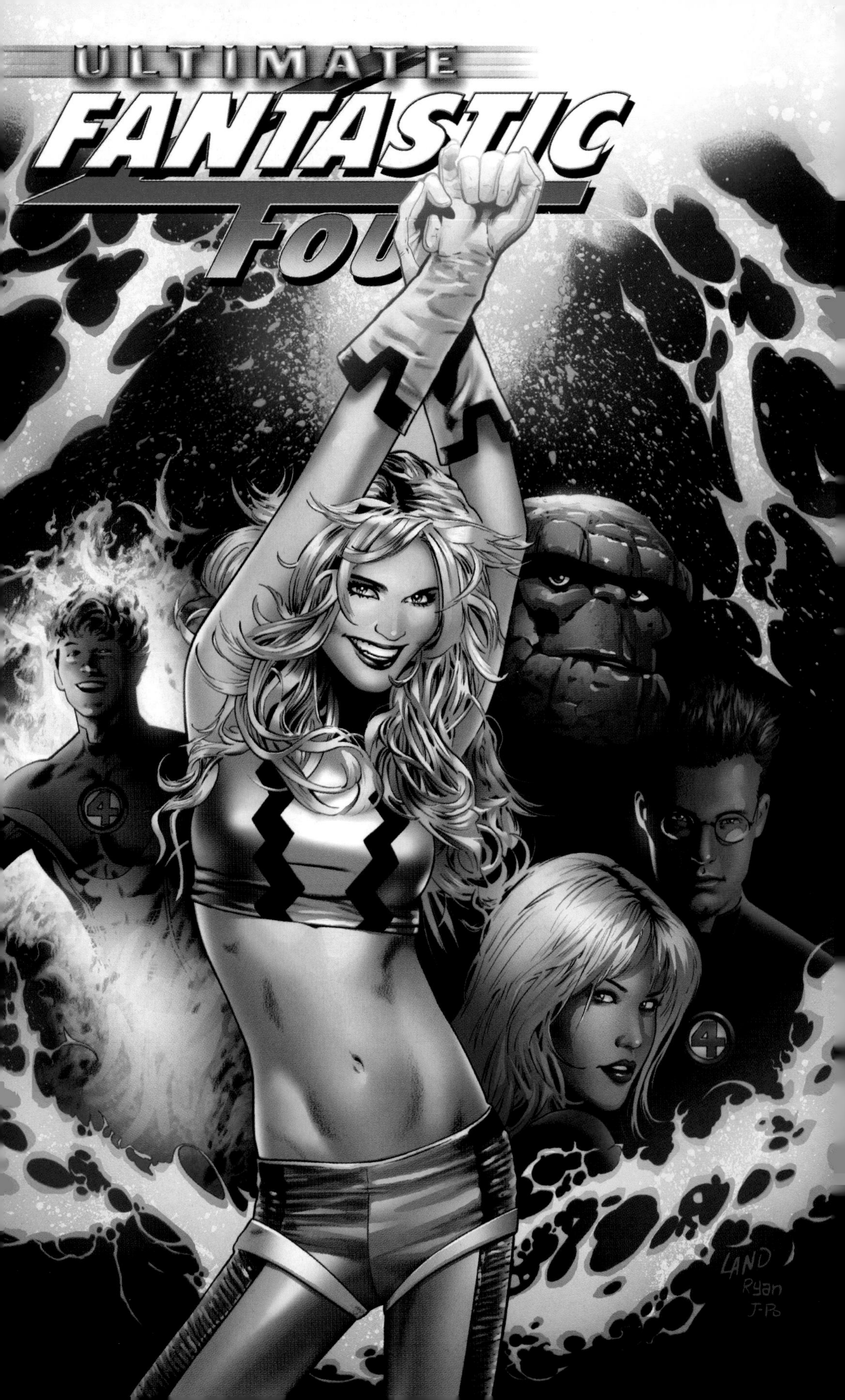
ULTIMATE
FANTASTIC
FOU
LAND
Ryan
J-Po

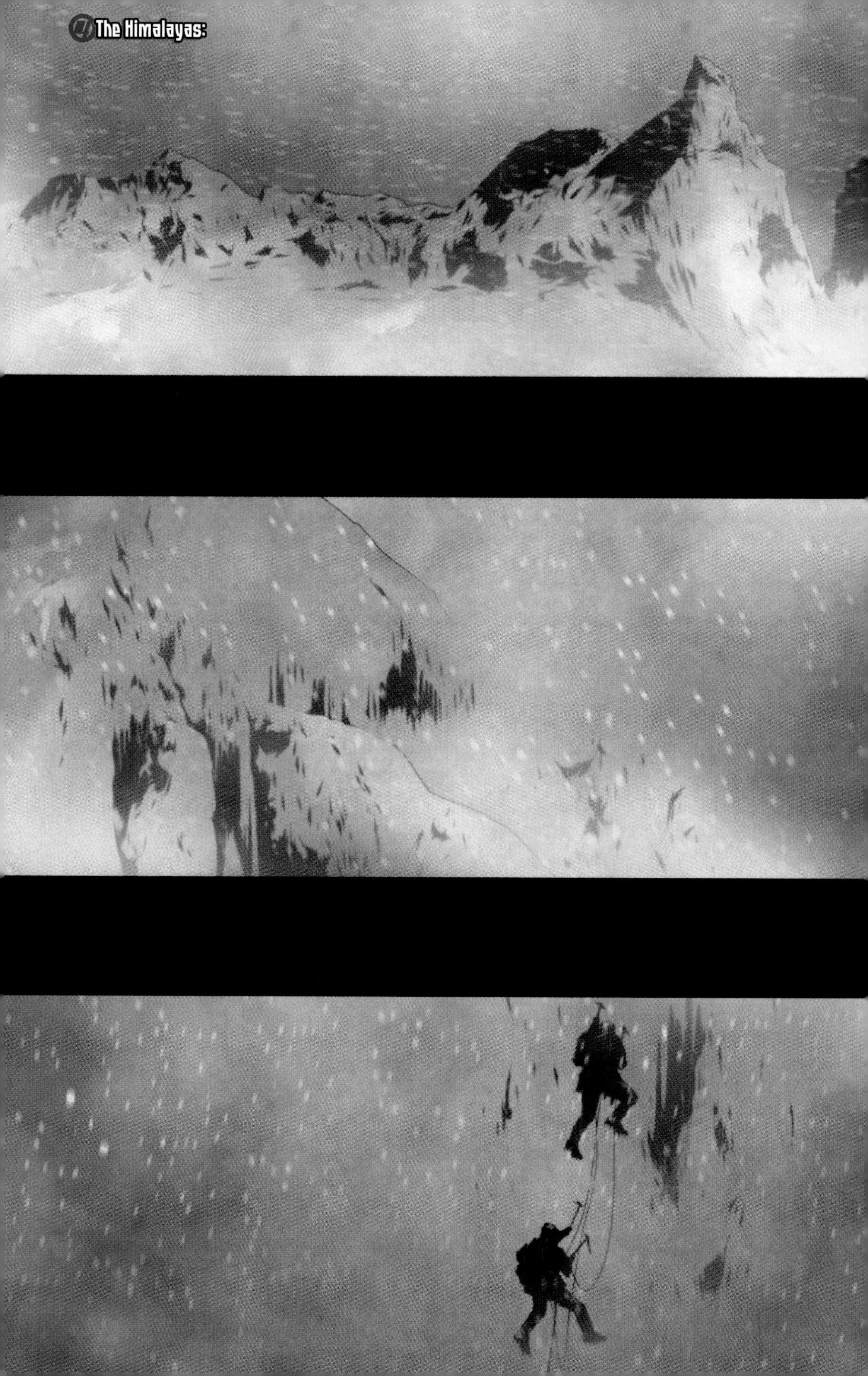
The Himalayas:

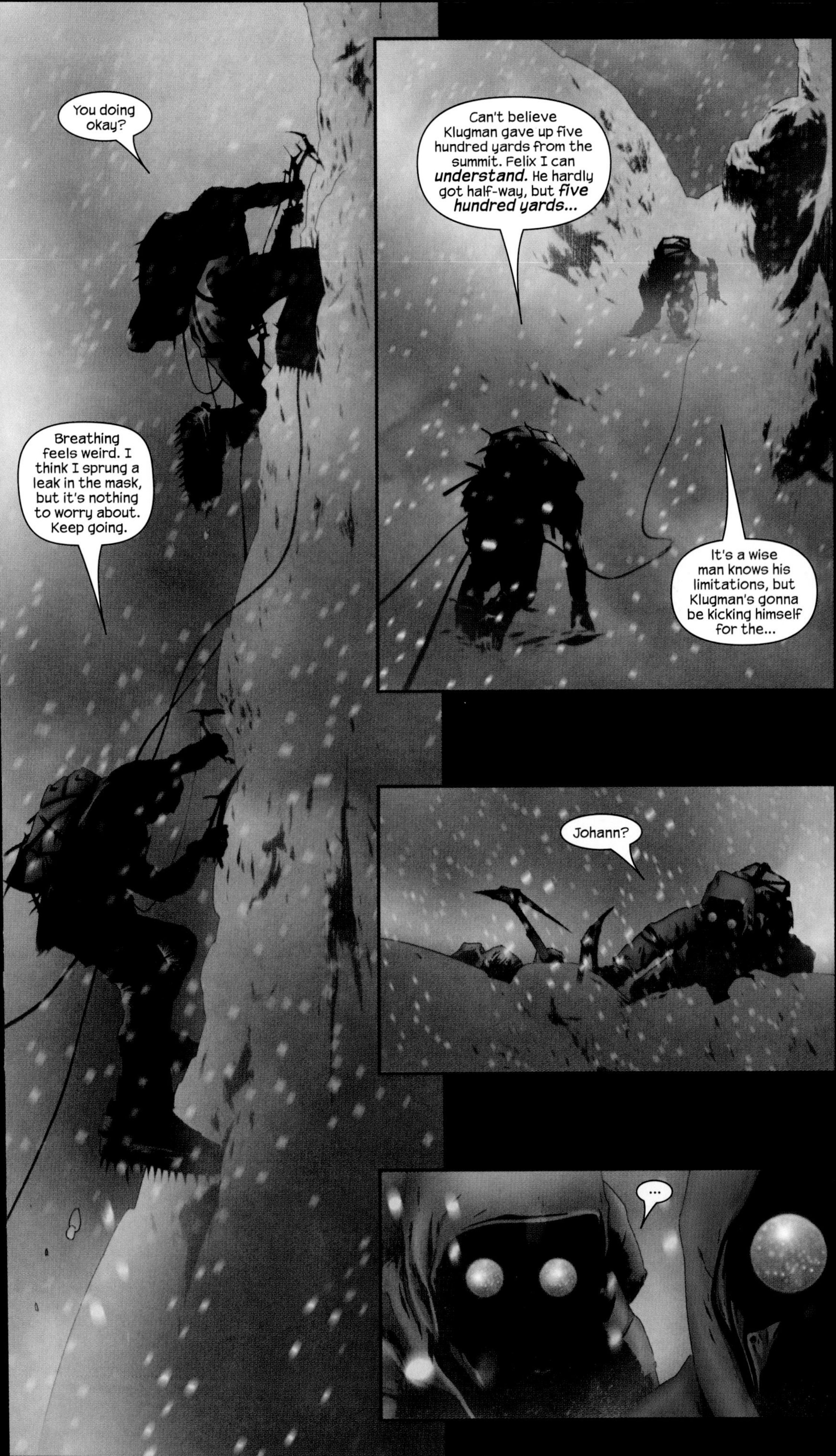
You doing okay?
Breathing feels weird. I think I sprung a leak in the mask, but it's nothing to worry about. Keep going.
Can't believe Klugman gave up five hundred yards from the summit. Felix I can *understand.* He hardly got half-way, but *five hundred yards...*
It's a wise man knows his limitations, but Klugman's gonna be kicking himself for the...
Johann?
...

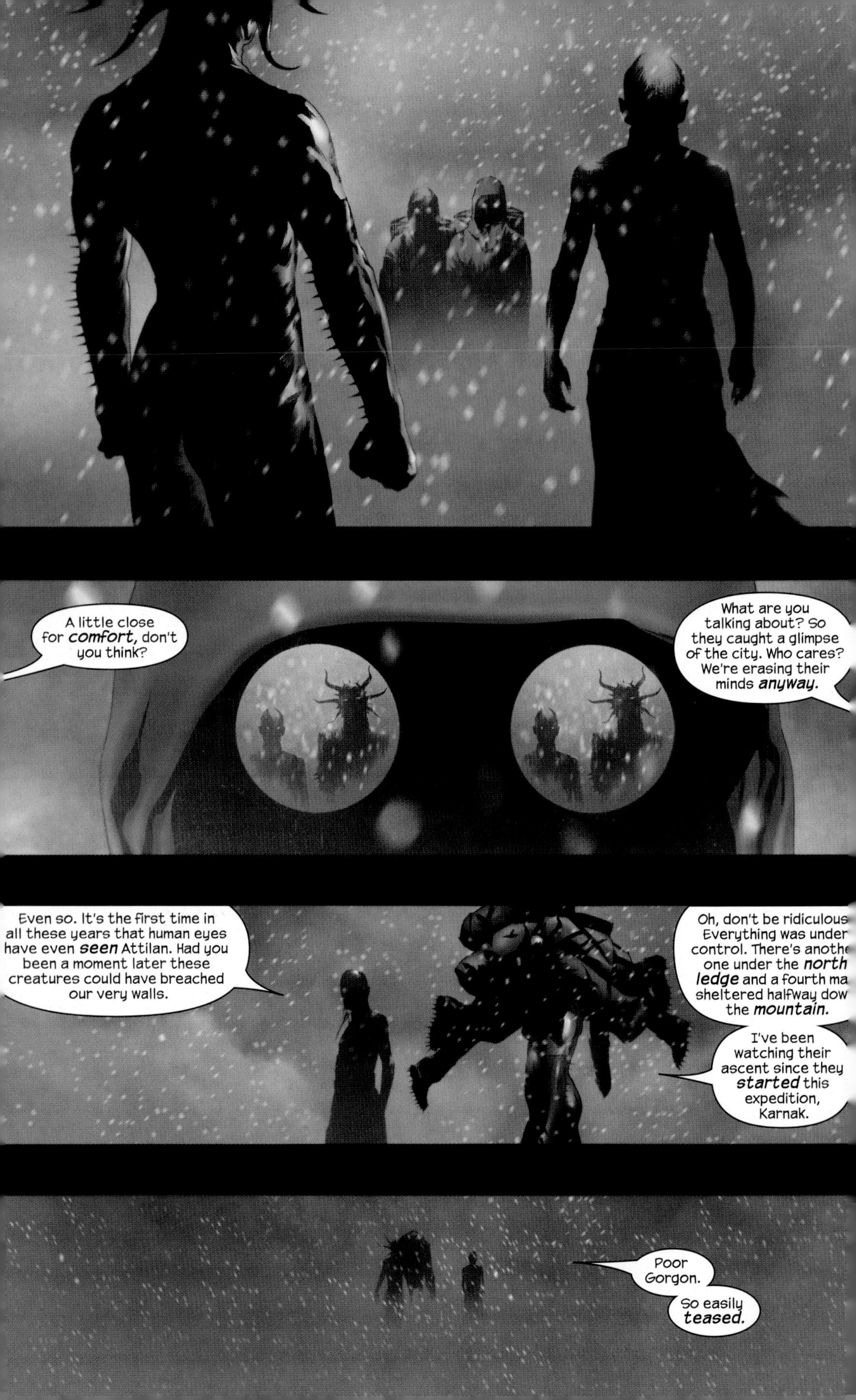

A little close for comfort, don't you think?
What are you talking about? So they caught a glimpse of the city. Who cares? We're erasing their minds anyway.
Even so. It's the first time in all these years that human eyes have even seen Attilan. Had you been a moment later these creatures could have breached our very walls.
Oh, don't be ridiculous Everything was under control. There's anoth one under the north ledge and a fourth ma sheltered halfway dow the mountain.
I've been watching their ascent since they started this expedition, Karnak.
Poor Gorgon.
So easily teased.

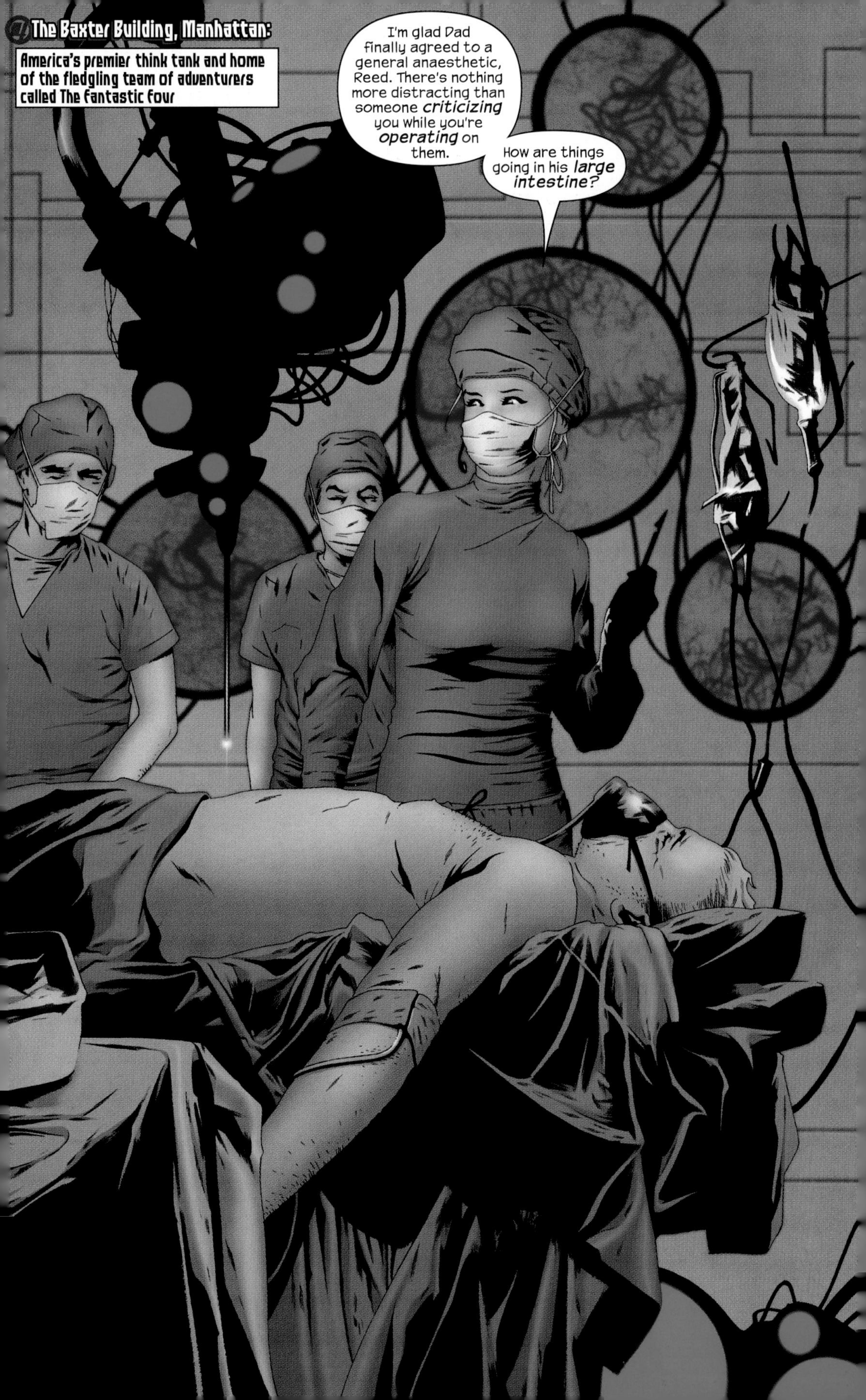

The Baxter Building, Manhattan:
America's premier think tank and home of the fledgling team of adventurers called The Fantastic Four
I'm glad Dad finally agreed to a general anaesthetic, Reed. There's nothing more distracting than someone criticizing you while you're operating on them.
How are things going in his large intestine?

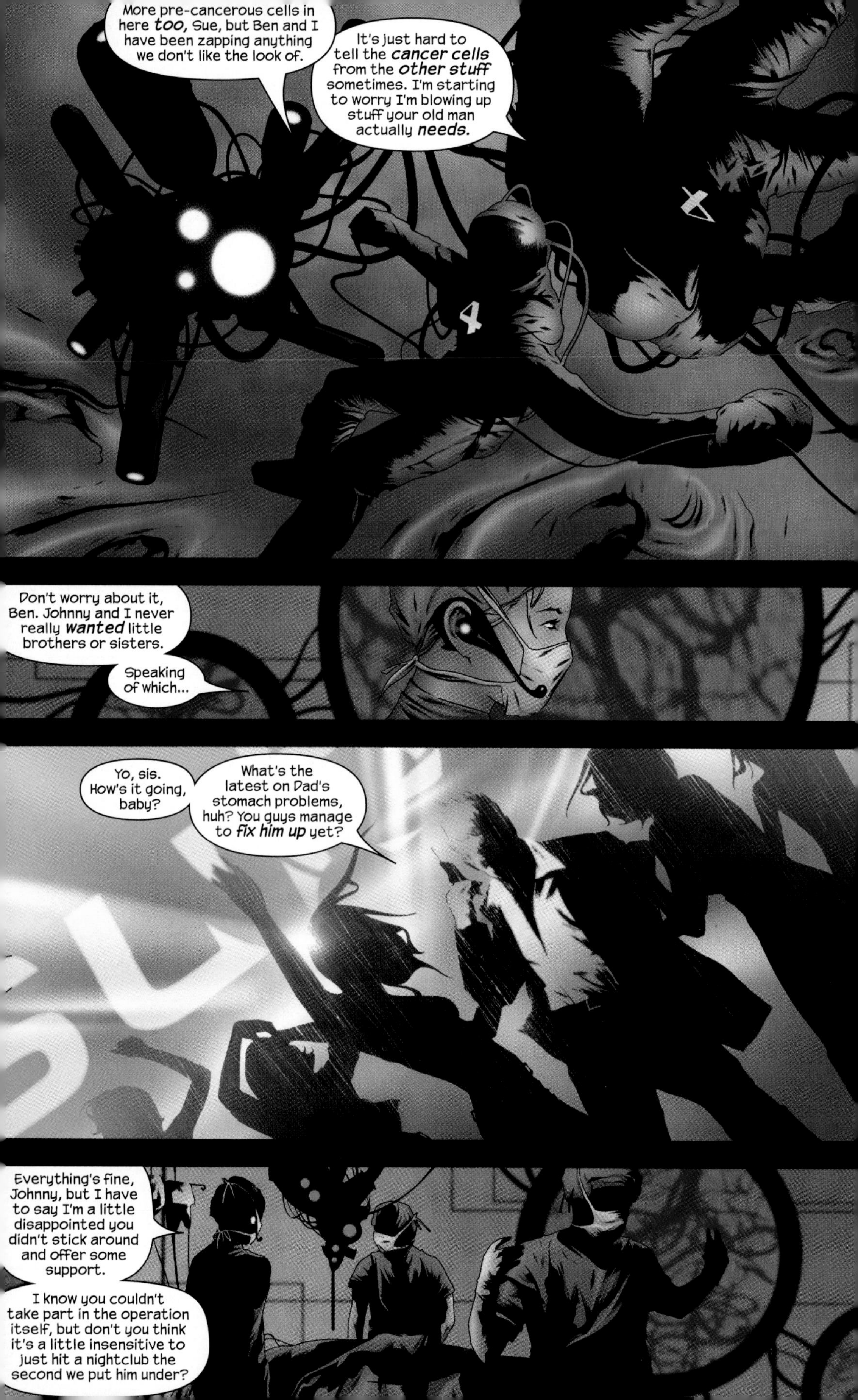
More pre-cancerous cells in here *too*, Sue, but Ben and I have been zapping anything we don't like the look of.
It's just hard to tell the *cancer cells* from the *other stuff* sometimes. I'm starting to worry I'm blowing up stuff your old man actually *needs.*
Don't worry about it, Ben. Johnny and I never really *wanted* little brothers or sisters.
Speaking of which...
Yo, sis. How's it going, baby?
What's the latest on Dad's stomach problems, huh? You guys manage to *fix him up* yet?
Everything's fine, Johnny, but I have to say I'm a little disappointed you didn't stick around and offer some support.
I know you couldn't take part in the operation itself, but don't you think it's a little insensitive to just hit a nightclub the second we put him under?

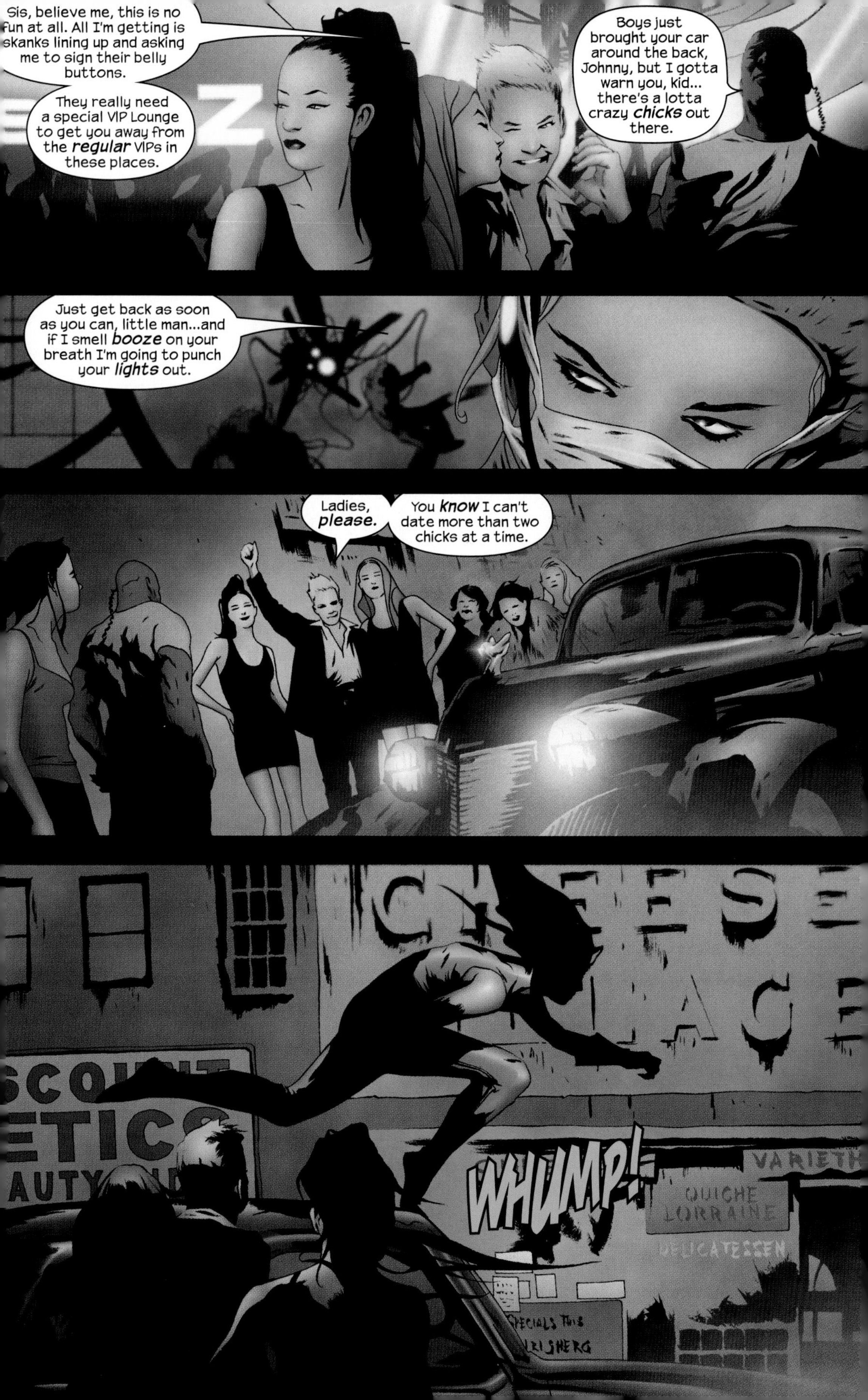

Sis, believe me, this is no fun at all. All I'm getting is skanks lining up and asking me to sign their belly buttons.
They really need a special VIP Lounge to get you away from the *regular* VIPs in these places.
Boys just brought your car around the back, Johnny, but I gotta warn you, kid... there's a lotta crazy *chicks* out there.
Just get back as soon as you can, little man...and if I smell *booze* on your breath I'm going to punch your *lights* out.
Ladies, *please.*
You *know* I can't date more than two chicks at a time.
WHUMP!
QUICHE LORRAINE
DELICATESSEN

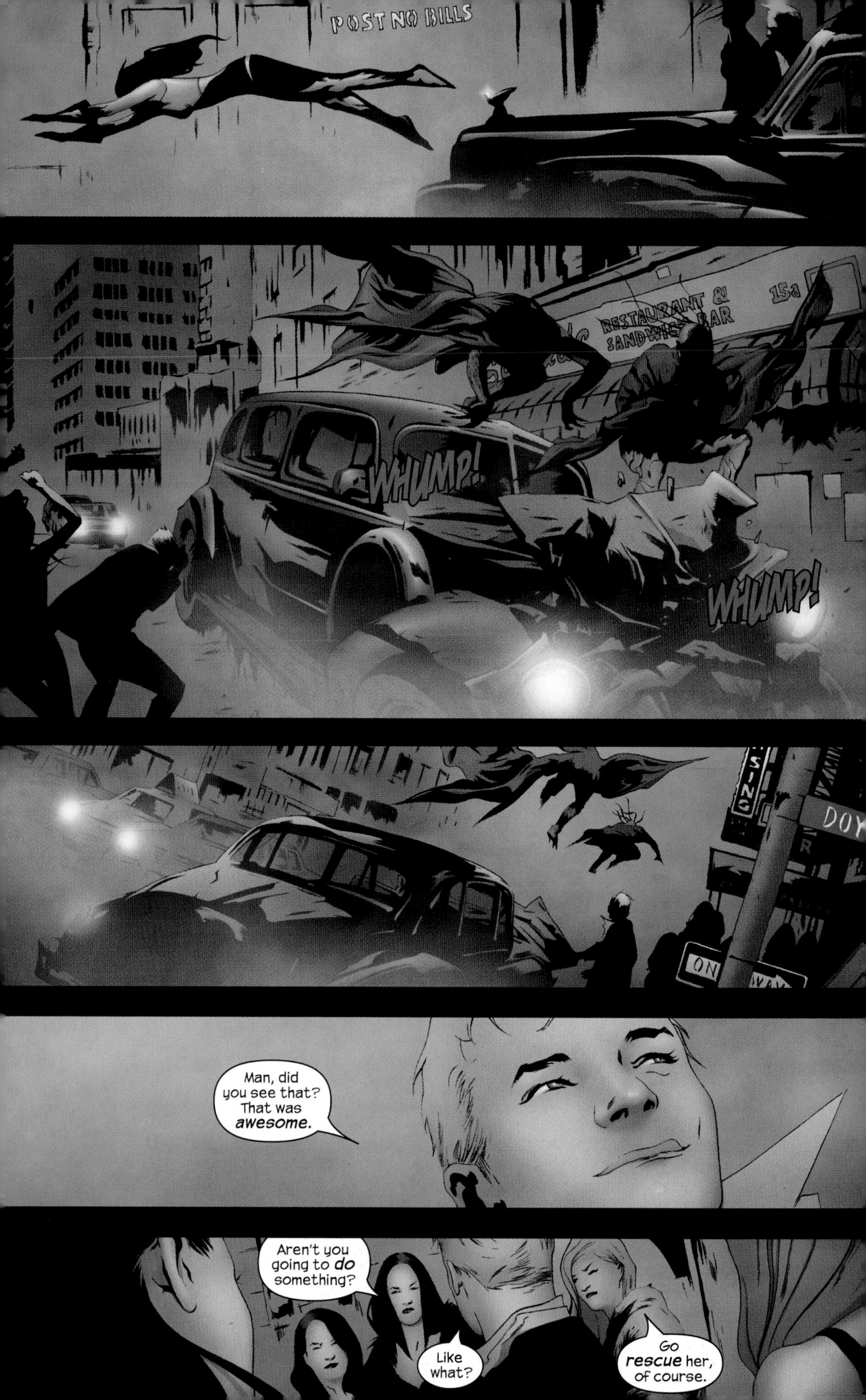
POST NO BILLS
RESTAURANT & SANDWICH BAR
15a
WHUMP!
WHUMP!
DOY
ONE WAY
Man, did you see that? That was *awesome.*
Aren't you going to *do* something?
Like what?
Go *rescue* her, of course.

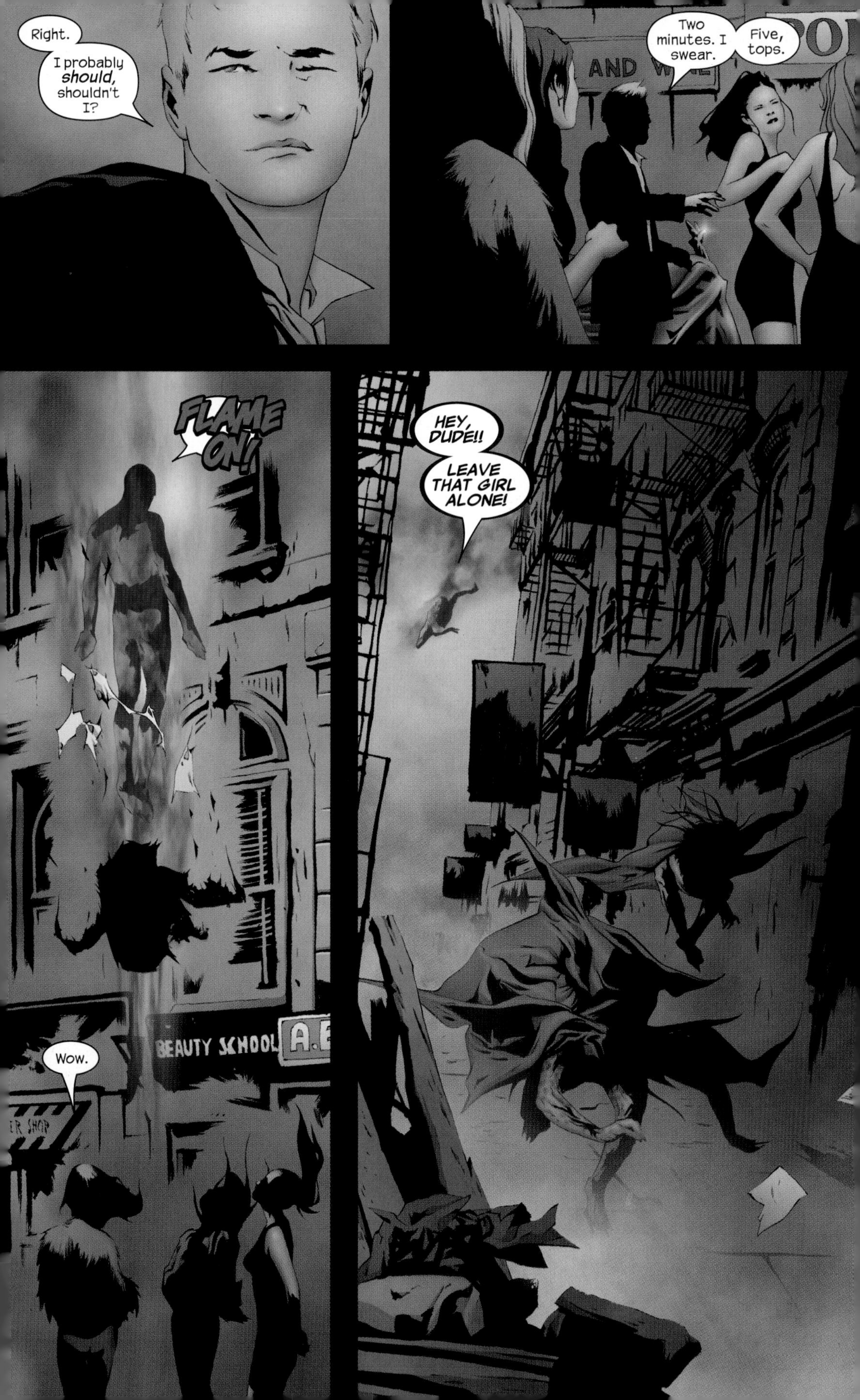
Right.
I probably should, shouldn't I?
Two minutes. I swear.
Five, tops.
AND
FLAME ON!
BEAUTY SCHOOL
A.
Wow.
HEY, DUDE!!
LEAVE THAT GIRL ALONE!

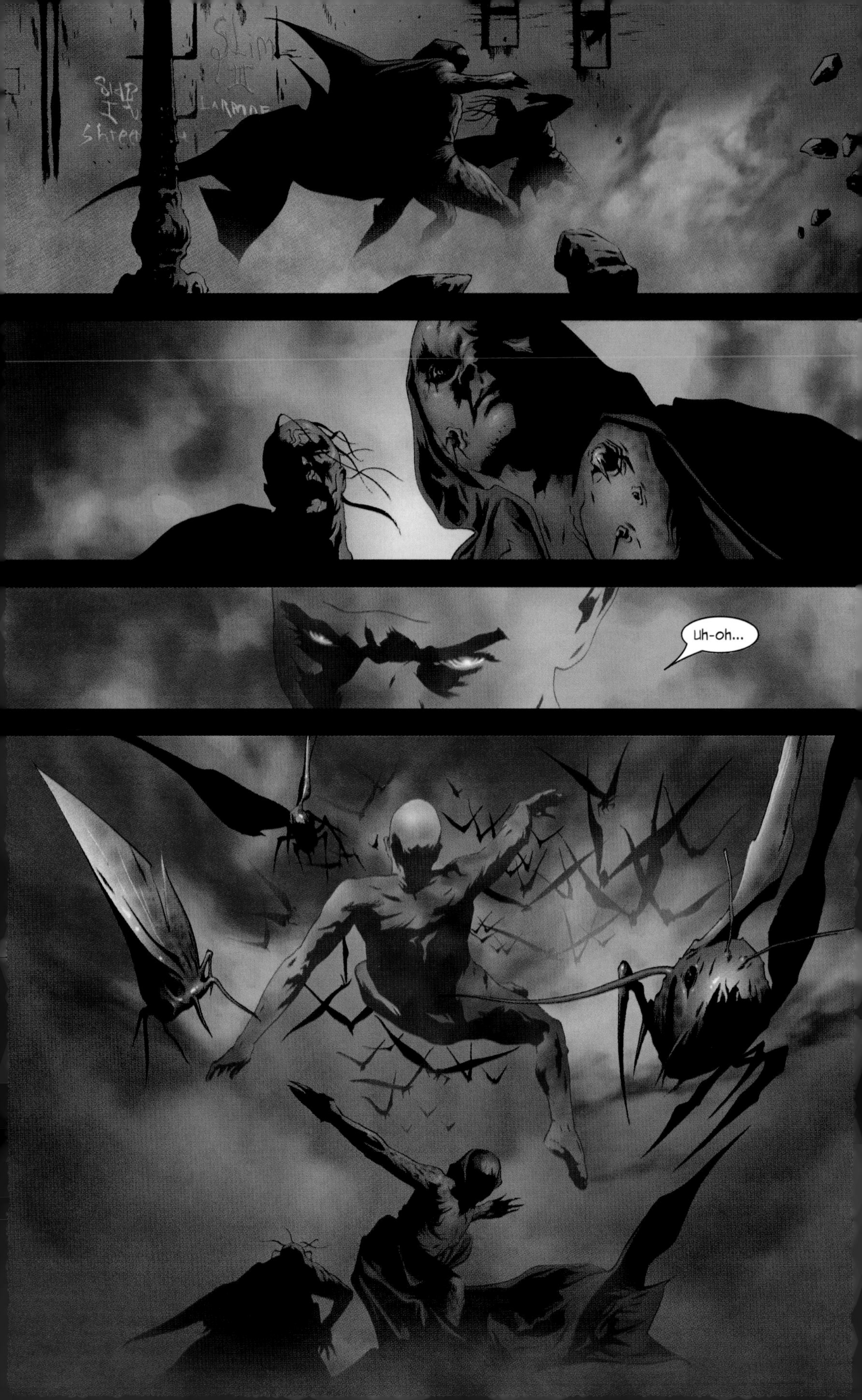
uh-oh...

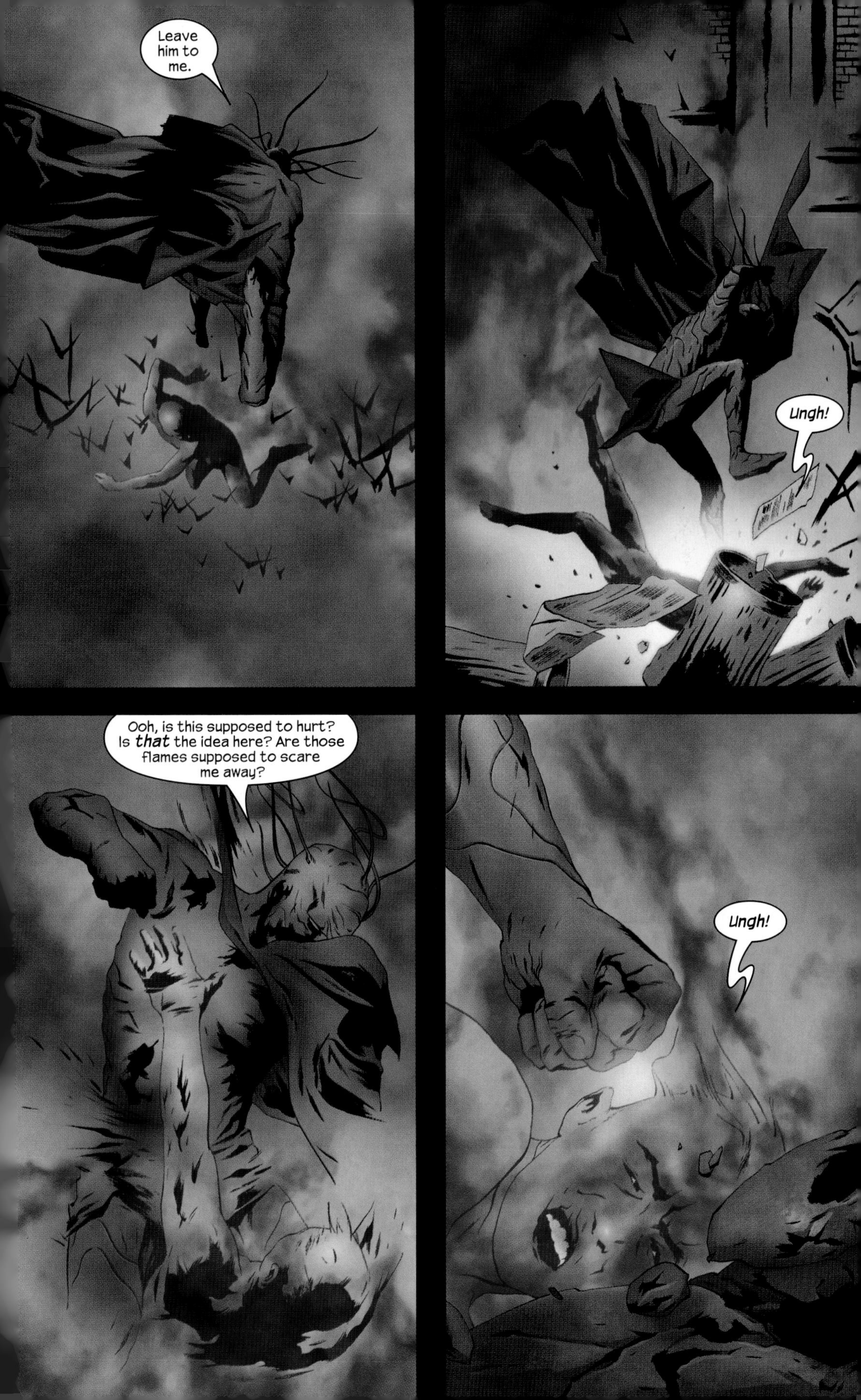
Leave him to me.
Ungh!
Ooh, is this supposed to hurt? Is *that* the idea here? Are those flames supposed to scare me away?
Ungh!

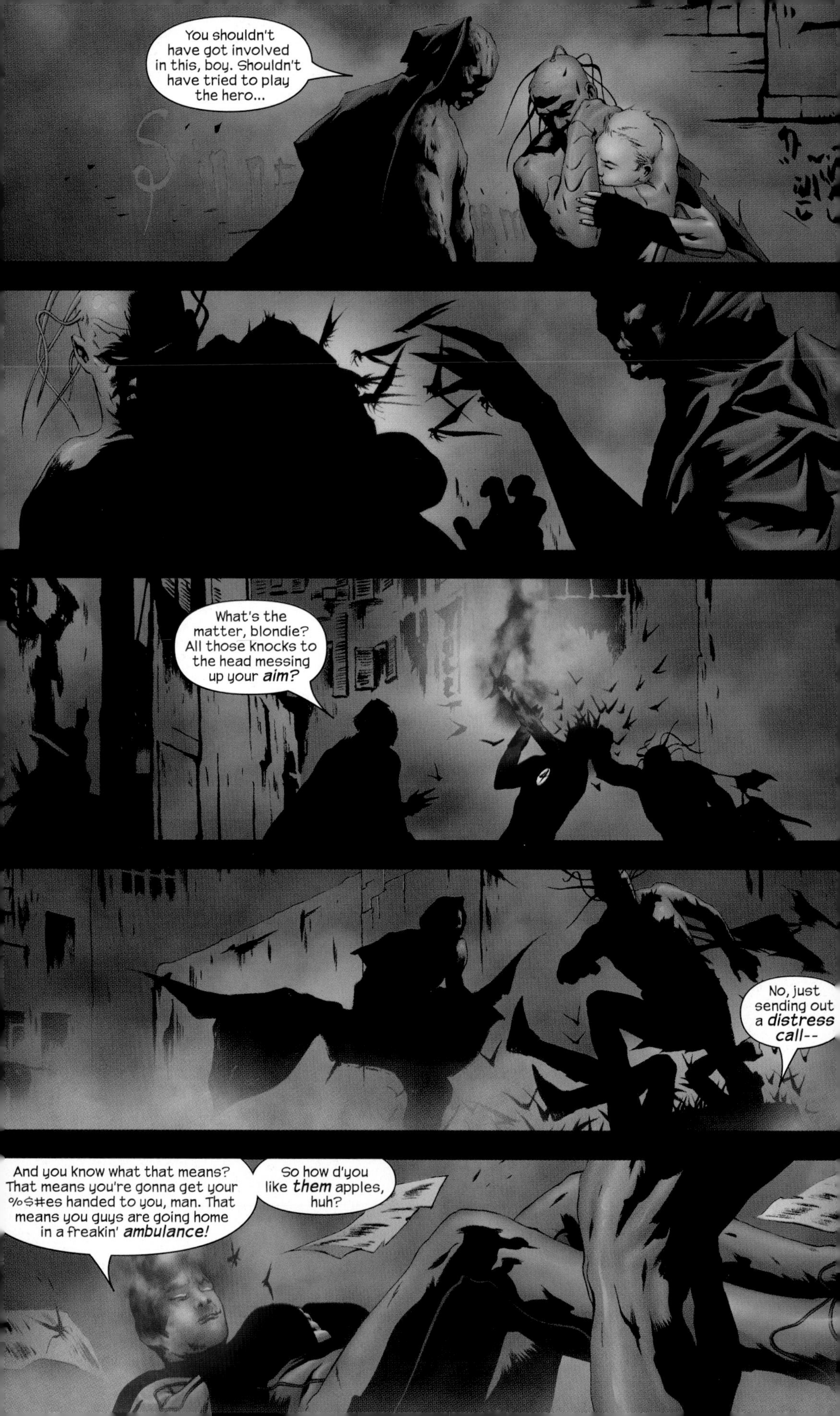
You shouldn't have got involved in this, boy. Shouldn't have tried to play the hero...
What's the matter, blondie? All those knocks to the head messing up your *aim?*
No, just sending out a *distress call--*
And you know what that means? That means you're gonna get your %$#es handed to you, man. That means you guys are going home in a freakin' *ambulance!*
So how d'you like *them* apples, huh?

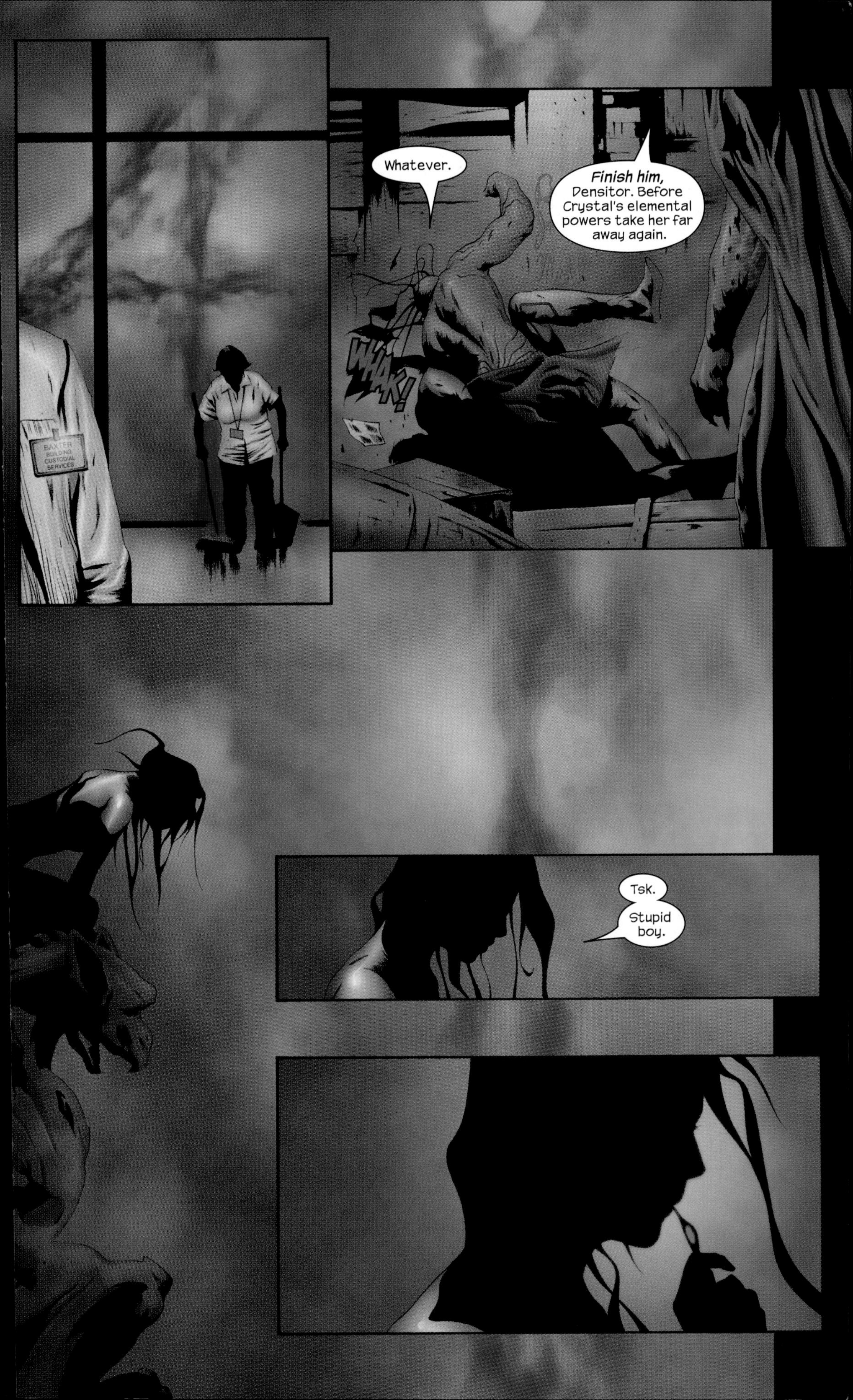
BAXTER BUILDING CUSTODIAL SERVICES
Whatever.
Finish him, Densitor. Before Crystal's elemental powers take her far away again.
WHAK!
Tsk.
Stupid boy.

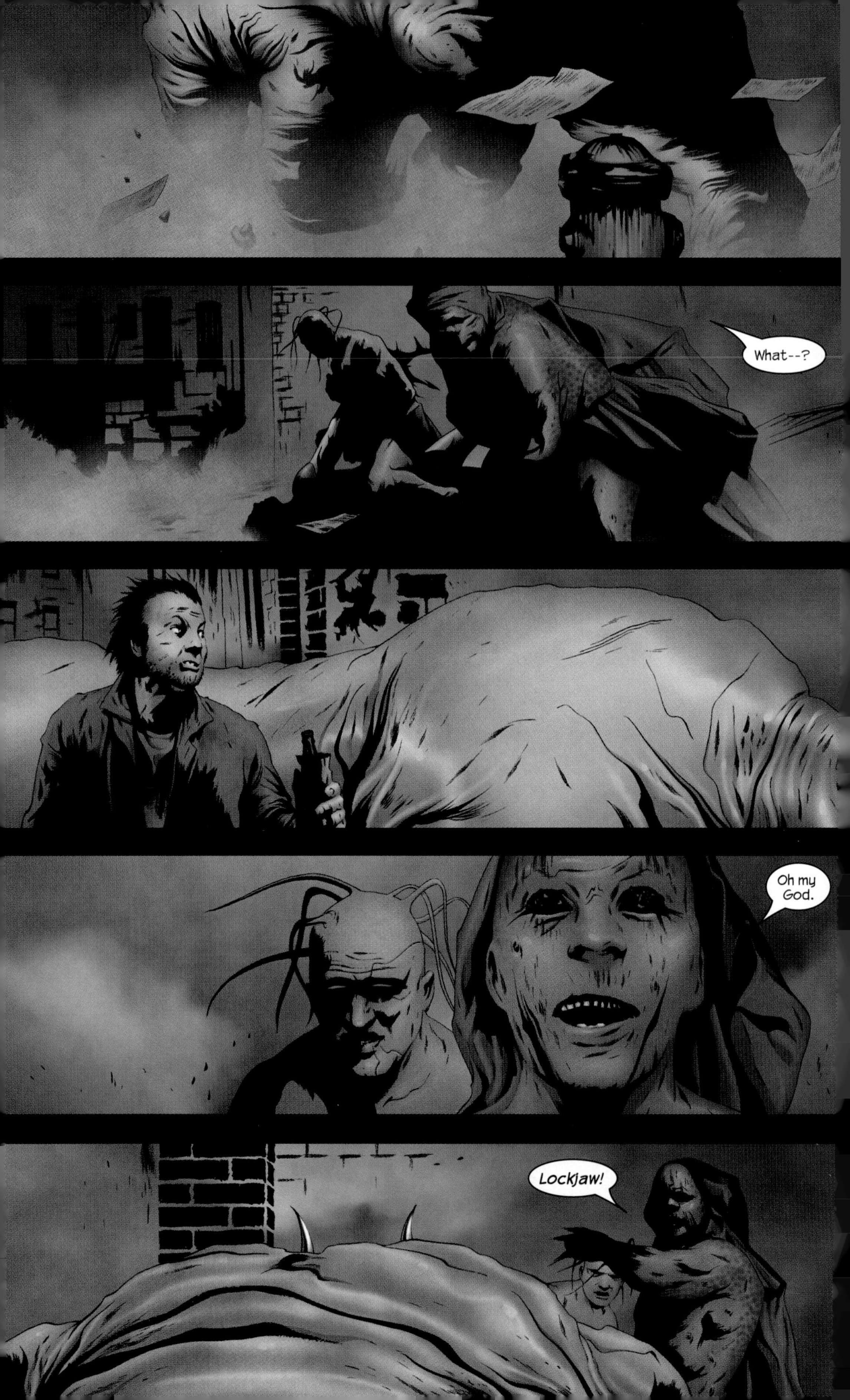
What--?
Oh my God.
Lockjaw!

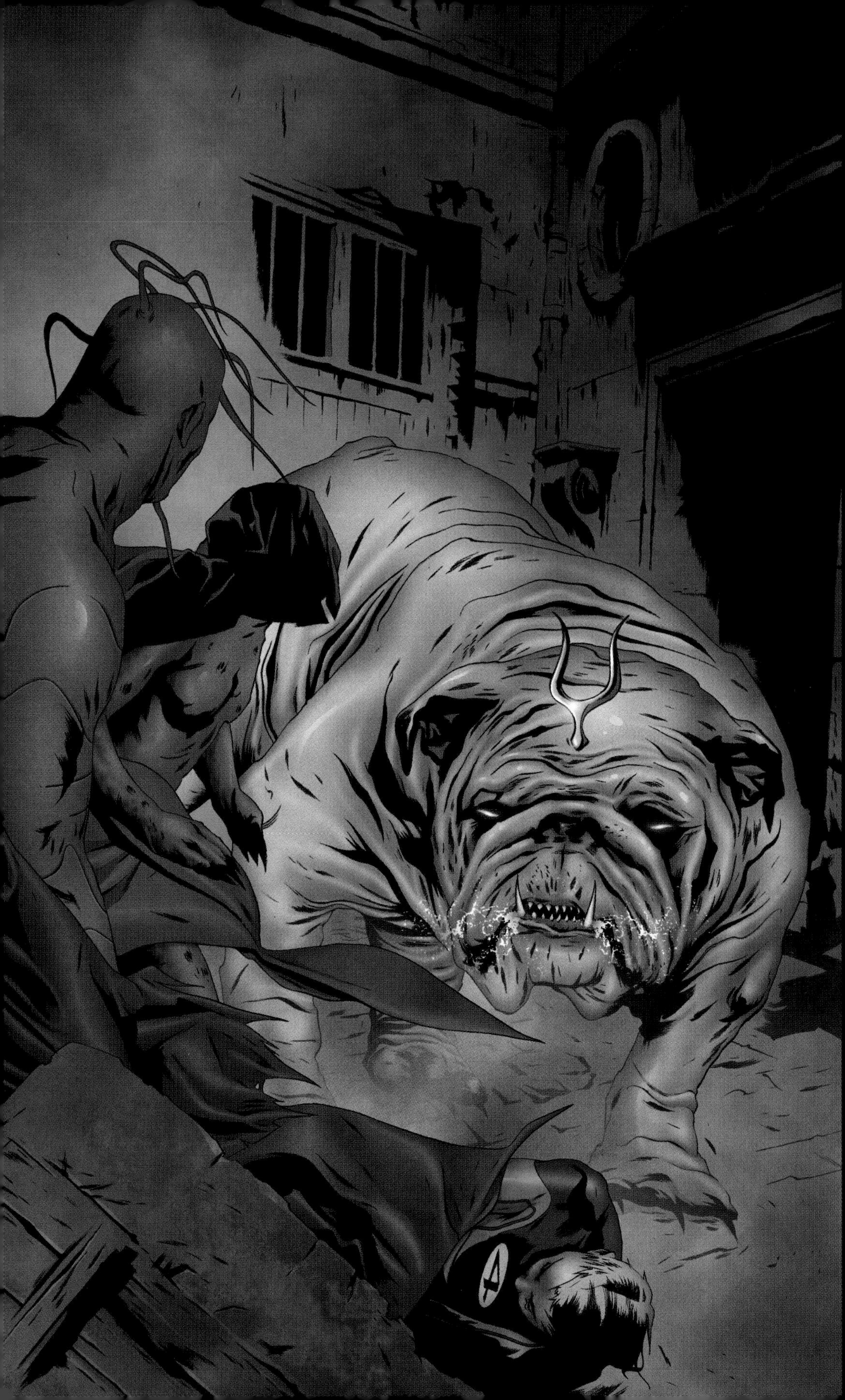

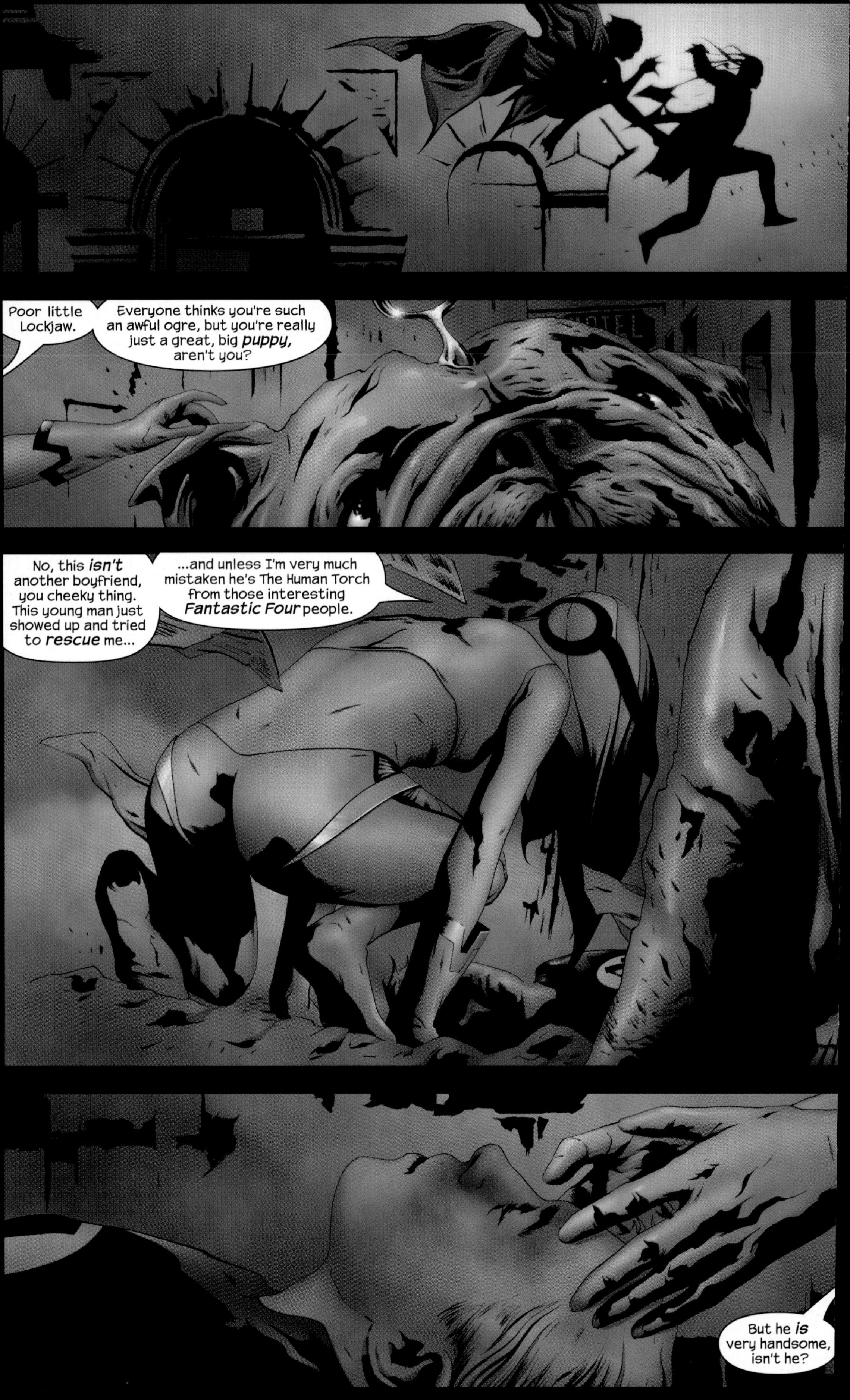
Poor little Lockjaw.
Everyone thinks you're such an awful ogre, but you're really just a great, big *puppy,* aren't you?
No, this *isn't* another boyfriend, you cheeky thing. This young man just showed up and tried to *rescue* me...
...and unless I'm very much mistaken he's The Human Torch from those interesting *Fantastic Four* people.
But he *is* very handsome, isn't he?

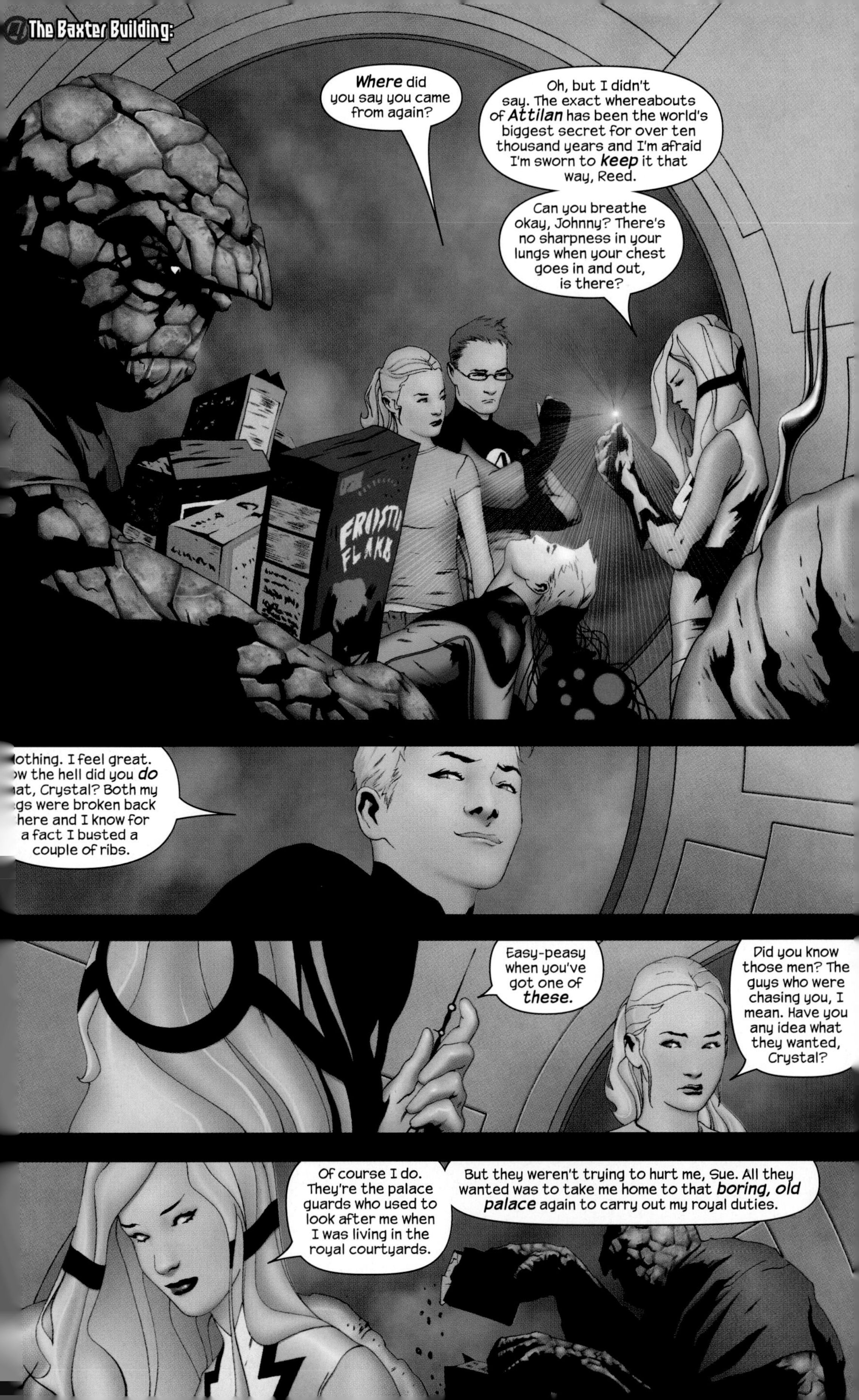
The Baxter Building:
Where did you say you came from again?
Oh, but I didn't say. The exact whereabouts of Attilan has been the world's biggest secret for over ten thousand years and I'm afraid I'm sworn to keep it that way, Reed.
Can you breathe okay, Johnny? There's no sharpness in your lungs when your chest goes in and out, is there?
FROSTI FLAKE
othing. I feel great. w the hell did you do at, Crystal? Both my gs were broken back here and I know for a fact I busted a couple of ribs.
Easy-peasy when you've got one of these.
Did you know those men? The guys who were chasing you, I mean. Have you any idea what they wanted, Crystal?
Of course I do. They're the palace guards who used to look after me when I was living in the royal courtyards.
But they weren't trying to hurt me, Sue. All they wanted was to take me home to that boring, old palace again to carry out my royal duties.

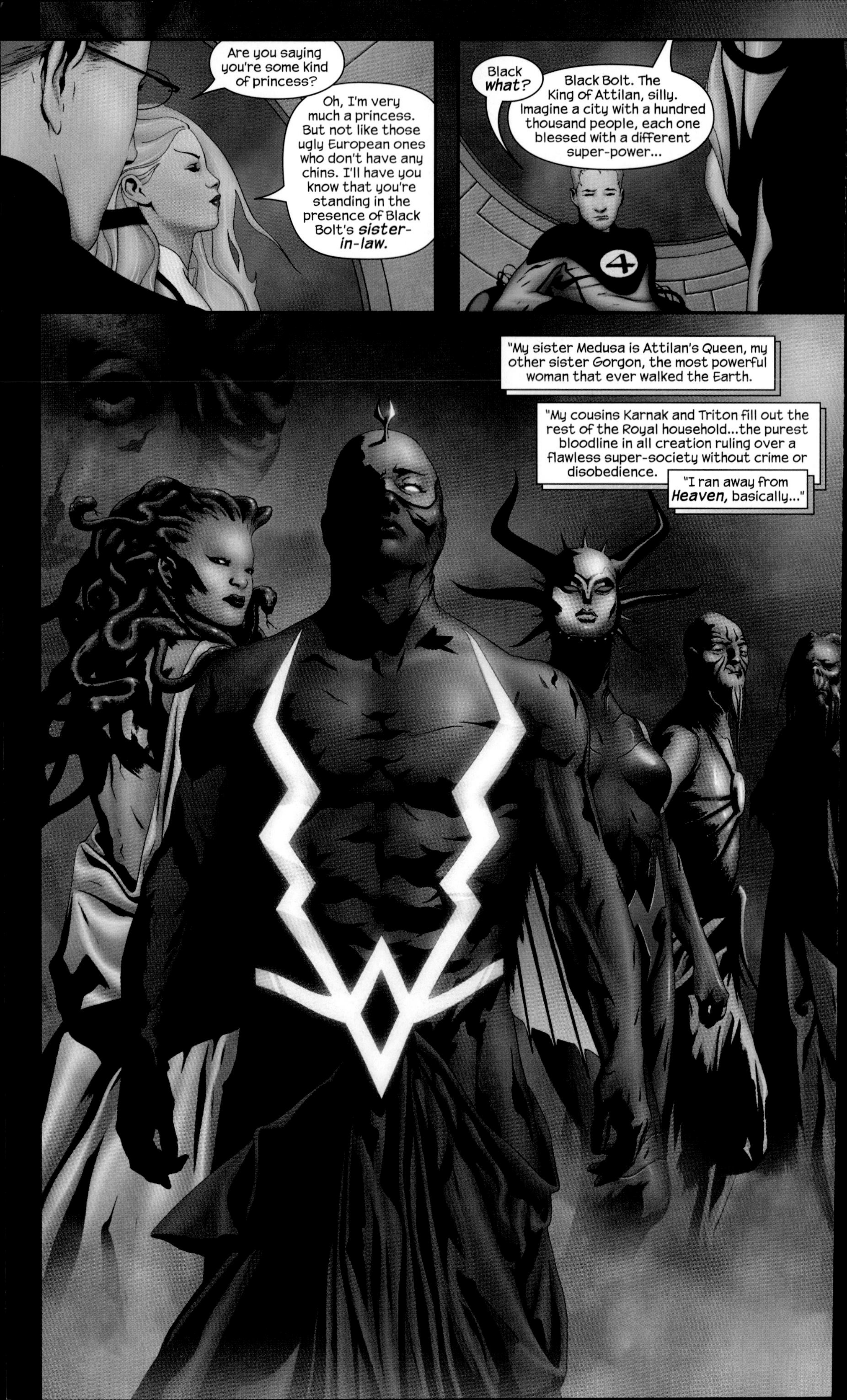
Are you saying you're some kind of princess?
Oh, I'm very much a princess. But not like those ugly European ones who don't have any chins. I'll have you know that you're standing in the presence of Black Bolt's *sister-in-law.*
Black *what?*
Black Bolt. The King of Attilan, silly. Imagine a city with a hundred thousand people, each one blessed with a different super-power...
"My sister Medusa is Attilan's Queen, my other sister Gorgon, the most powerful woman that ever walked the Earth.
"My cousins Karnak and Triton fill out the rest of the Royal household...the purest bloodline in all creation ruling over a flawless super-society without crime or disobedience.
"I ran away from *Heaven,* basically..."

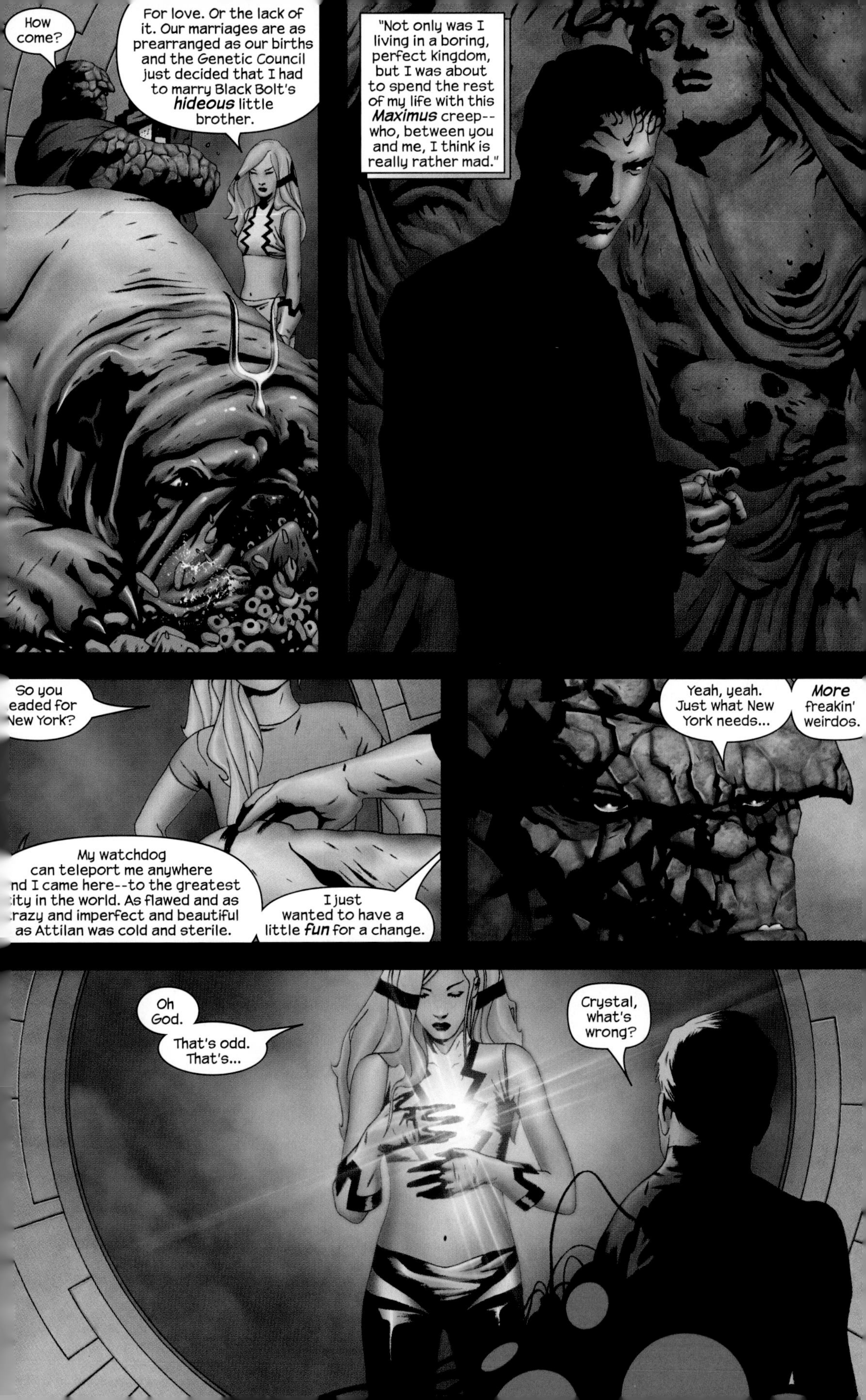
How come?
For love. Or the lack of it. Our marriages are as prearranged as our births and the Genetic Council just decided that I had to marry Black Bolt's *hideous* little brother.
"Not only was I living in a boring, perfect kingdom, but I was about to spend the rest of my life with this *Maximus* creep--who, between you and me, I think is really rather mad."
So you eaded for New York?
My watchdog can teleport me anywhere nd I came here--to the greatest ity in the world. As flawed and as razy and imperfect and beautiful as Attilan was cold and sterile.
I just wanted to have a little *fun* for a change.
Yeah, yeah. Just what New York needs...
More freakin' weirdos.
Oh God.
That's odd. That's...
Crystal, what's wrong?

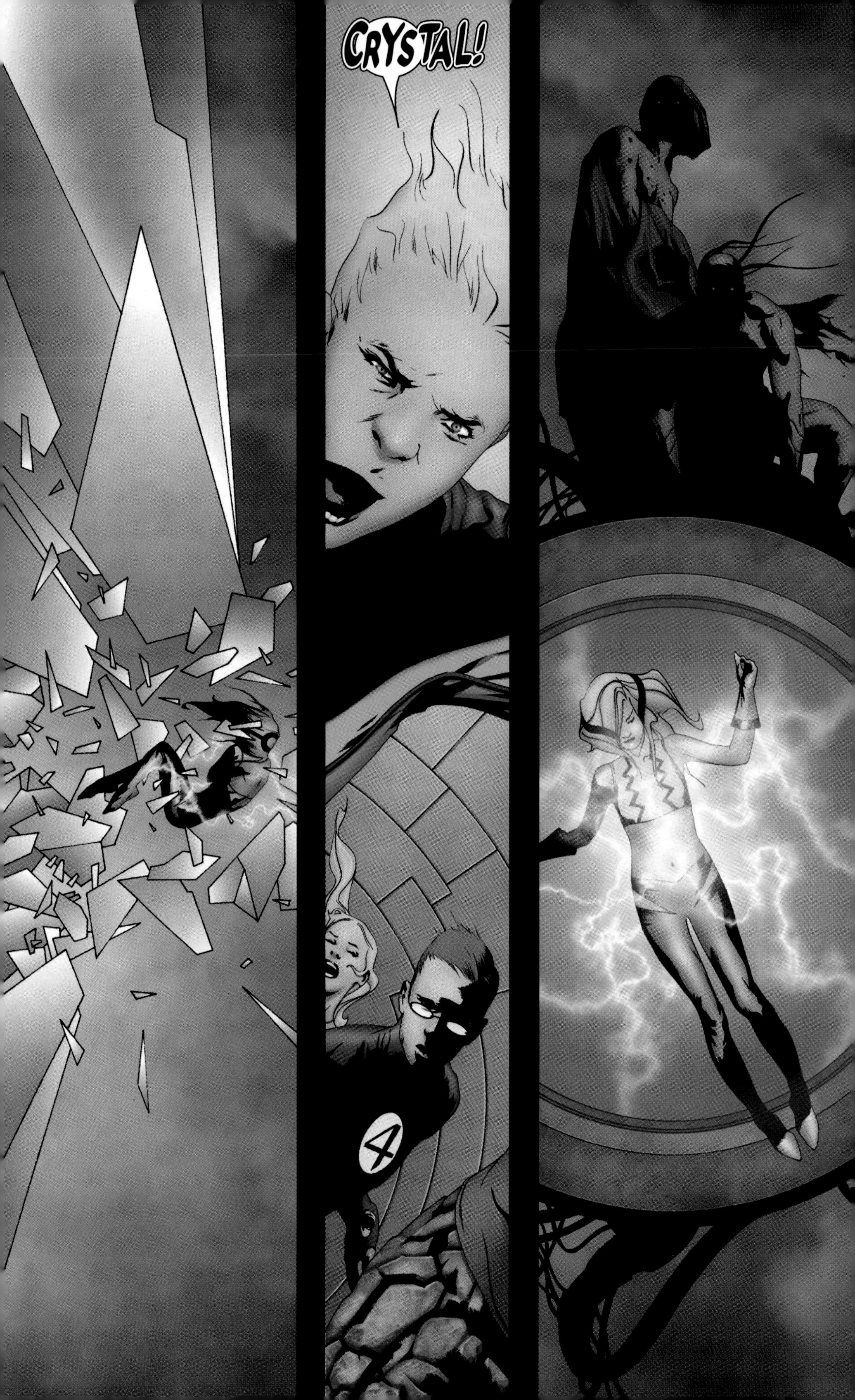
CRYSTAL!

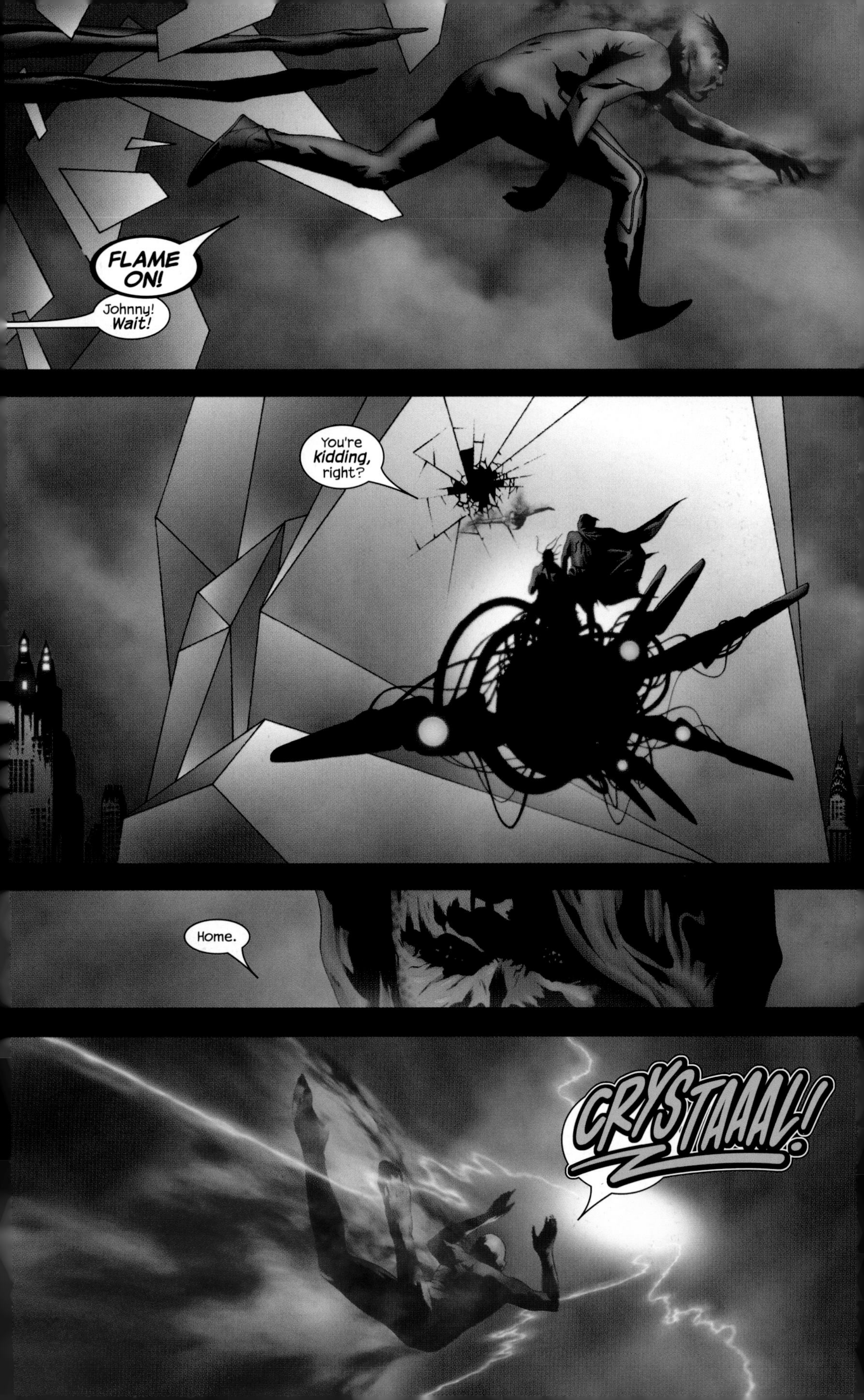
FLAME ON!
Johnny! Wait!
You're kidding, right?
Home.
CRYSTAAAL!

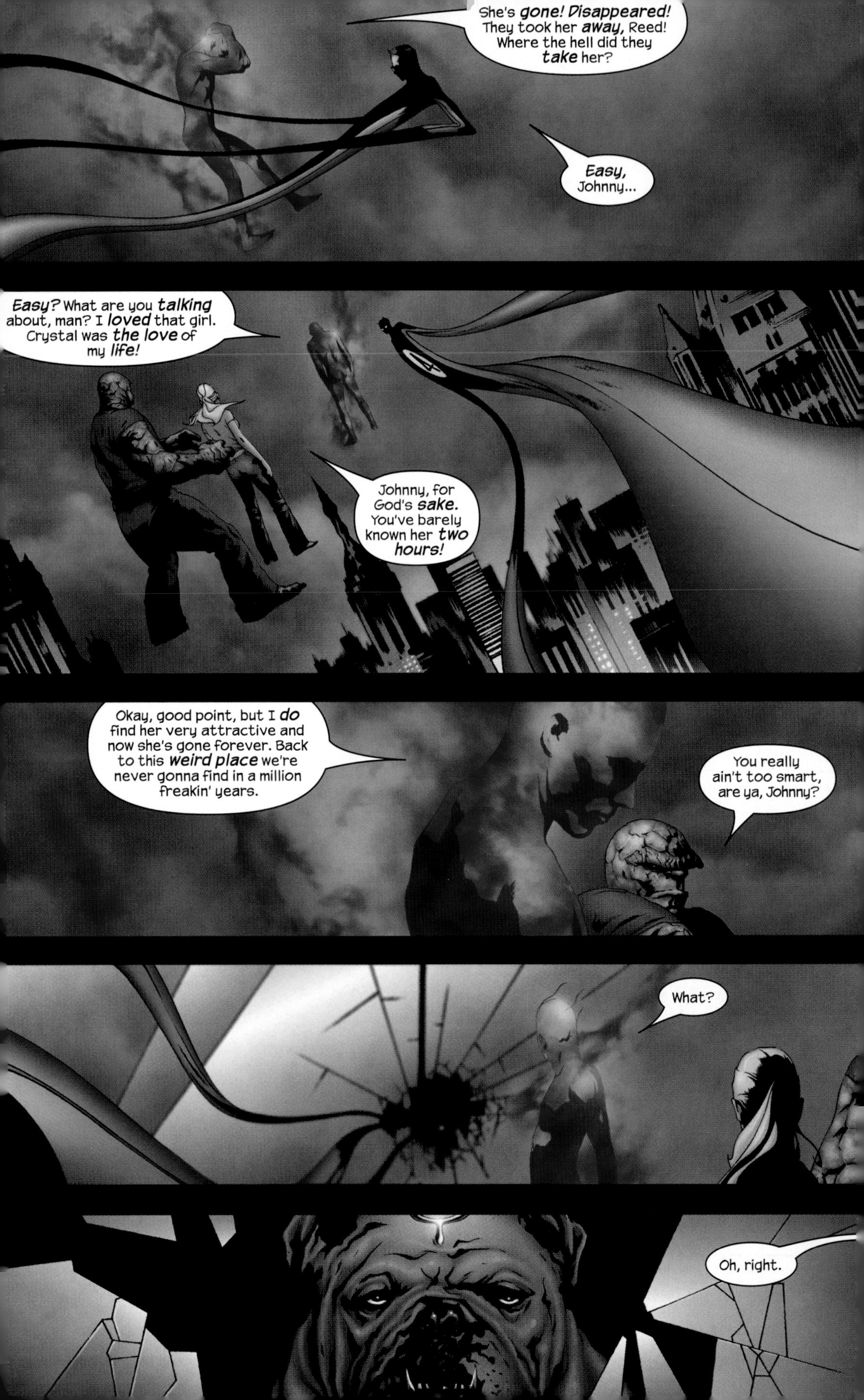
She's gone! Disappeared! They took her away, Reed! Where the hell did they take her?
Easy, Johnny...
Easy? What are you talking about, man? I loved that girl. Crystal was the love of my life!
Johnny, for God's sake. You've barely known her two hours!
Okay, good point, but I do find her very attractive and now she's gone forever. Back to this weird place we're never gonna find in a million freakin' years.
You really ain't too smart, are ya, Johnny?
What?
Oh, right.

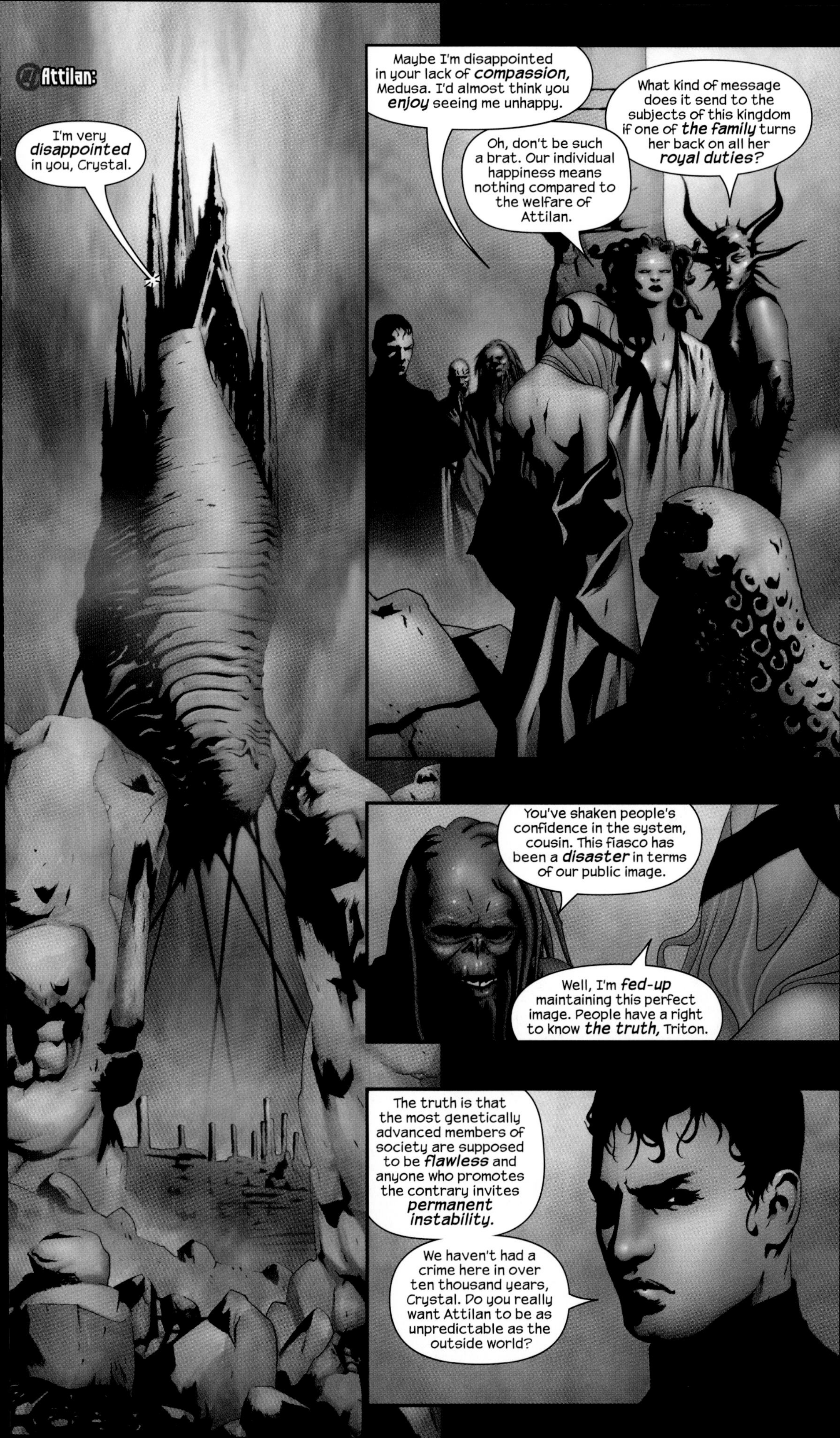
Attilan:
I'm very disappointed in you, Crystal.
Maybe I'm disappointed in your lack of compassion, Medusa. I'd almost think you enjoy seeing me unhappy.
Oh, don't be such a brat. Our individual happiness means nothing compared to the welfare of Attilan.
What kind of message does it send to the subjects of this kingdom if one of the family turns her back on all her royal duties?
You've shaken people's confidence in the system, cousin. This fiasco has been a disaster in terms of our public image.
Well, I'm fed-up maintaining this perfect image. People have a right to know the truth, Triton.
The truth is that the most genetically advanced members of society are supposed to be flawless and anyone who promotes the contrary invites permanent instability.
We haven't had a crime here in over ten thousand years, Crystal. Do you really want Attilan to be as unpredictable as the outside world?

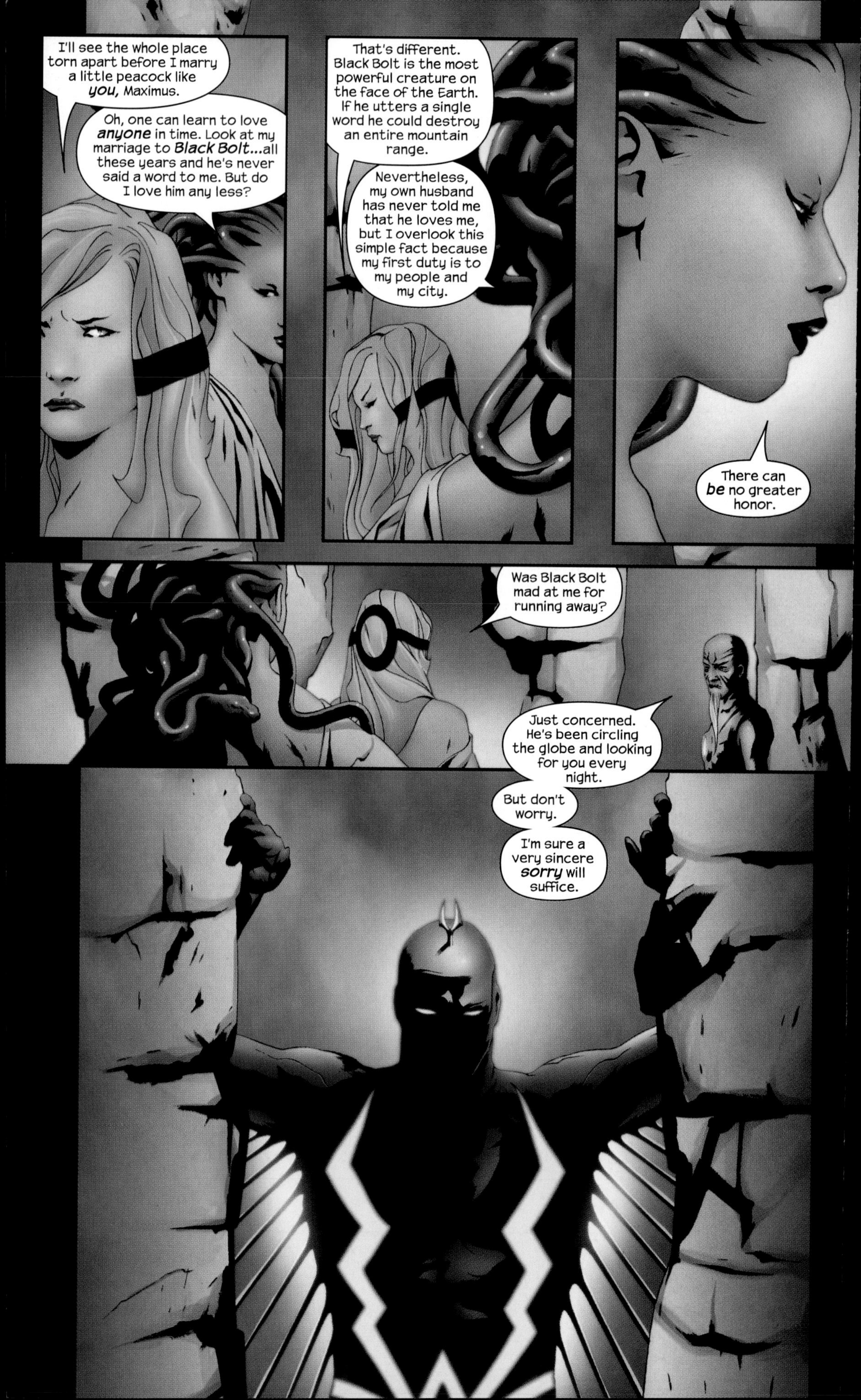
I'll see the whole place torn apart before I marry a little peacock like you, Maximus.
Oh, one can learn to love anyone in time. Look at my marriage to Black Bolt...all these years and he's never said a word to me. But do I love him any less?
That's different. Black Bolt is the most powerful creature on the face of the Earth. If he utters a single word he could destroy an entire mountain range.
Nevertheless, my own husband has never told me that he loves me, but I overlook this simple fact because my first duty is to my people and my city.
There can be no greater honor.
Was Black Bolt mad at me for running away?
Just concerned. He's been circling the globe and looking for you every night.
But don't worry.
I'm sure a very sincere sorry will suffice.

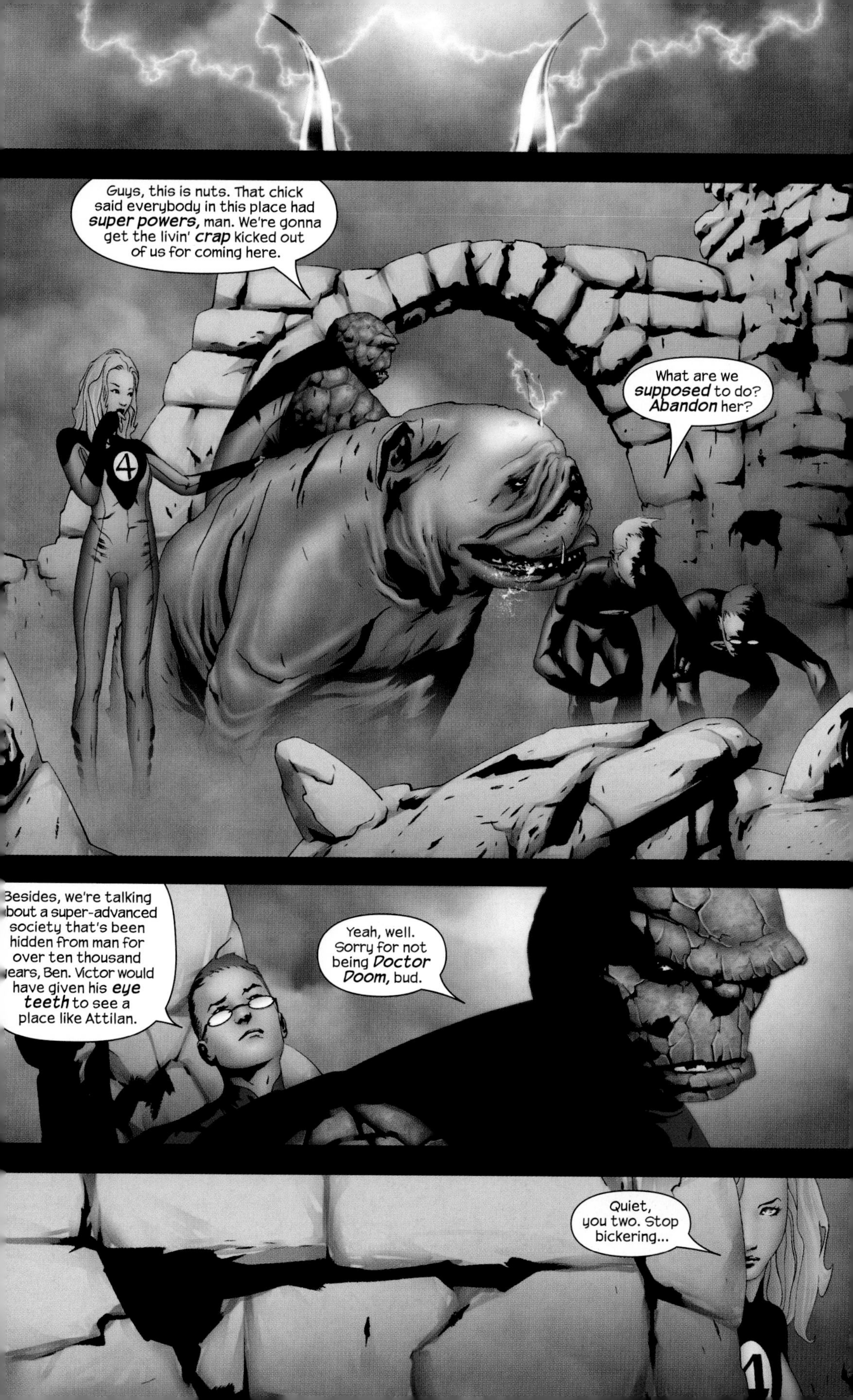

Guys, this is nuts. That chick said everybody in this place had **super powers,** man. We're gonna get the livin' ***crap*** kicked out of us for coming here.
What are we ***supposed*** to do? ***Abandon*** her?
Besides, we're talking about a super-advanced society that's been hidden from man for over ten thousand years, Ben. Victor would have given his ***eye teeth*** to see a place like Attilan.
Yeah, well. Sorry for not being ***Doctor Doom,*** bud.
Quiet, you two. Stop bickering...

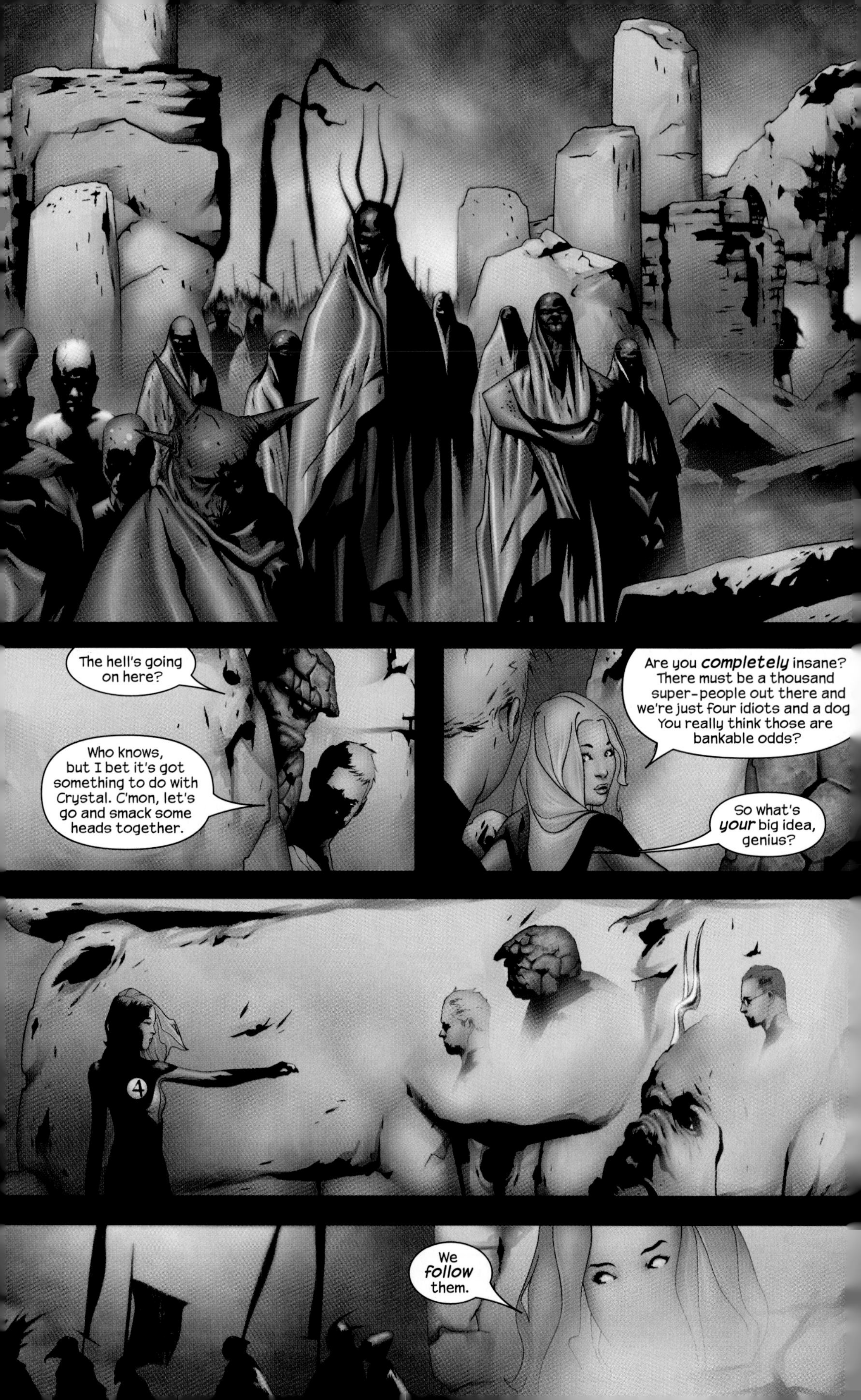
The hell's going on here?
Who knows, but I bet it's got something to do with Crystal. C'mon, let's go and smack some heads together.
Are you *completely* insane? There must be a thousand super-people out there and we're just four idiots and a dog You really think those are bankable odds?
So what's *your* big idea, genius?
We *follow* them.

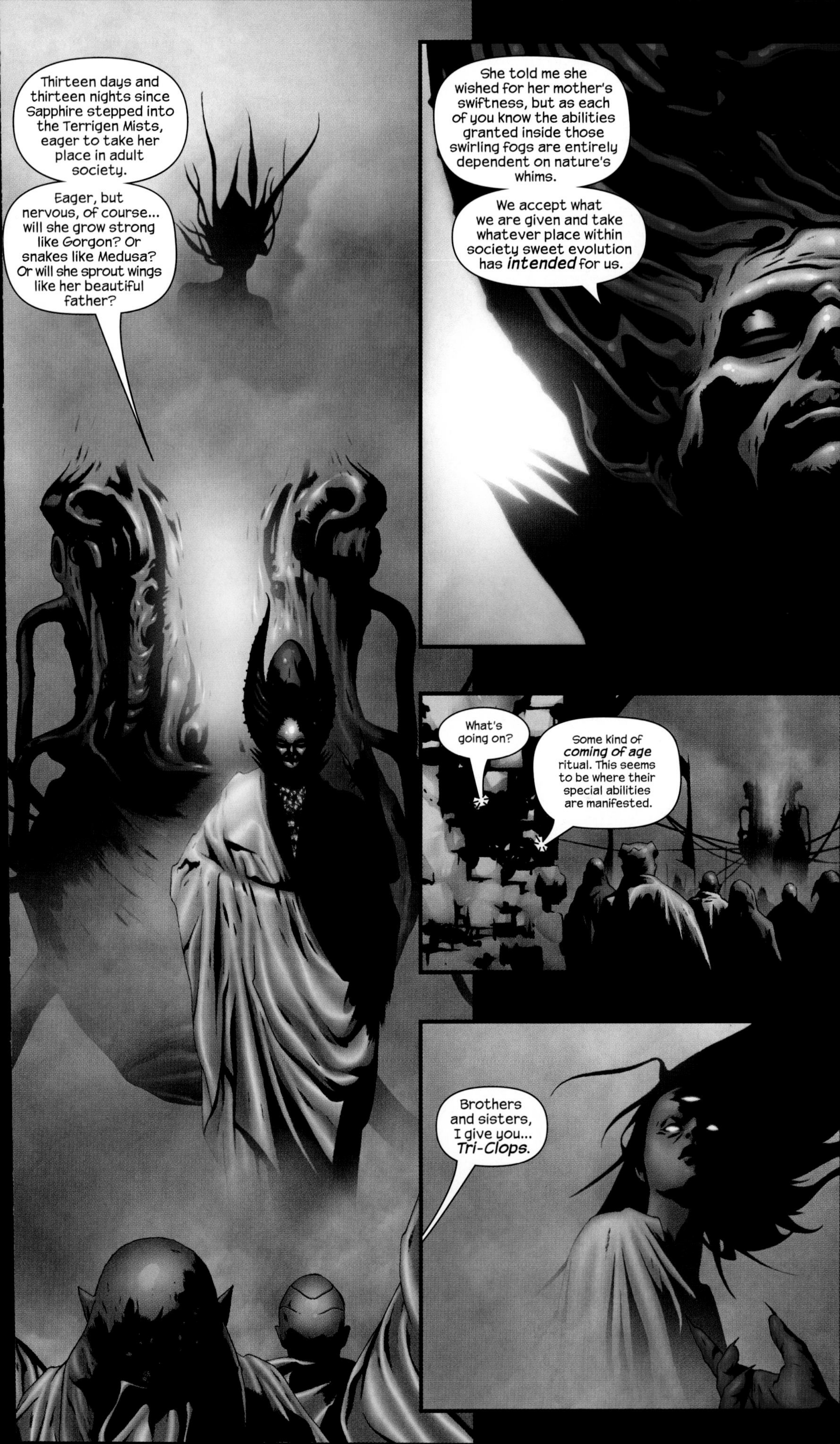
Thirteen days and thirteen nights since Sapphire stepped into the Terrigen Mists, eager to take her place in adult society.
Eager, but nervous, of course... will she grow strong like Gorgon? Or snakes like Medusa? Or will she sprout wings like her beautiful father?
She told me she wished for her mother's swiftness, but as each of you know the abilities granted inside those swirling fogs are entirely dependent on nature's whims.
We accept what we are given and take whatever place within society sweet evolution has *intended* for us.
What's going on?
Some kind of *coming of age* ritual. This seems to be where their special abilities are manifested.
Brothers and sisters, I give you... *Tri-Clops*.

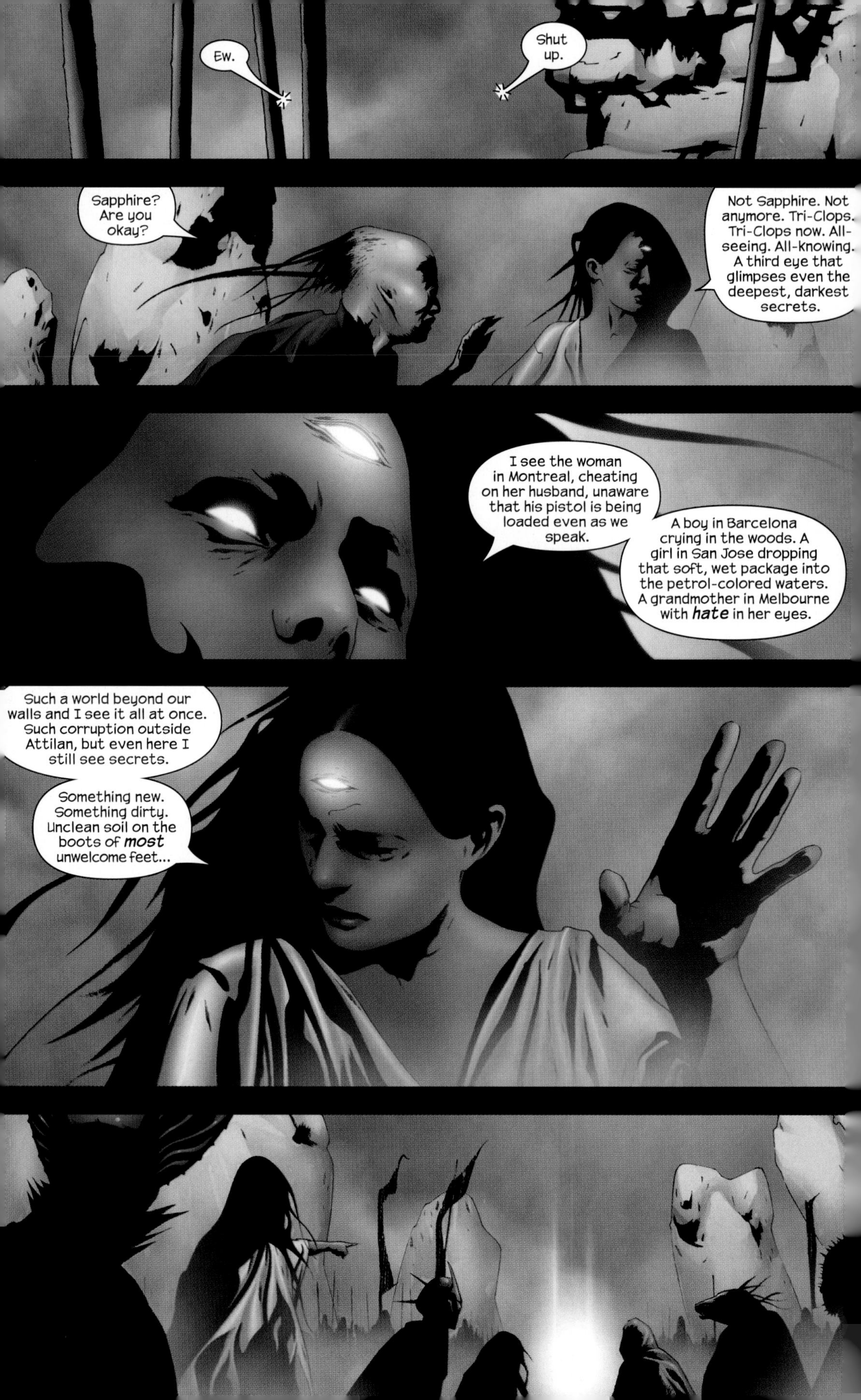
Ew.
Shut up.
Sapphire? Are you okay?
Not Sapphire. Not anymore. Tri-Clops. Tri-Clops now. All-seeing. All-knowing. A third eye that glimpses even the deepest, darkest secrets.
I see the woman in Montreal, cheating on her husband, unaware that his pistol is being loaded even as we speak.
A boy in Barcelona crying in the woods. A girl in San Jose dropping that soft, wet package into the petrol-colored waters. A grandmother in Melbourne with *hate* in her eyes.
Such a world beyond our walls and I see it all at once. Such corruption outside Attilan, but even here I still see secrets.
Something new. Something dirty. Unclean soil on the boots of *most* unwelcome feet...

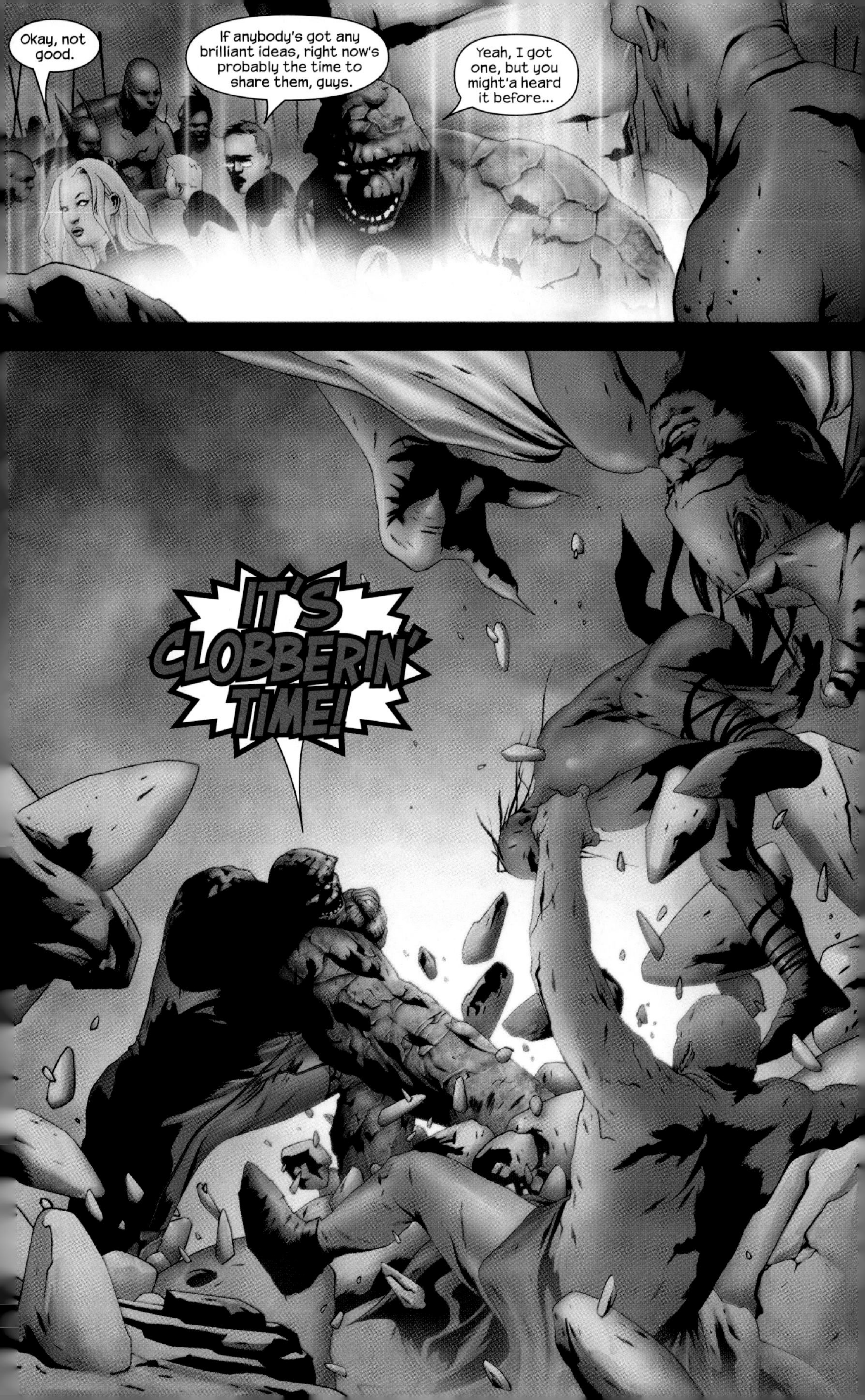
Okay, not good.
If anybody's got any brilliant ideas, right now's probably the time to share them, guys.
Yeah, I got one, but you might'a heard it before...
IT'S CLOBBERIN' TIME!

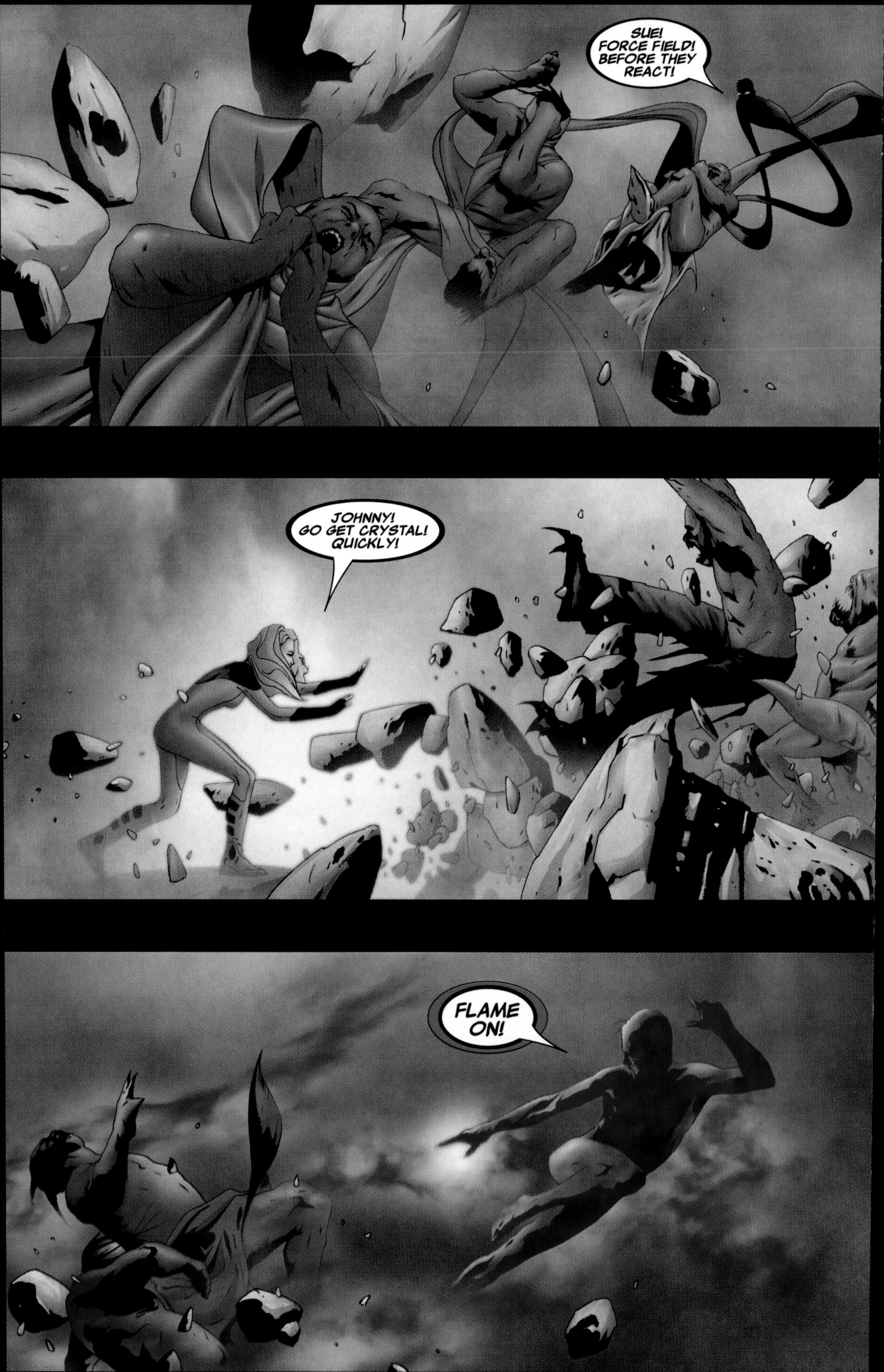
SUE! FORCE FIELD! BEFORE THEY REACT!
JOHNNY! GO GET CRYSTAL! QUICKLY!
FLAME ON!

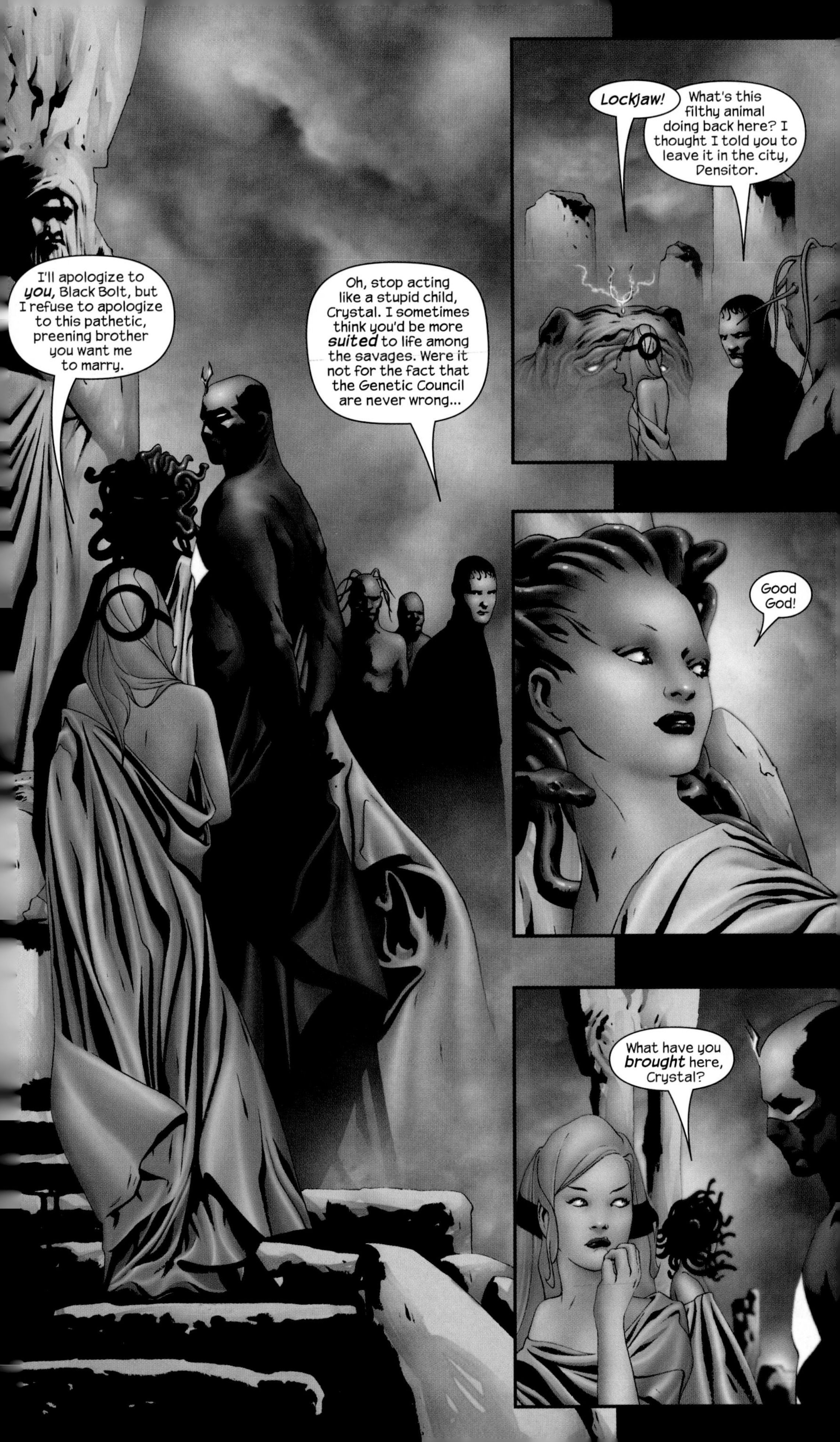
I'll apologize to *you*, Black Bolt, but I refuse to apologize to this pathetic, preening brother you want me to marry.
Oh, stop acting like a stupid child, Crystal. I sometimes think you'd be more *suited* to life among the savages. Were it not for the fact that the Genetic Council are never wrong...
Lockjaw!
What's this filthy animal doing back here? I thought I told you to leave it in the city, Densitor.
Good God!
What have you *brought* here, Crystal?

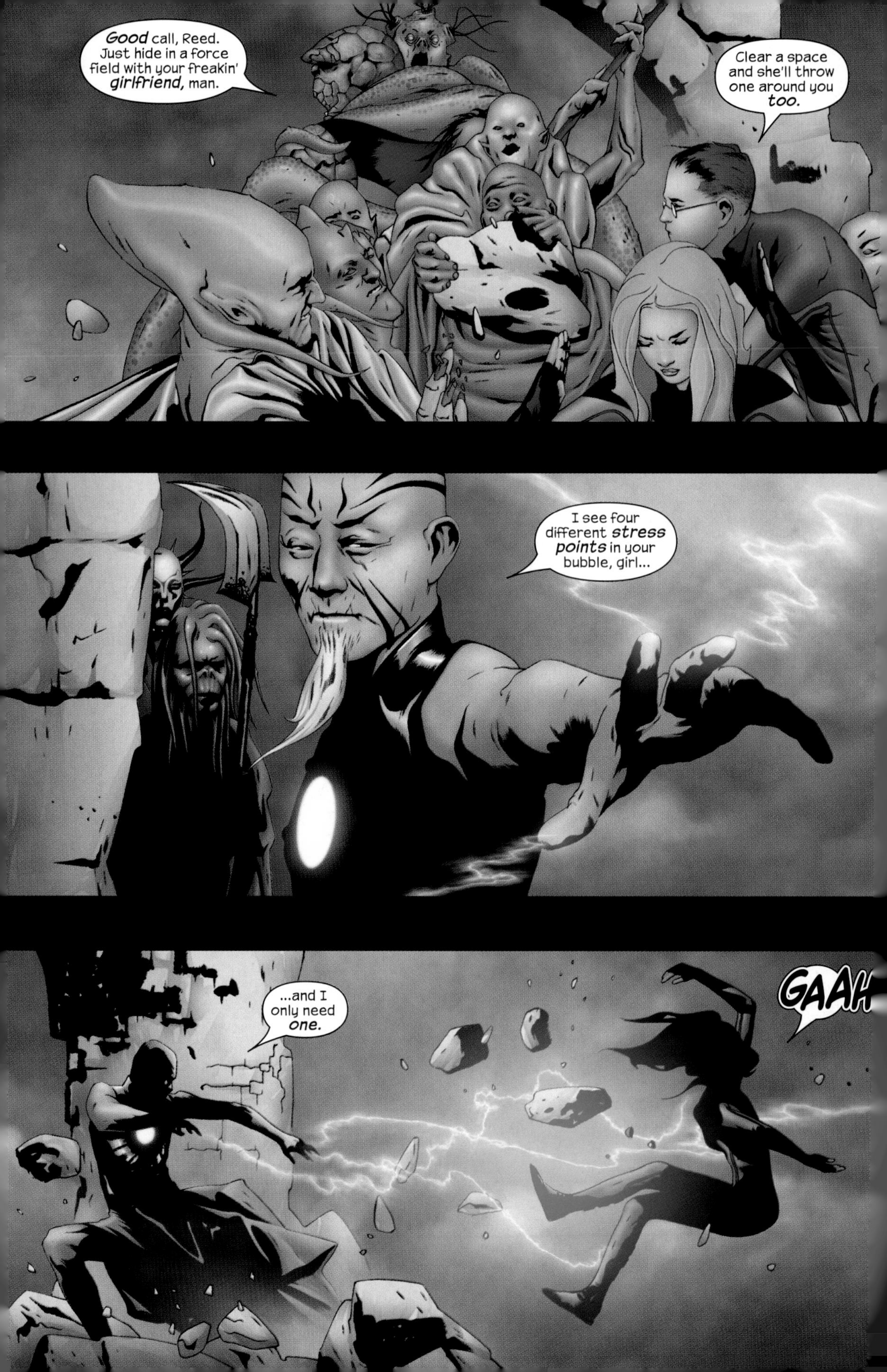
Good call, Reed. Just hide in a force field with your freakin' girlfriend, man.
Clear a space and she'll throw one around you too.
I see four different stress points in your bubble, girl...
...and I only need one.
GAAH

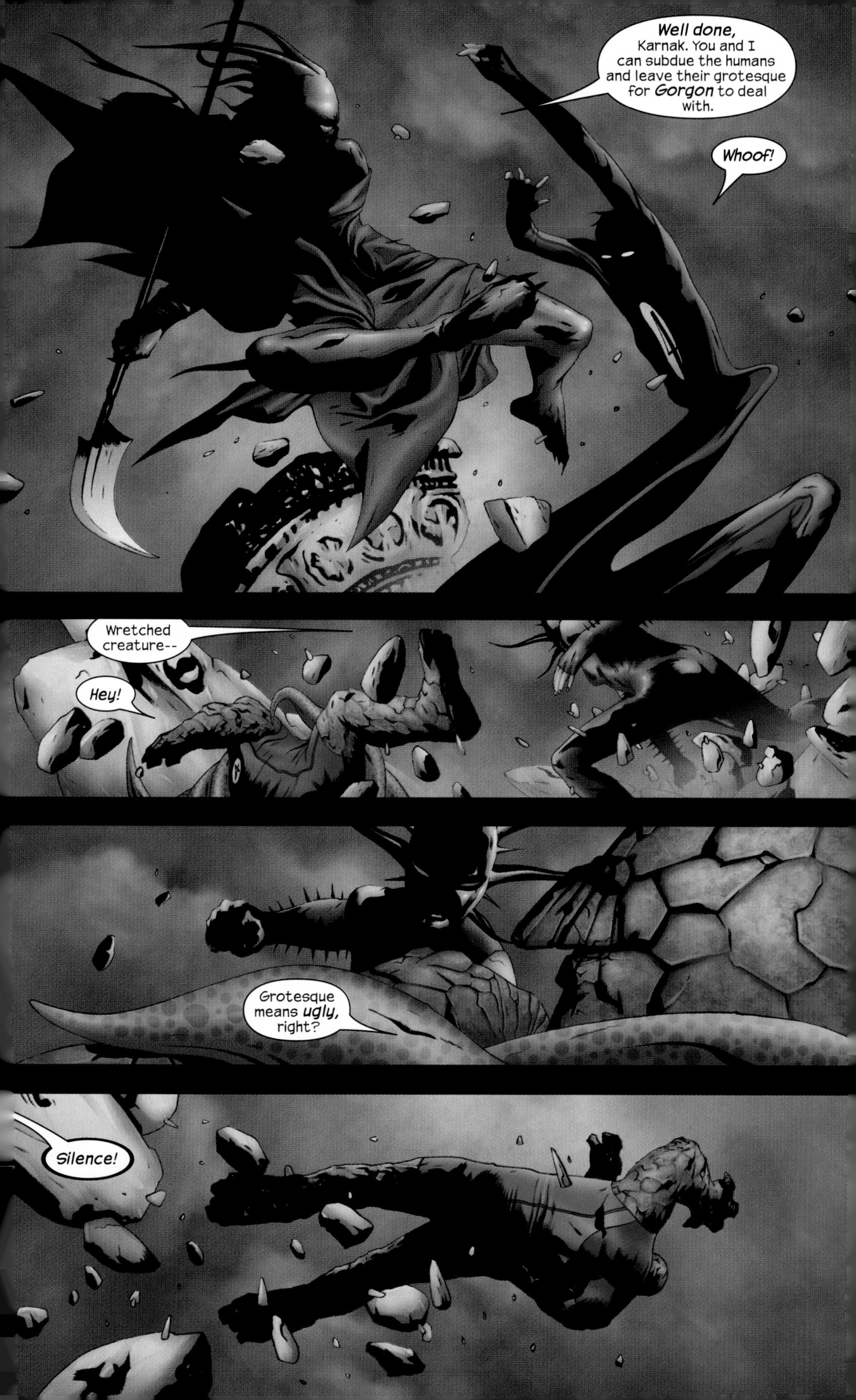

Well done, Karnak. You and I can subdue the humans and leave their grotesque for Gorgon to deal with.
Whoof!
Wretched creature--
Hey!
Grotesque means ugly, right?
Silence!

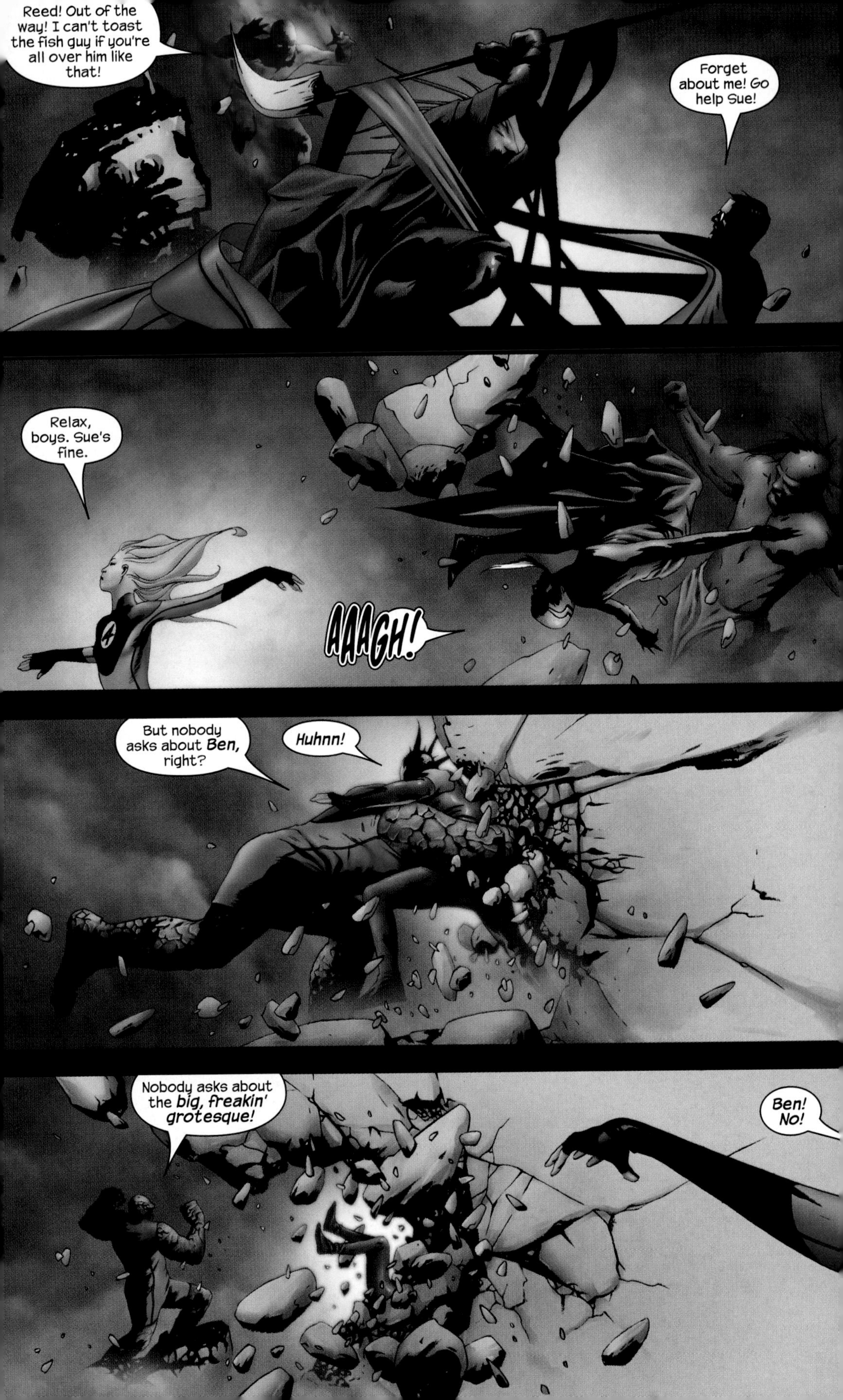

Reed! Out of the way! I can't toast the fish guy if you're all over him like that!
Forget about me! Go help Sue!
Relax, boys. Sue's fine.
AAAGH!
But nobody asks about Ben, right?
Huhnn!
Nobody asks about the big, freakin' grotesque!
Ben! No!

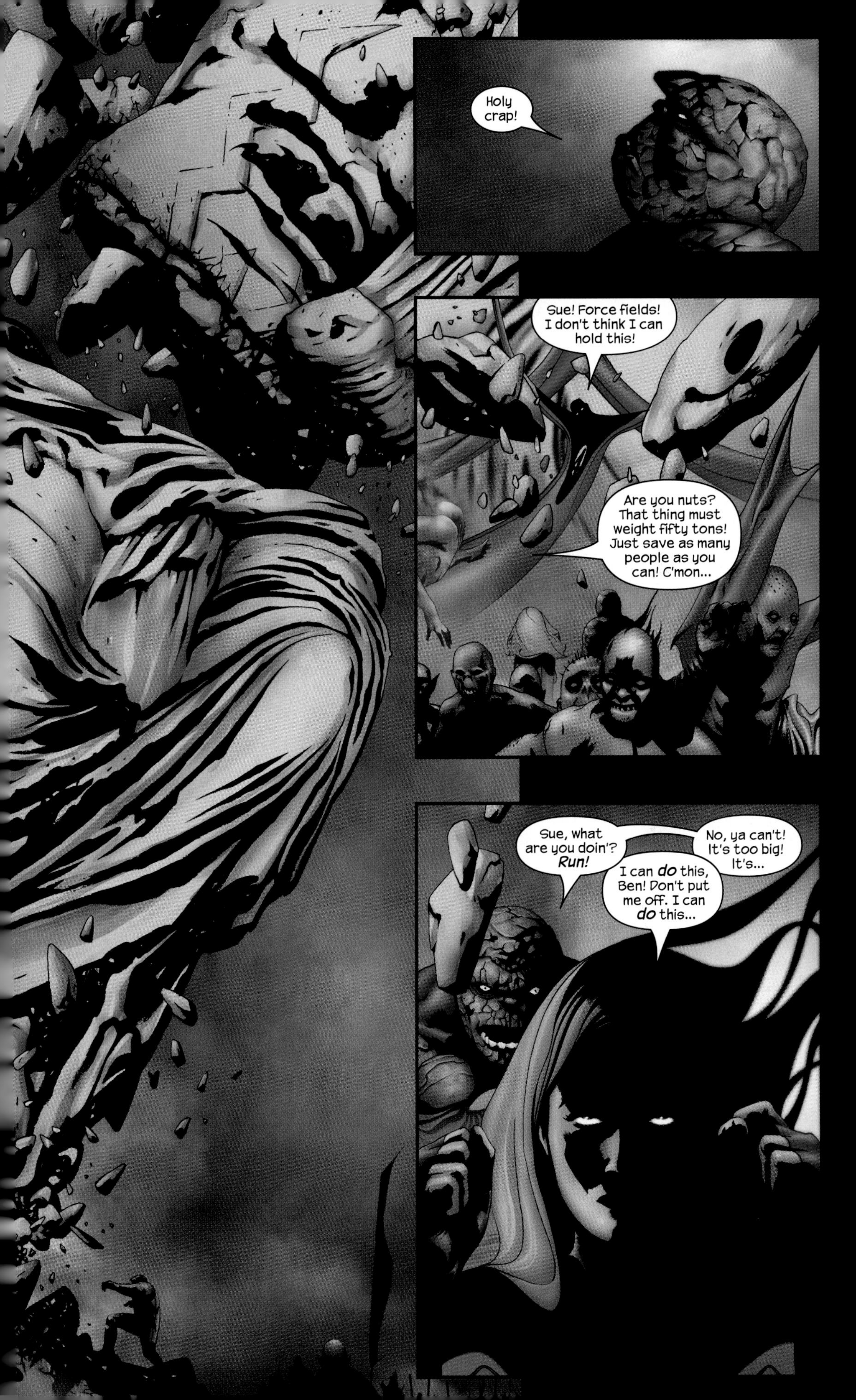
Holy crap!
Sue! Force fields! I don't think I can hold this!
Are you nuts? That thing must weight fifty tons! Just save as many people as you can! C'mon...
Sue, what are you doin'? Run!
I can do this, Ben! Don't put me off. I can do this...
No, ya can't! It's too big! It's...

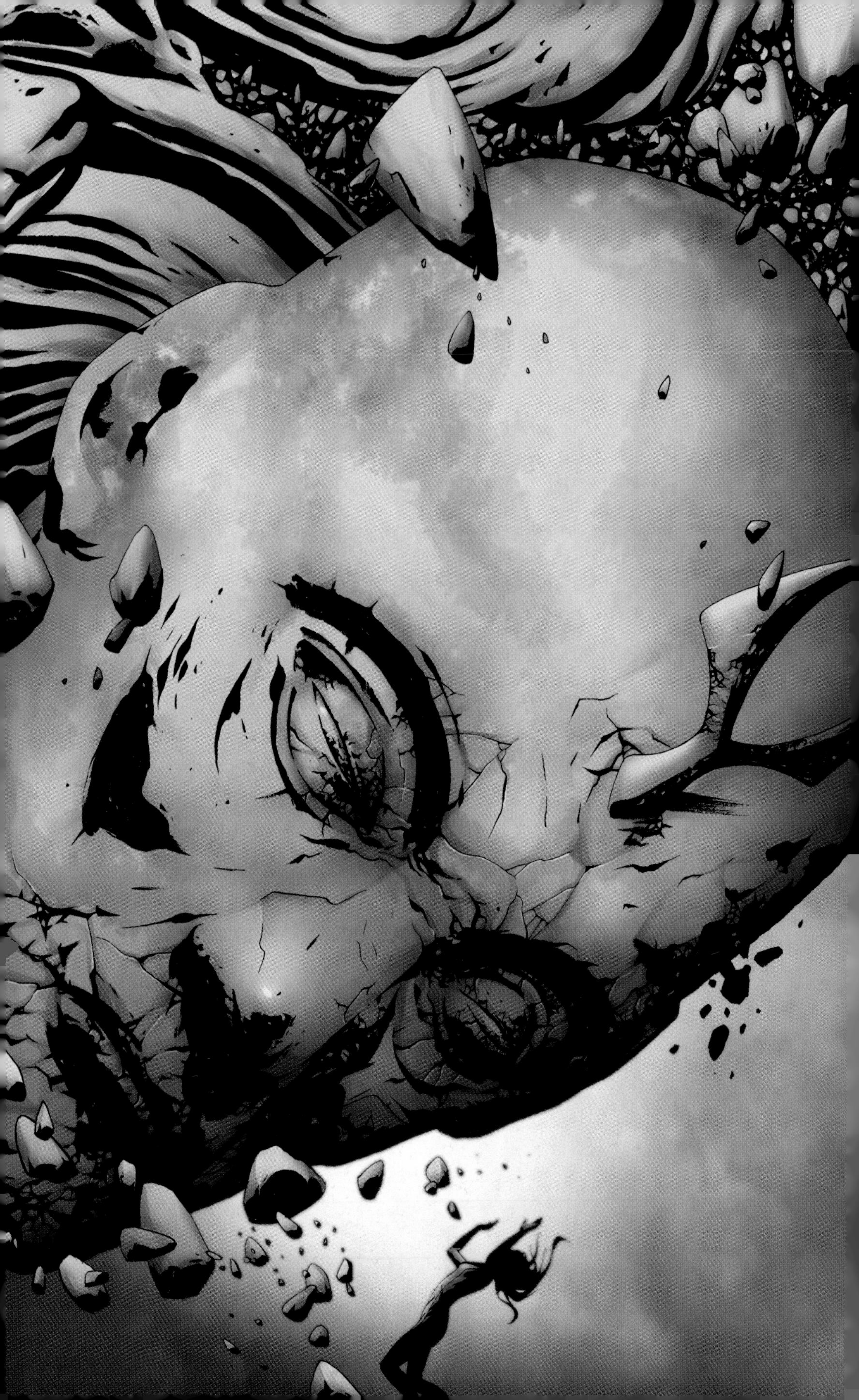

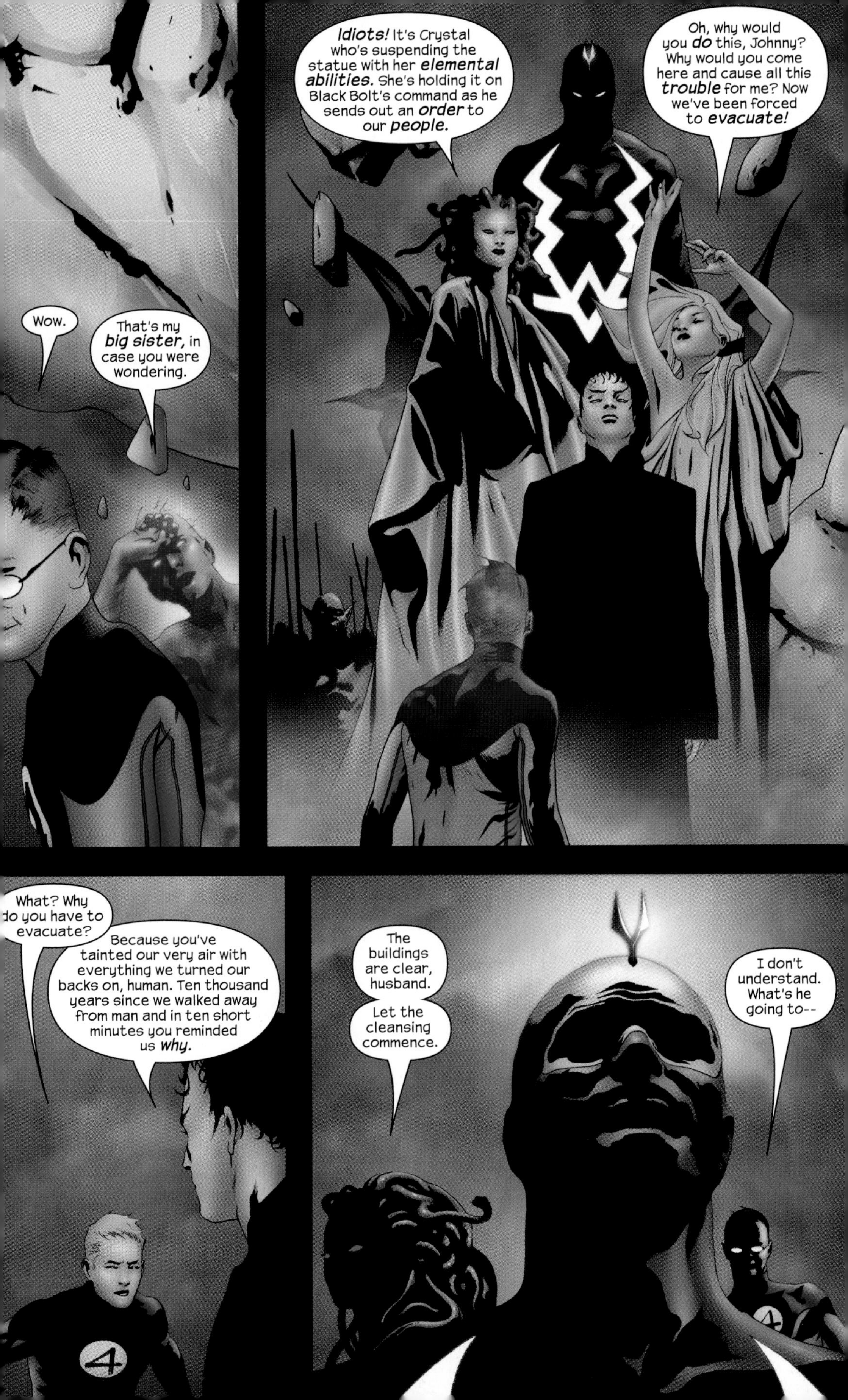
Wow.
That's my **big sister,** in case you were wondering.
Idiots! It's Crystal who's suspending the statue with her **elemental abilities.** She's holding it on Black Bolt's command as he sends out an **order** to our **people.**
Oh, why would you **do** this, Johnny? Why would you come here and cause all this **trouble** for me? Now we've been forced to **evacuate!**
What? Why do you have to evacuate?
Because you've tainted our very air with everything we turned our backs on, human. Ten thousand years since we walked away from man and in ten short minutes you reminded us **why.**
The buildings are clear, husband.
Let the cleansing commence.
I don't understand. What's he going to--

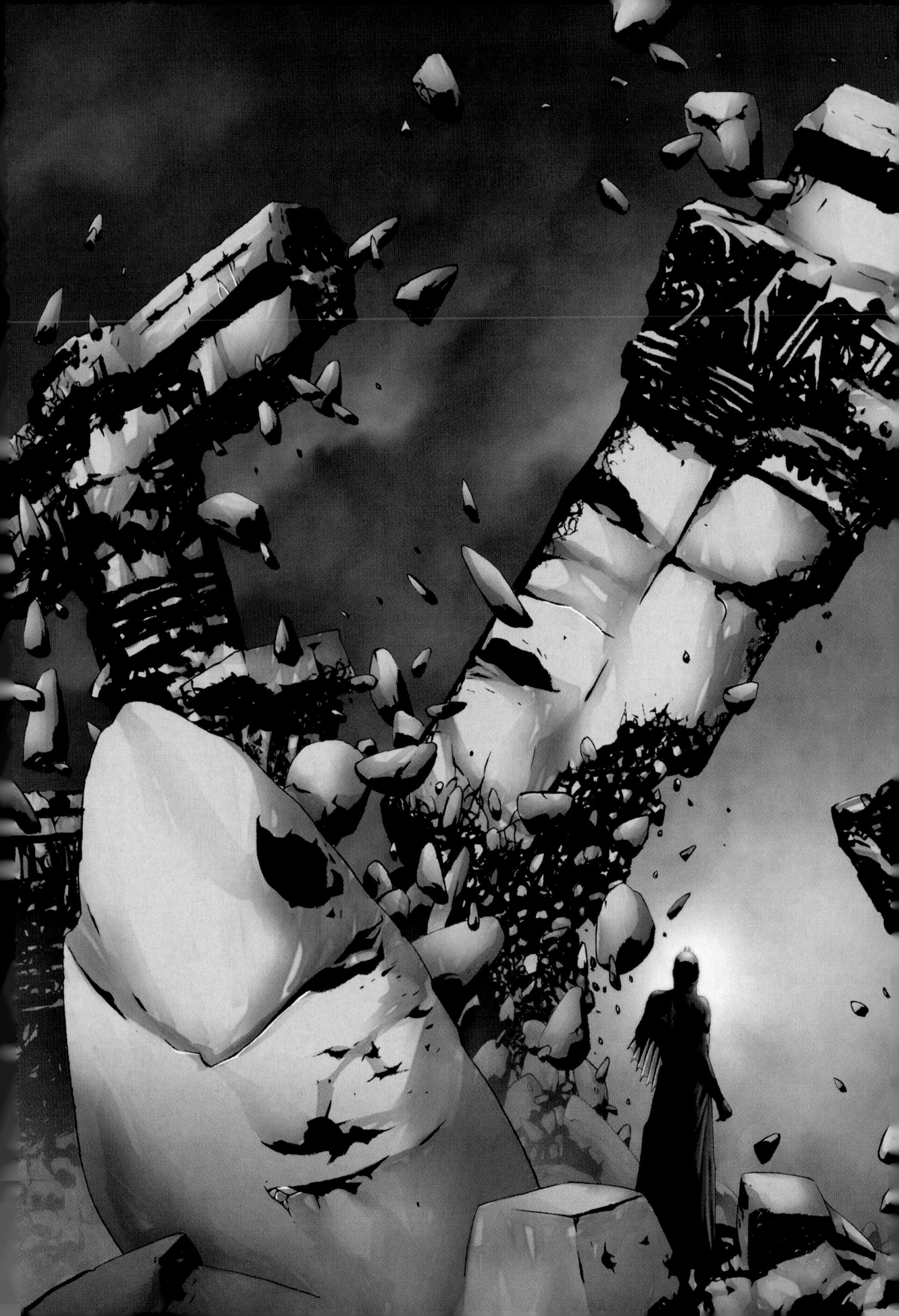

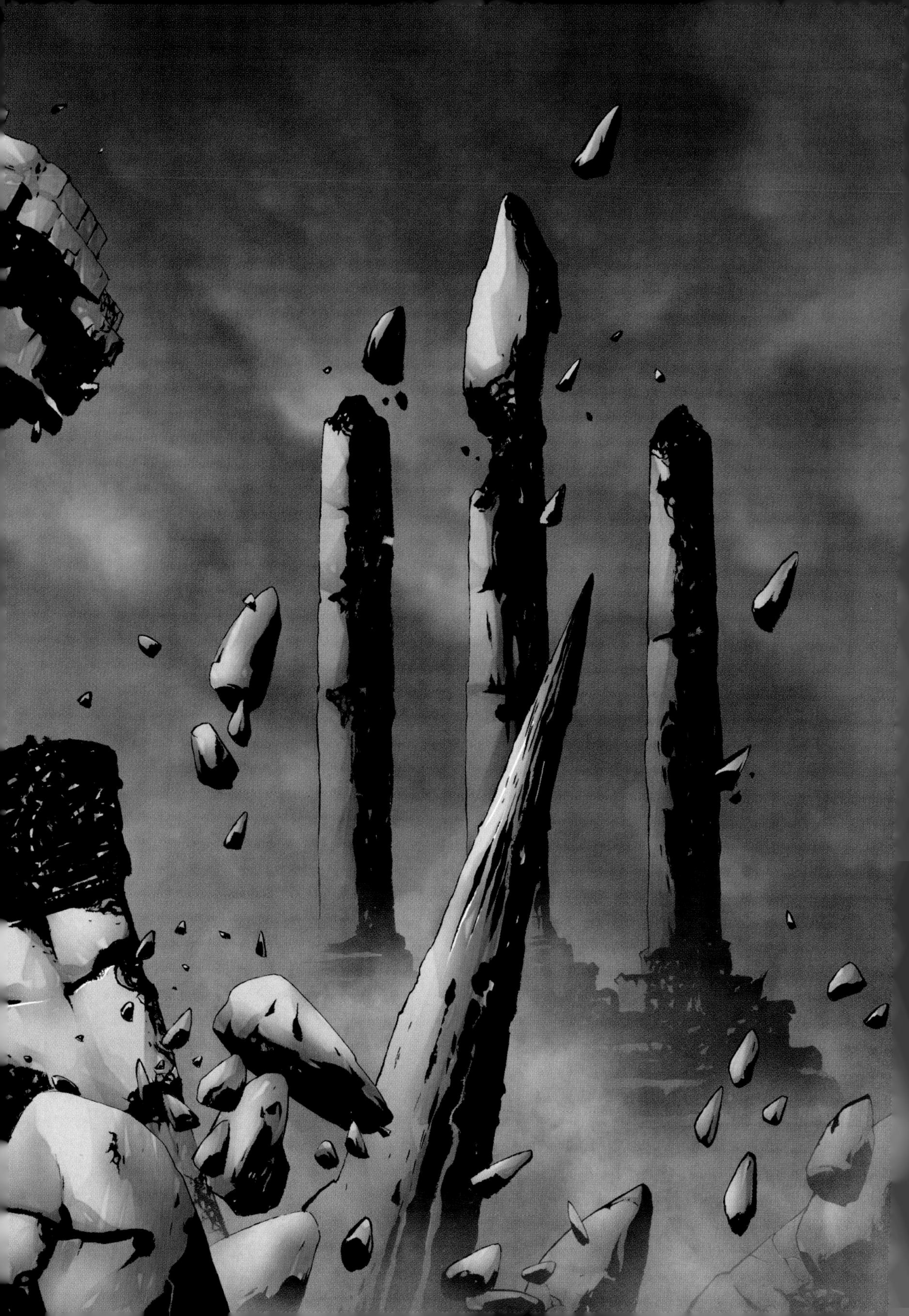

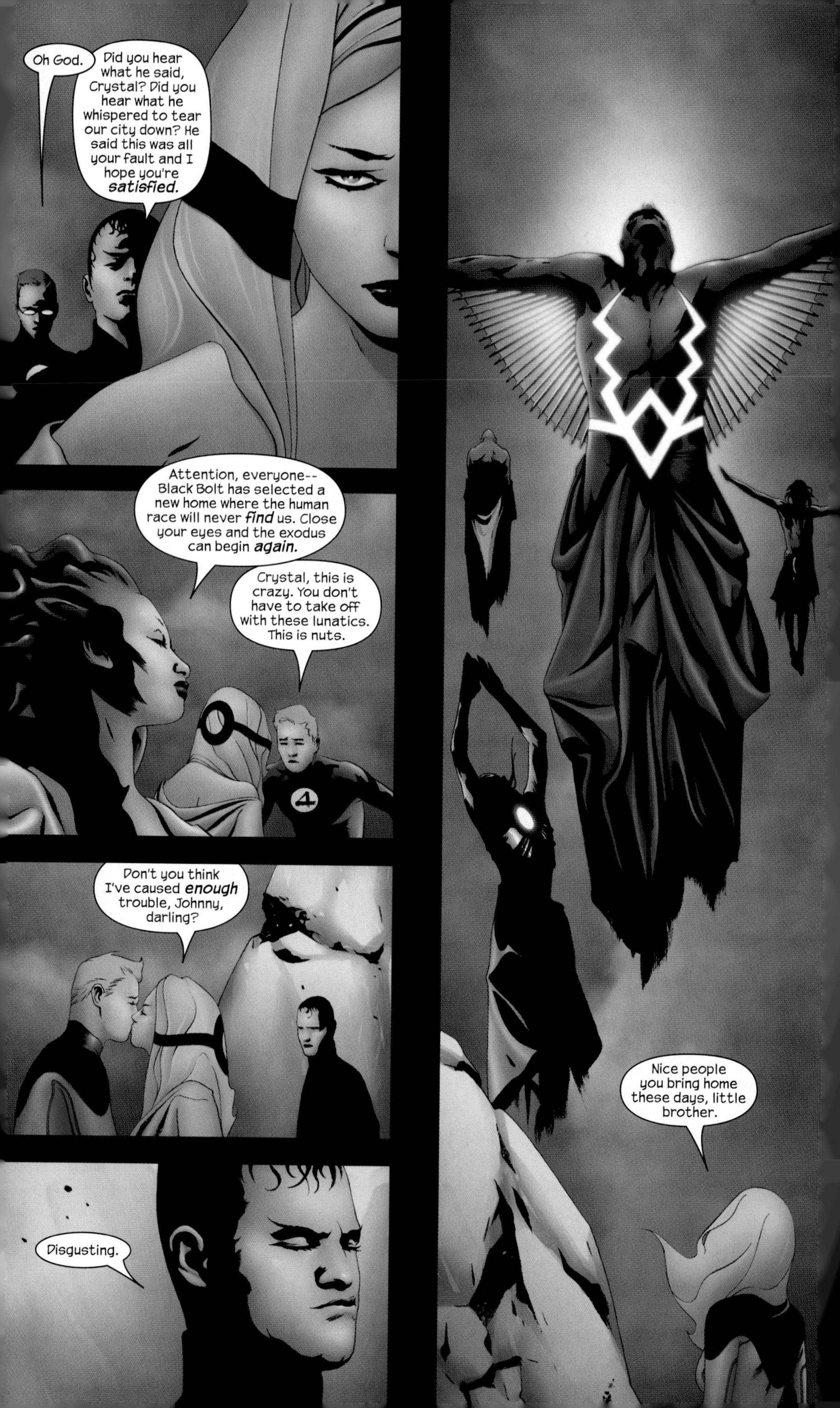
Oh God.
Did you hear what he said, Crystal? Did you hear what he whispered to tear our city down? He said this was all your fault and I hope you're *satisfied.*
Attention, everyone-- Black Bolt has selected a new home where the human race will never *find* us. Close your eyes and the exodus can begin *again.*
Crystal, this is crazy. You don't have to take off with these lunatics. This is nuts.
Don't you think I've caused *enough* trouble, Johnny, darling?
Disgusting.
Nice people you bring home these days, little brother.

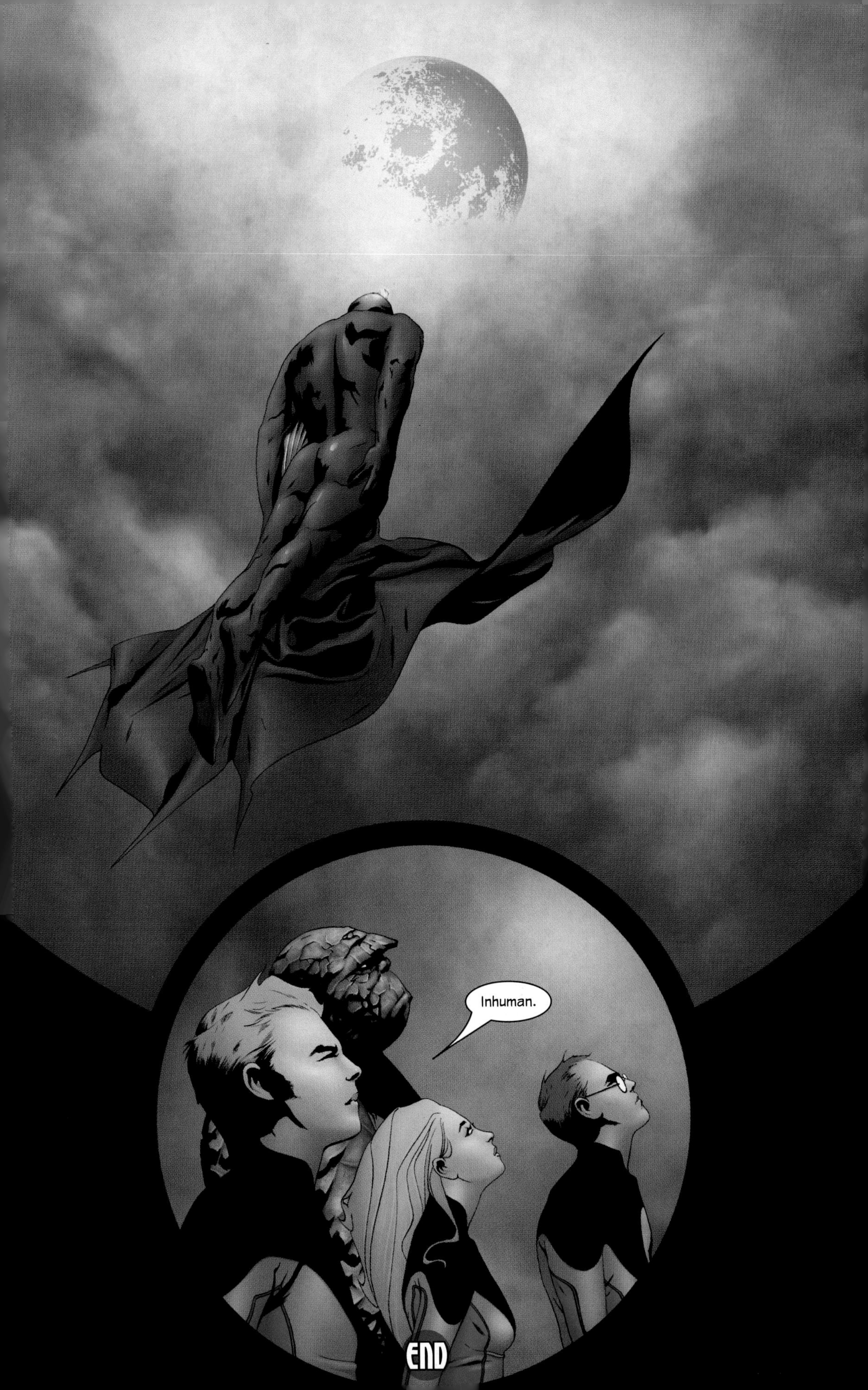
Inhuman.
END

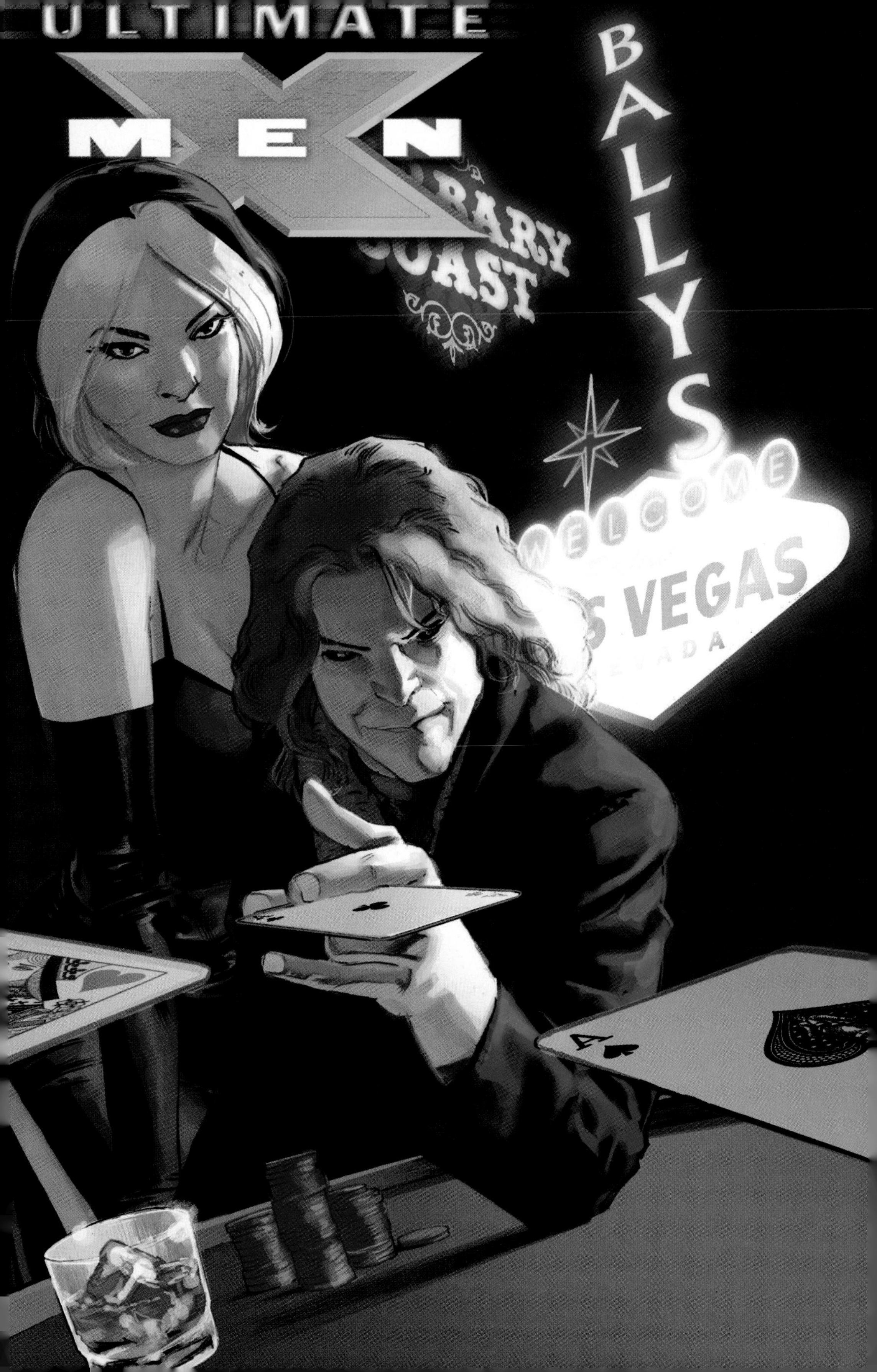
ULTIMATE
X-MEN
BALLYS
WELCOME
S VEGAS
ADA

PREVIOUSLY IN ULTIMATE X-MEN:

Born with strange and amazing abilities, the X-Men are young mutant heroes,
sworn to protect a world that fears and hates them.

One of their recent recruits is Rogue, a teenage girl and reformed acolyte of the mutant terrorist
Magneto. Forced to absorb the memories and abilities of whomever she touches, Rogue has
always had a difficult time getting close to others.

But after being manipulated by the billionaire industrialists known as fenris, Rogue decided to run
off with a dashing mutant thief named Gambit, who convinced the young woman to leave her
teammates and pursue her own destiny.

Congratulations,
X-Men.

You have the
honor of being
escorted into
oblivion by none
other than... the
Green Goblin.

ULTIMATE SACRIFICE

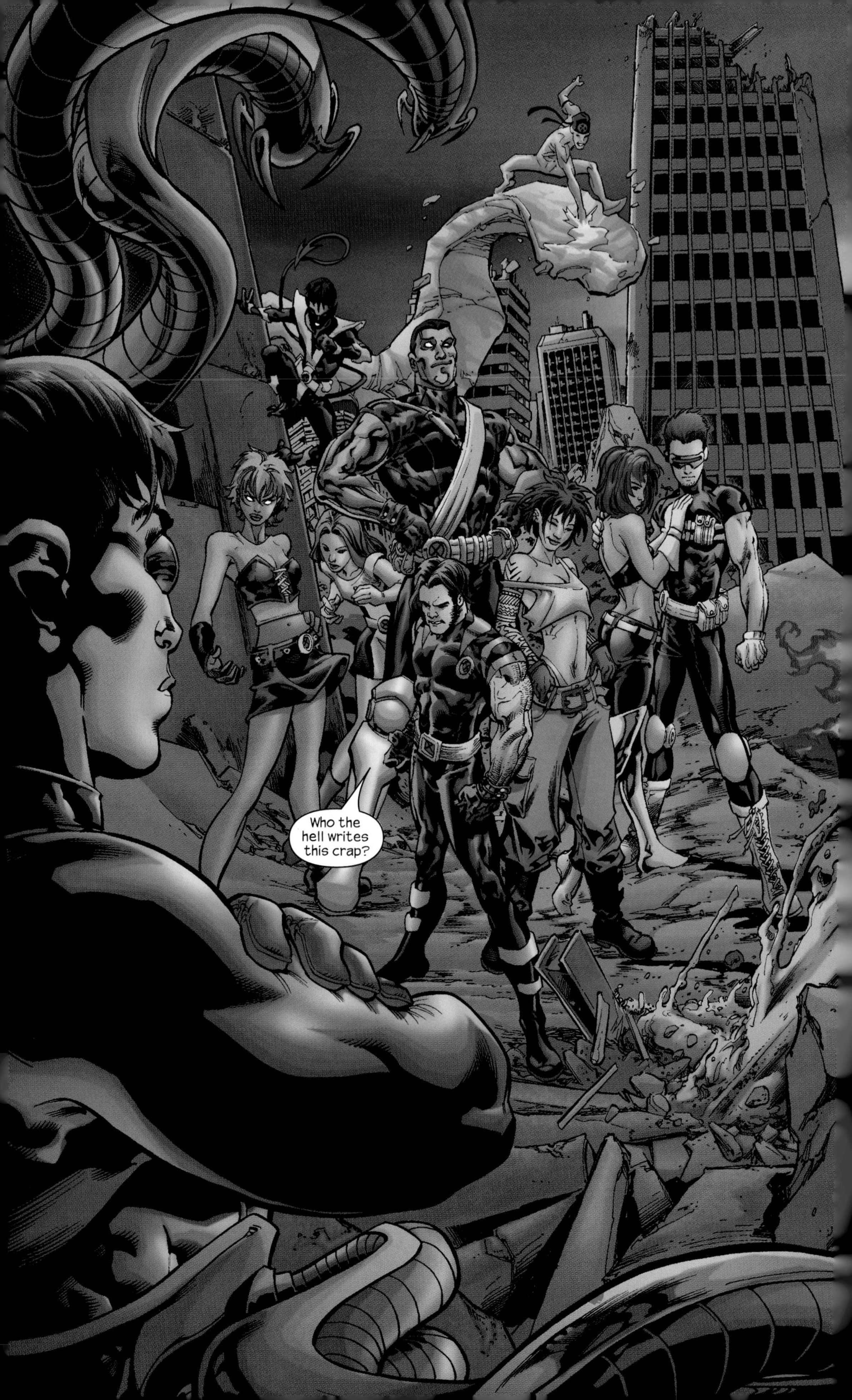
Who the hell writes this crap?

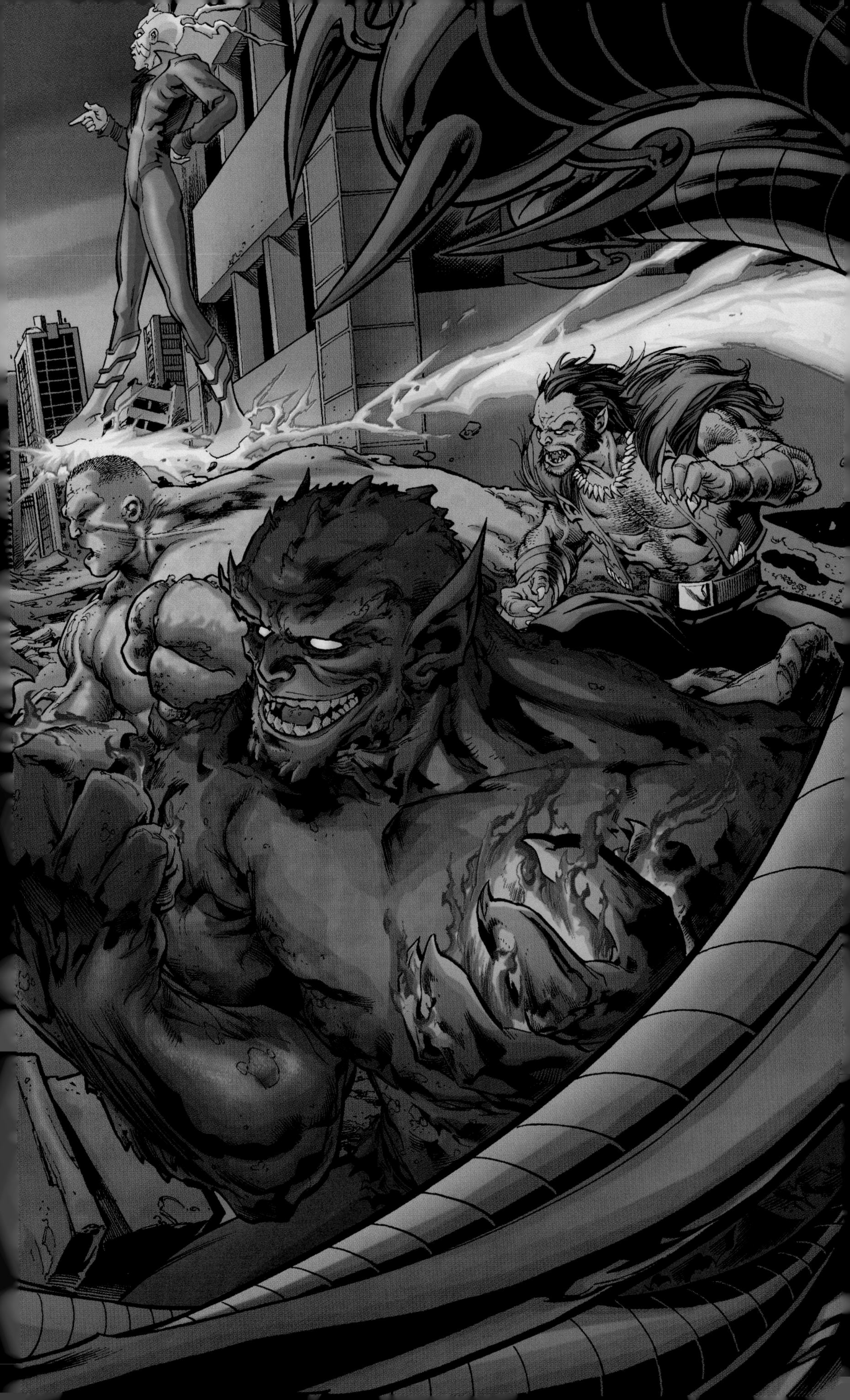

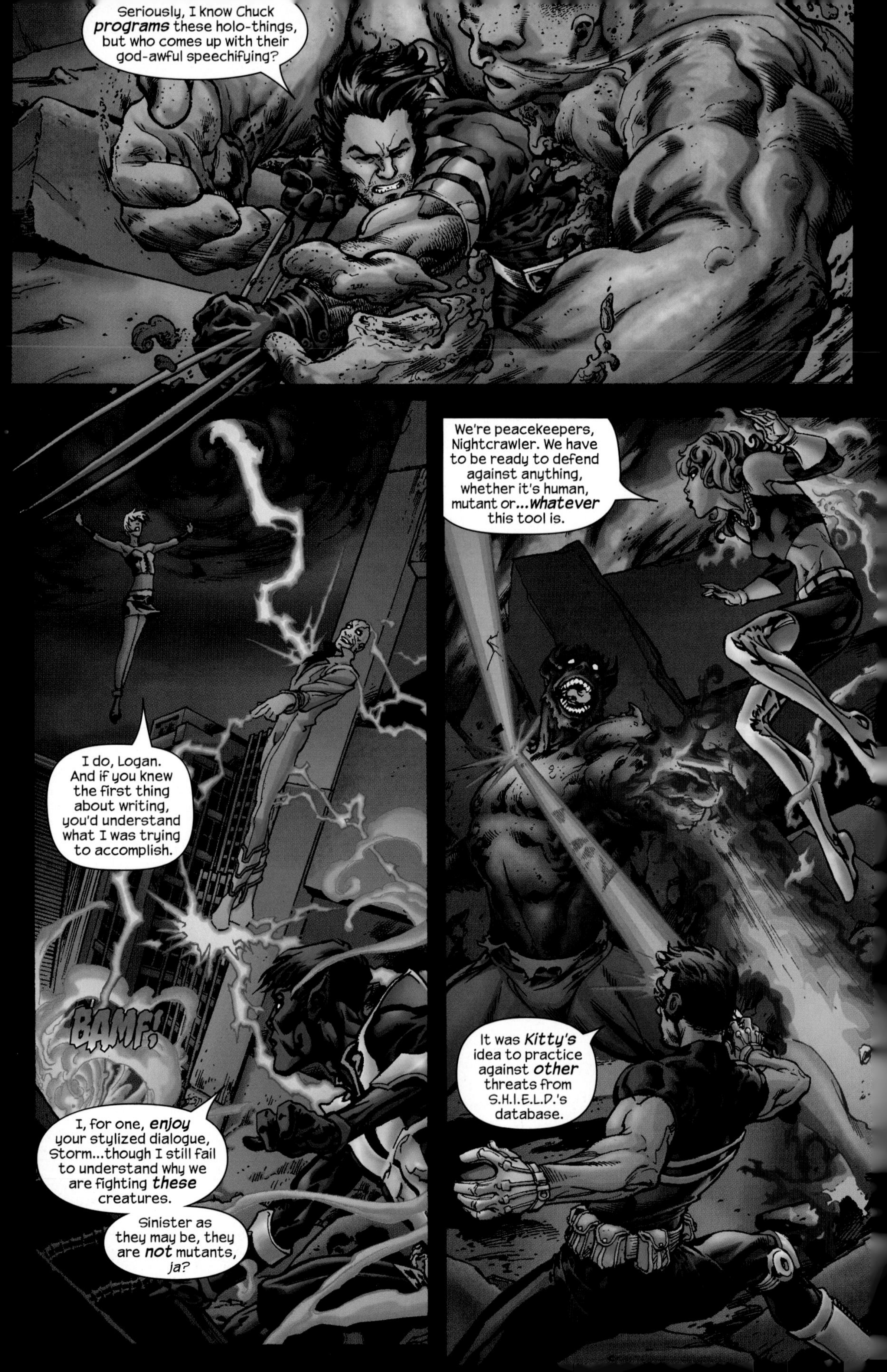

Seriously, I know Chuck **programs** these holo-things, but who comes up with their god-awful speechifying?
I do, Logan. And if you knew the first thing about writing, you'd understand what I was trying to accomplish.
BAMF!
I, for one, **enjoy** your stylized dialogue, Storm...though I still fail to understand why we are fighting **these** creatures.
Sinister as they may be, they are **not** mutants, *ja?*
We're peacekeepers, Nightcrawler. We have to be ready to defend against anything, whether it's human, mutant or...**whatever** this tool is.
It was **Kitty's** idea to practice against **other** threats from S.H.I.E.L.D.'s database.

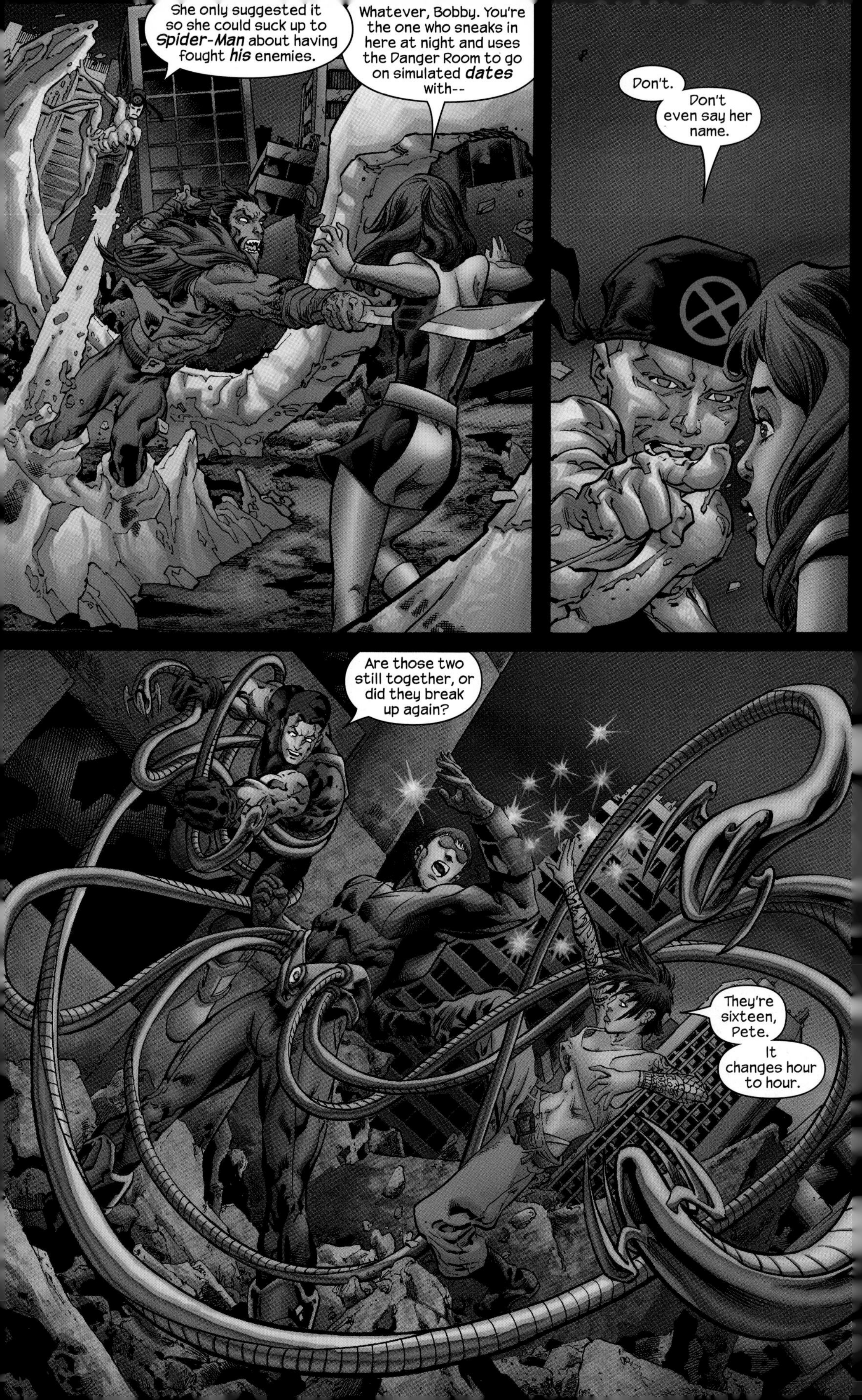
She only suggested it so she could suck up to Spider-Man about having fought his enemies.
Whatever, Bobby. You're the one who sneaks in here at night and uses the Danger Room to go on simulated dates with--
Don't.
Don't even say her name.
Are those two still together, or did they break up again?
They're sixteen, Pete.
It changes hour to hour.

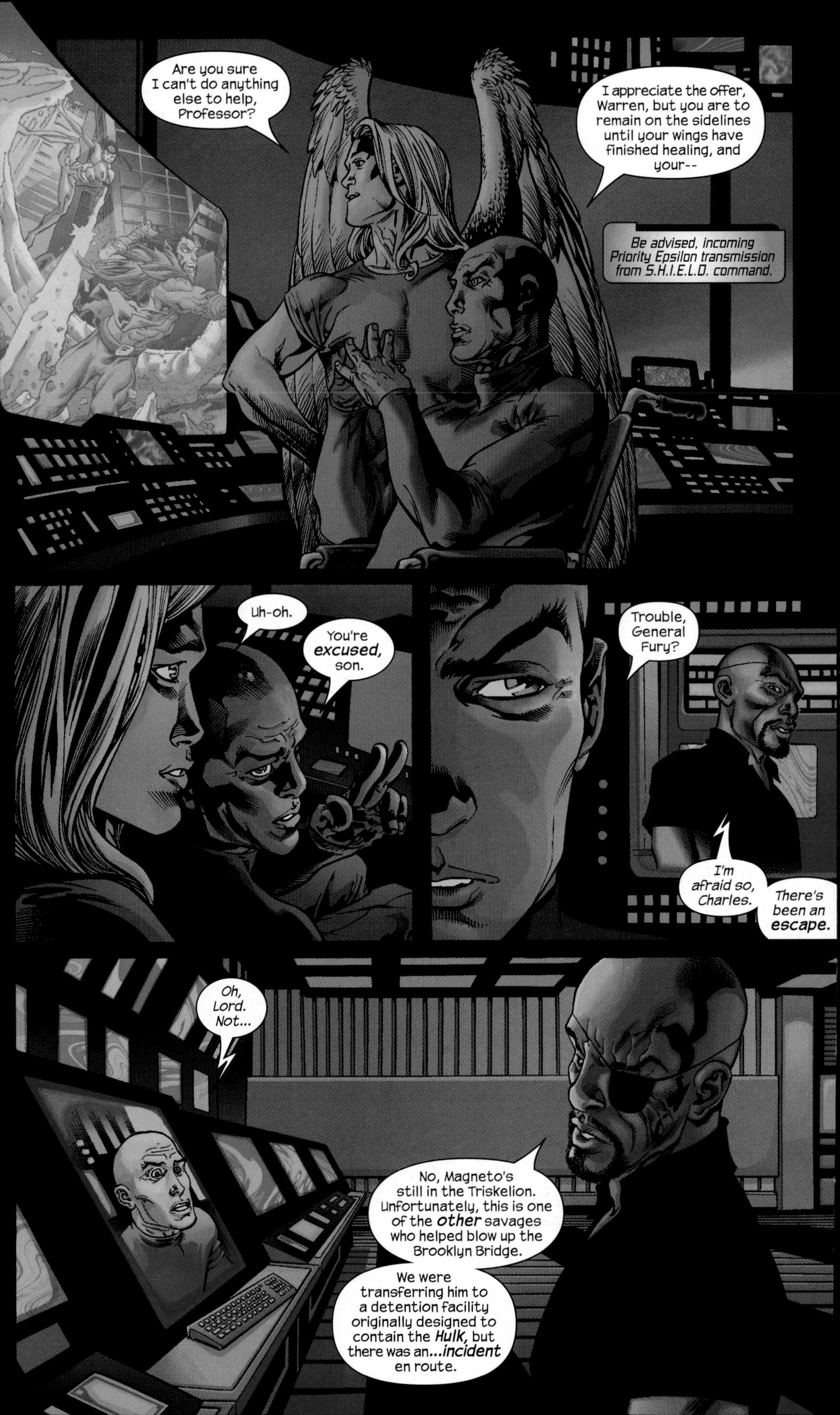
Are you sure I can't do anything else to help, Professor?
I appreciate the offer, Warren, but you are to remain on the sidelines until your wings have finished healing, and your--
Be advised, incoming Priority Epsilon transmission from S.H.I.E.L.D. command.
Uh-oh.
You're *excused,* son.
Trouble, General Fury?
I'm afraid so, Charles.
There's been an **escape.**
Oh, Lord. Not...
No, Magneto's still in the Triskelion. Unfortunately, this is one of the *other* savages who helped blow up the Brooklyn Bridge.
We were transferring him to a detention facility originally designed to contain the *Hulk,* but there was an...*incident* en route.

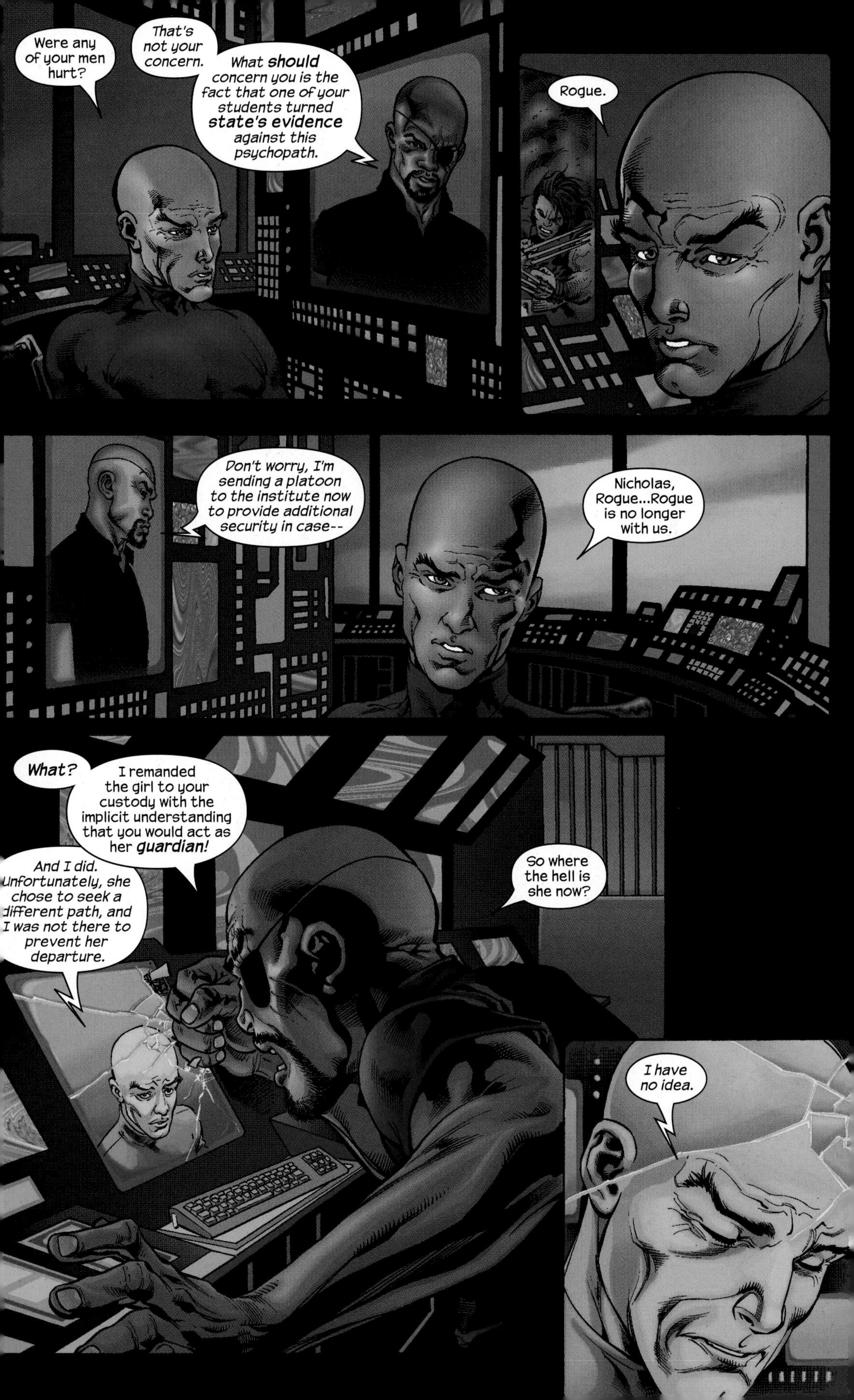

Were any of your men hurt?
That's not your concern.
What **should** concern you is the fact that one of your students turned **state's evidence** against this psychopath.
Rogue.
Don't worry, I'm sending a platoon to the institute now to provide additional security in case--
Nicholas, Rogue...Rogue is no longer with us.
What?
I remanded the girl to your custody with the implicit understanding that you would act as her **guardian!**
And I did. Unfortunately, she chose to seek a different path, and I was not there to prevent her departure.
So where the hell is she now?
I have no idea.

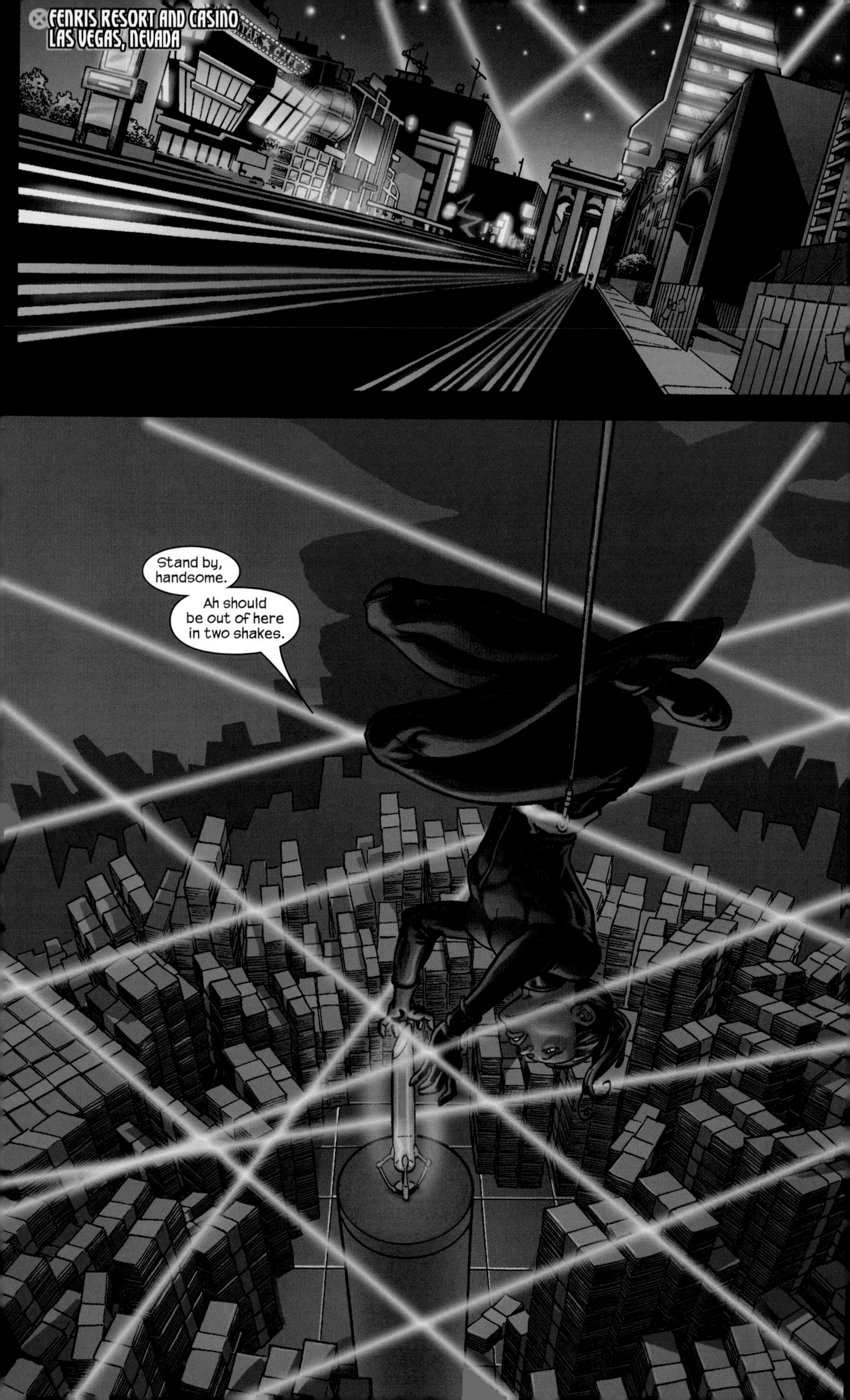
FENRIS RESORT AND CASINO
LAS VEGAS, NEVADA
Stand by, handsome.
Ah should be out of here in two shakes.

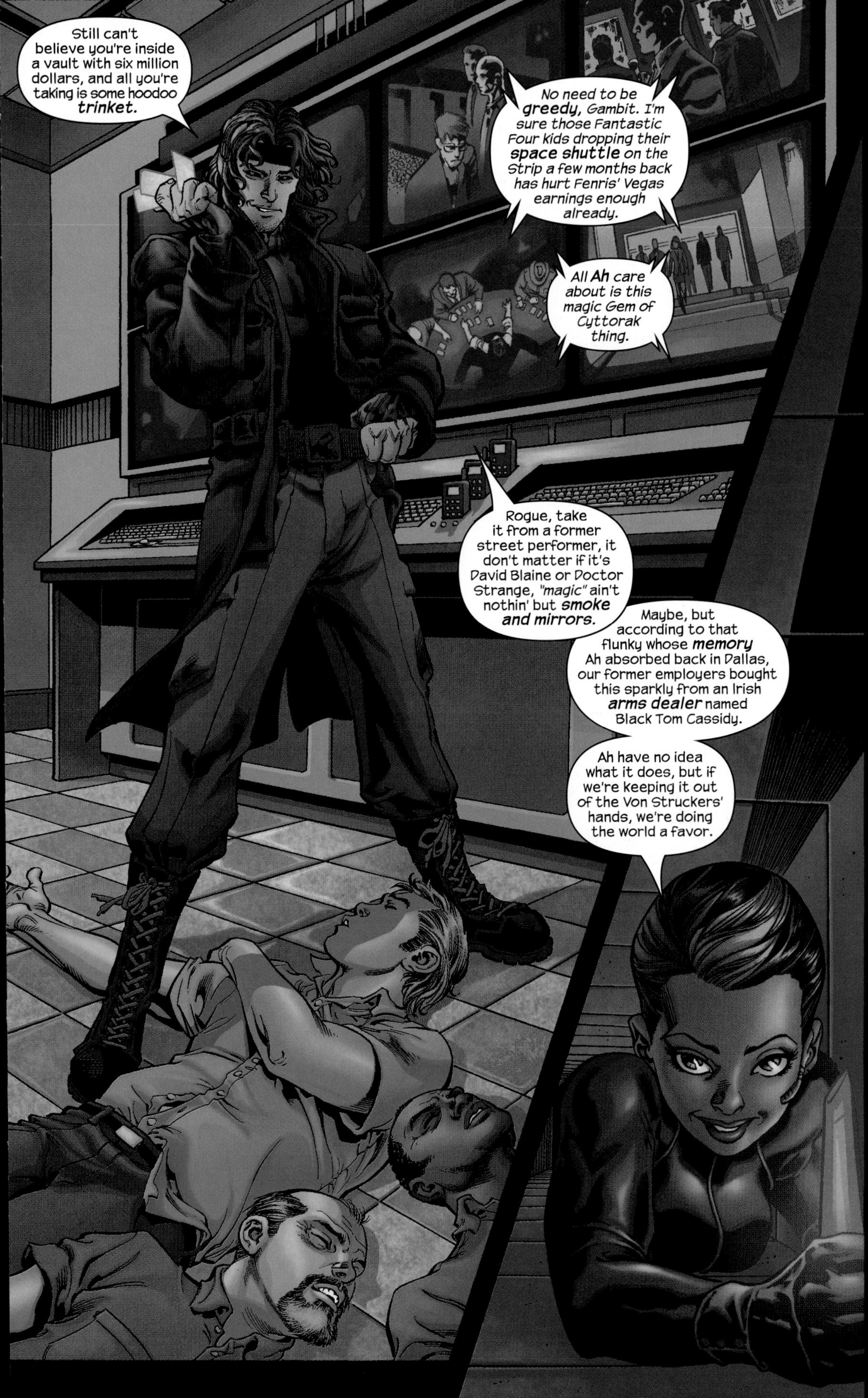
Still can't believe you're inside a vault with six million dollars, and all you're taking is some hoodoo trinket.
No need to be greedy, Gambit. I'm sure those Fantastic Four kids dropping their space shuttle on the Strip a few months back has hurt Fenris' Vegas earnings enough already.
All Ah care about is this magic Gem of Cyttorak thing.
Rogue, take it from a former street performer, it don't matter if it's David Blaine or Doctor Strange, "magic" ain't nothin' but smoke and mirrors.
Maybe, but according to that flunky whose memory Ah absorbed back in Dallas, our former employers bought this sparkly from an Irish arms dealer named Black Tom Cassidy.
Ah have no idea what it does, but if we're keeping it out of the Von Struckers' hands, we're doing the world a favor.

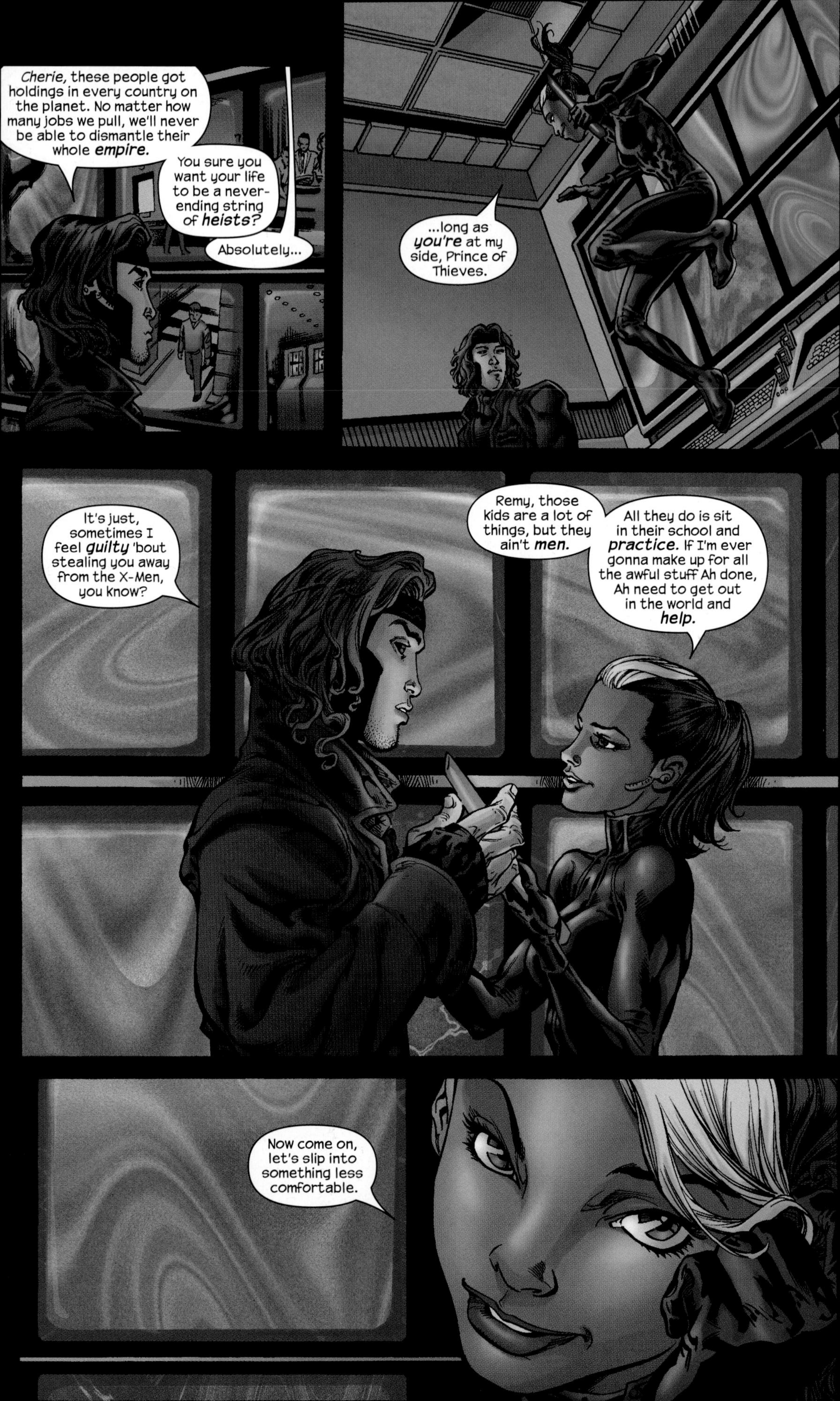
Cherie, these people got holdings in every country on the planet. No matter how many jobs we pull, we'll never be able to dismantle their whole empire.
You sure you want your life to be a never-ending string of heists?
Absolutely...
...long as you're at my side, Prince of Thieves.
It's just, sometimes I feel guilty 'bout stealing you away from the X-Men, you know?
Remy, those kids are a lot of things, but they ain't men.
All they do is sit in their school and practice. If I'm ever gonna make up for all the awful stuff Ah done, Ah need to get out in the world and help.
Now come on, let's slip into something less comfortable.

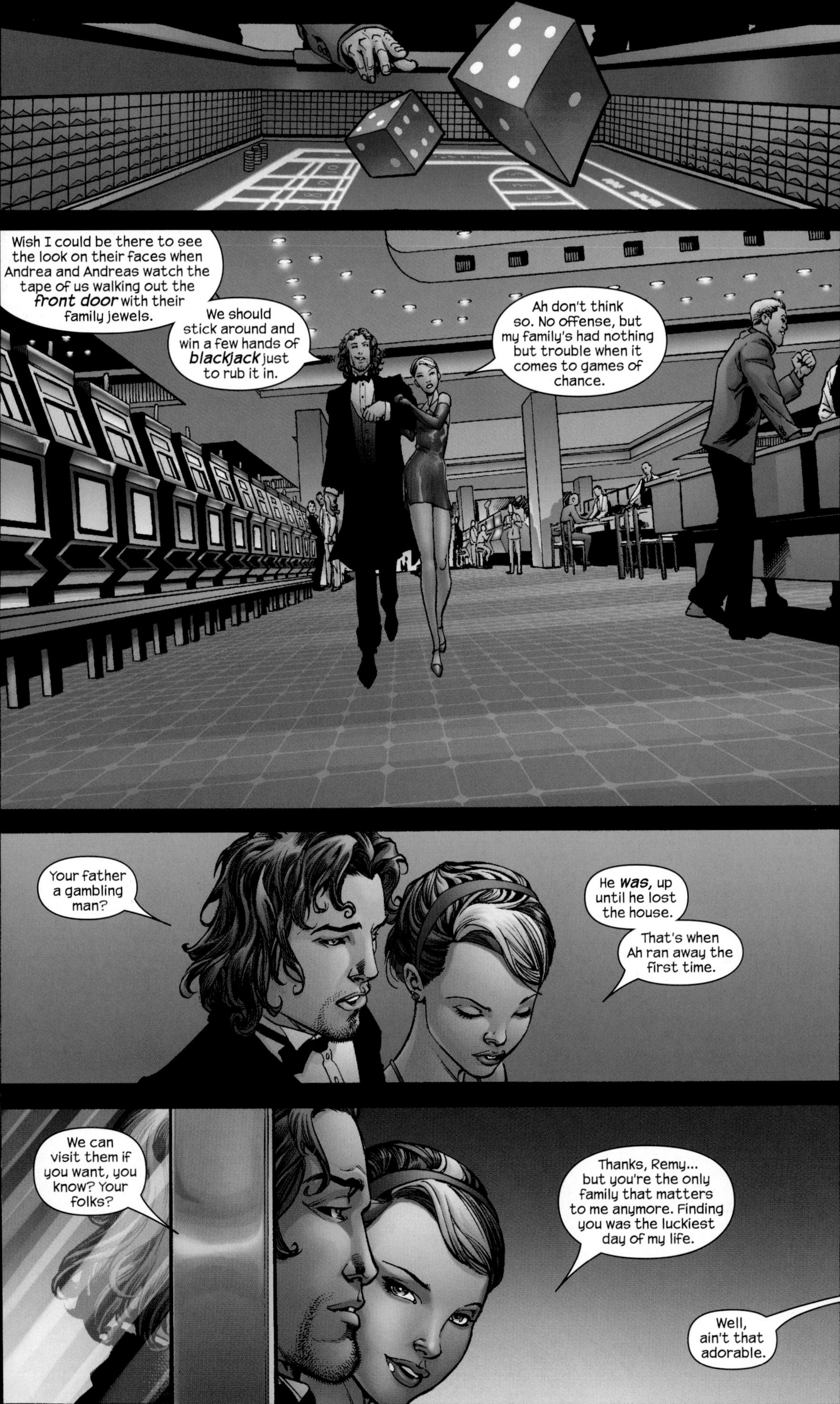

Wish I could be there to see the look on their faces when Andrea and Andreas watch the tape of us walking out the *front door* with their family jewels.
We should stick around and win a few hands of *blackjack* just to rub it in.
Ah don't think so. No offense, but my family's had nothing but trouble when it comes to games of chance.
Your father a gambling man?
He *was,* up until he lost the house.
That's when Ah ran away the first time.
We can visit them if you want, you know? Your folks?
Thanks, Remy... but you're the only family that matters to me anymore. Finding you was the luckiest day of my life.
Well, ain't that adorable.

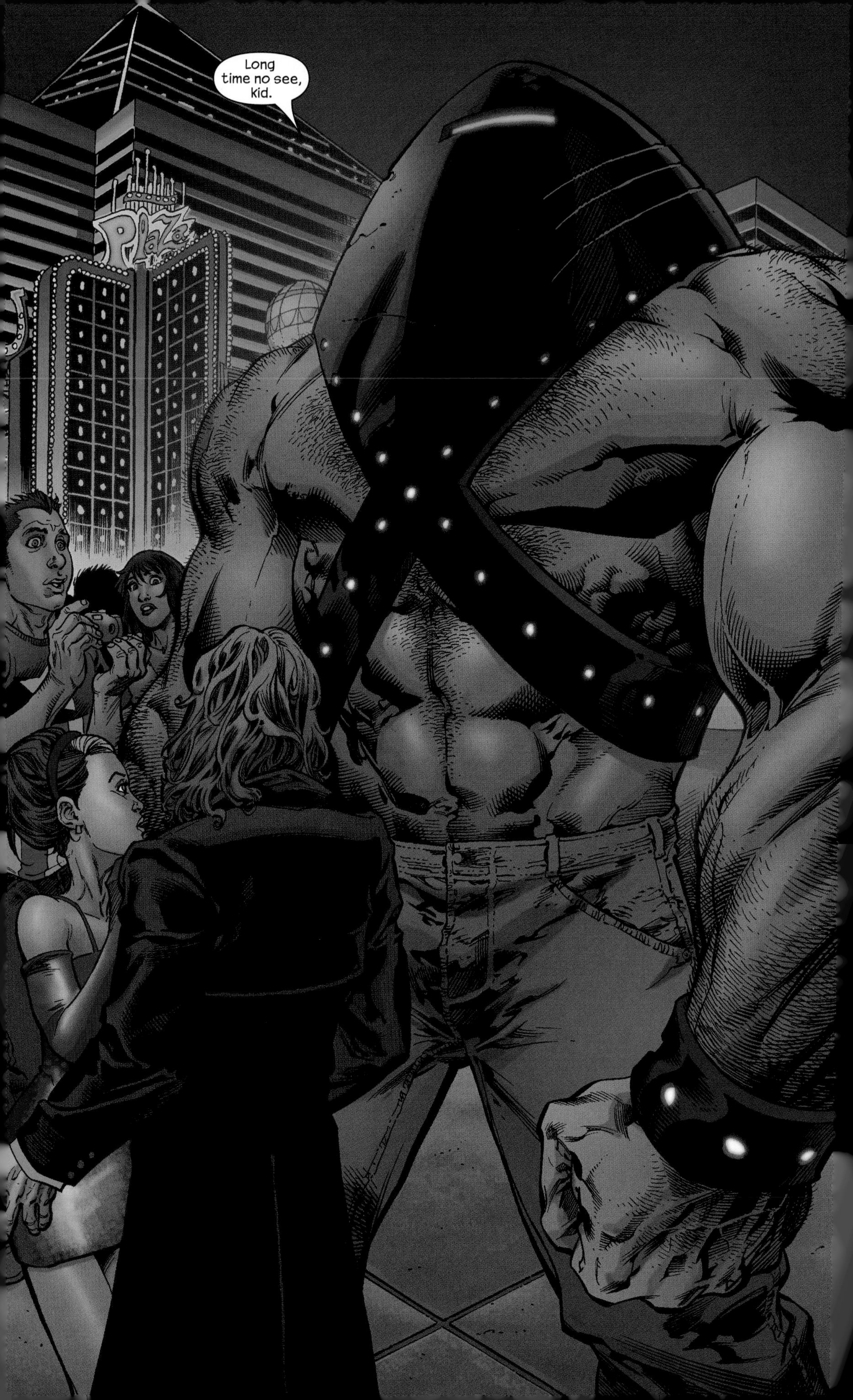
Long time no see, kid.

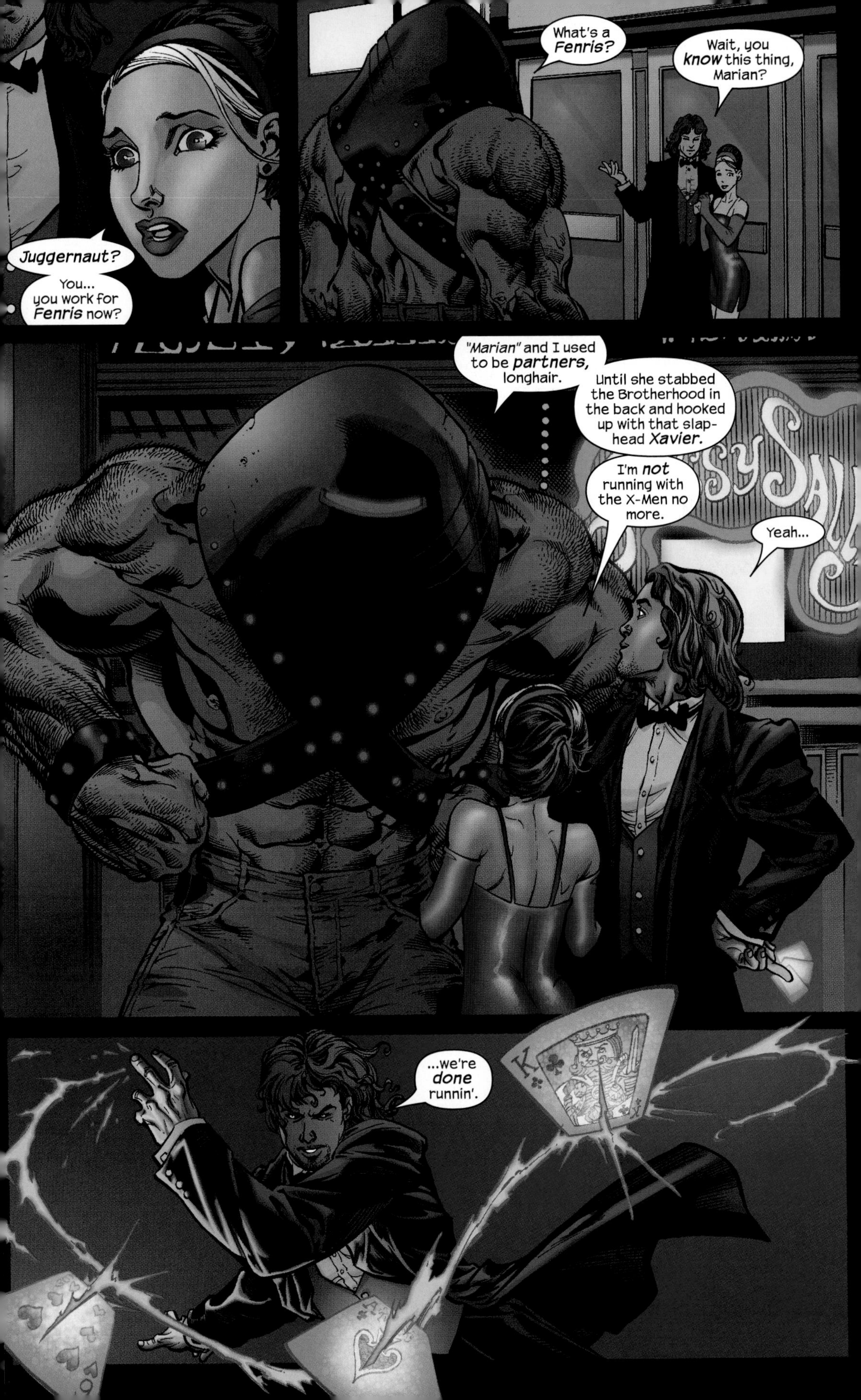
Juggernaut?
You... you work for *Fenris* now?
What's a *Fenris?*
Wait, you *know* this thing, Marian?
"Marian" and I used to be *partners,* longhair.
Until she stabbed the Brotherhood in the back and hooked up with that slap-head *Xavier.*
I'm *not* running with the X-Men no more.
Yeah...
...we're *done* runnin'.

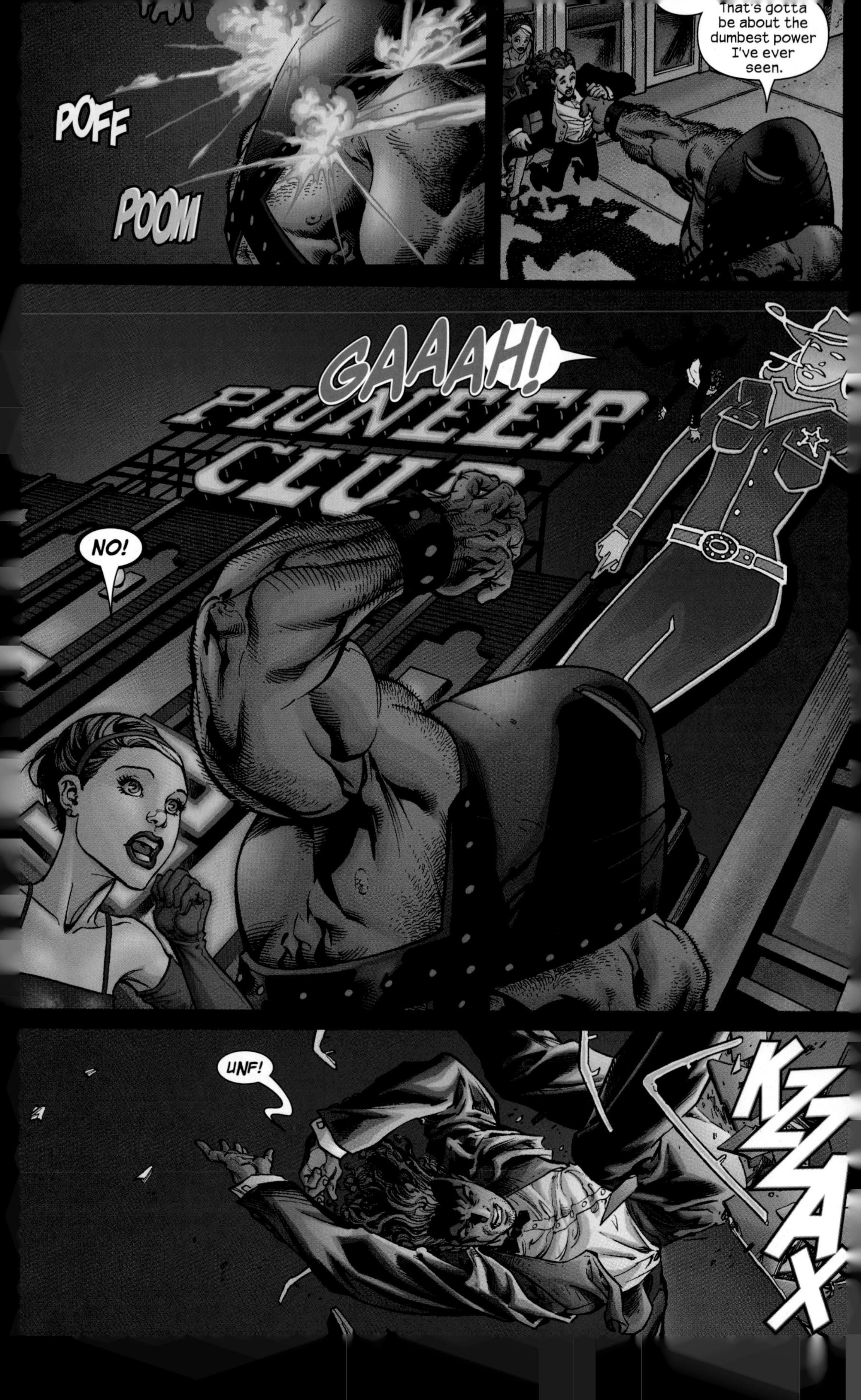
POFF
POOM
That's gotta be about the dumbest power I've ever seen.
GAAAH!
NO!
UNF!
KZZAX

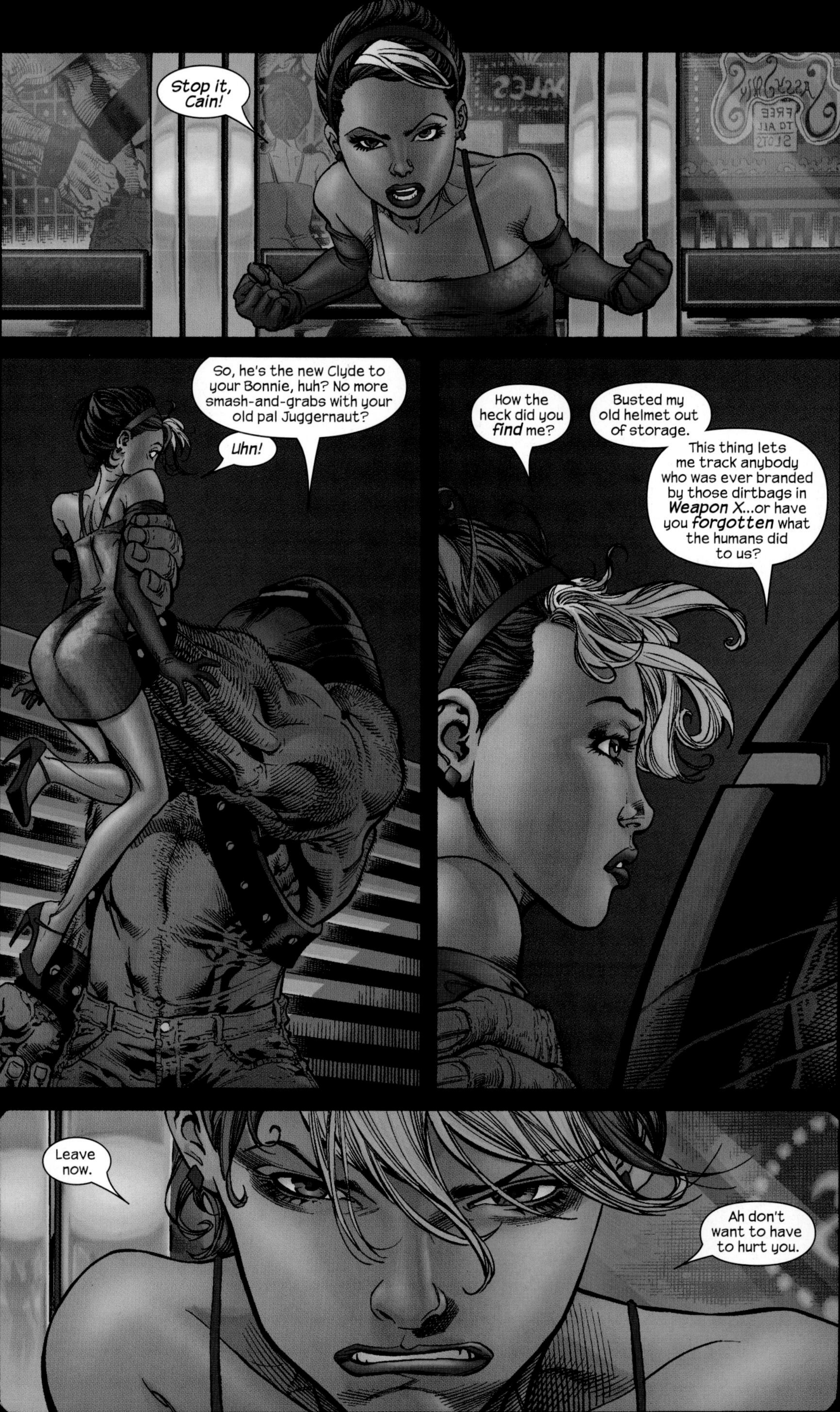
Stop it, Cain!
So, he's the new Clyde to your Bonnie, huh? No more smash-and-grabs with your old pal Juggernaut?
Uhn!
How the heck did you find me?
Busted my old helmet out of storage.
This thing lets me track anybody who was ever branded by those dirtbags in Weapon X...or have you forgotten what the humans did to us?
Leave now.
Ah don't want to have to hurt you.

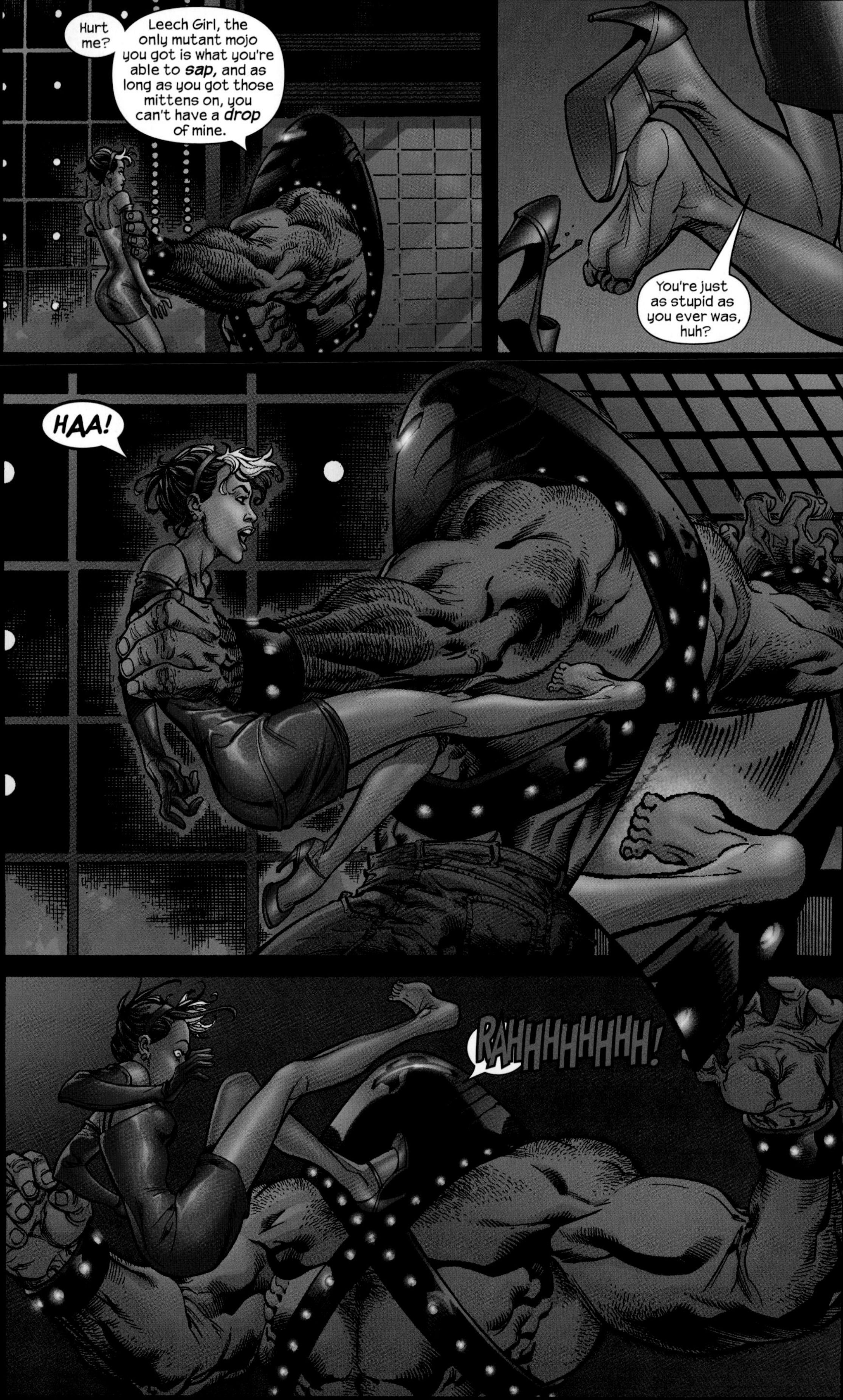
Hurt me?
Leech Girl, the only mutant mojo you got is what you're able to *sap*, and as long as you got those mittens on, you can't have a *drop* of mine.
You're just as stupid as you ever was, huh?
HAA!
RAHHHHHHHH!

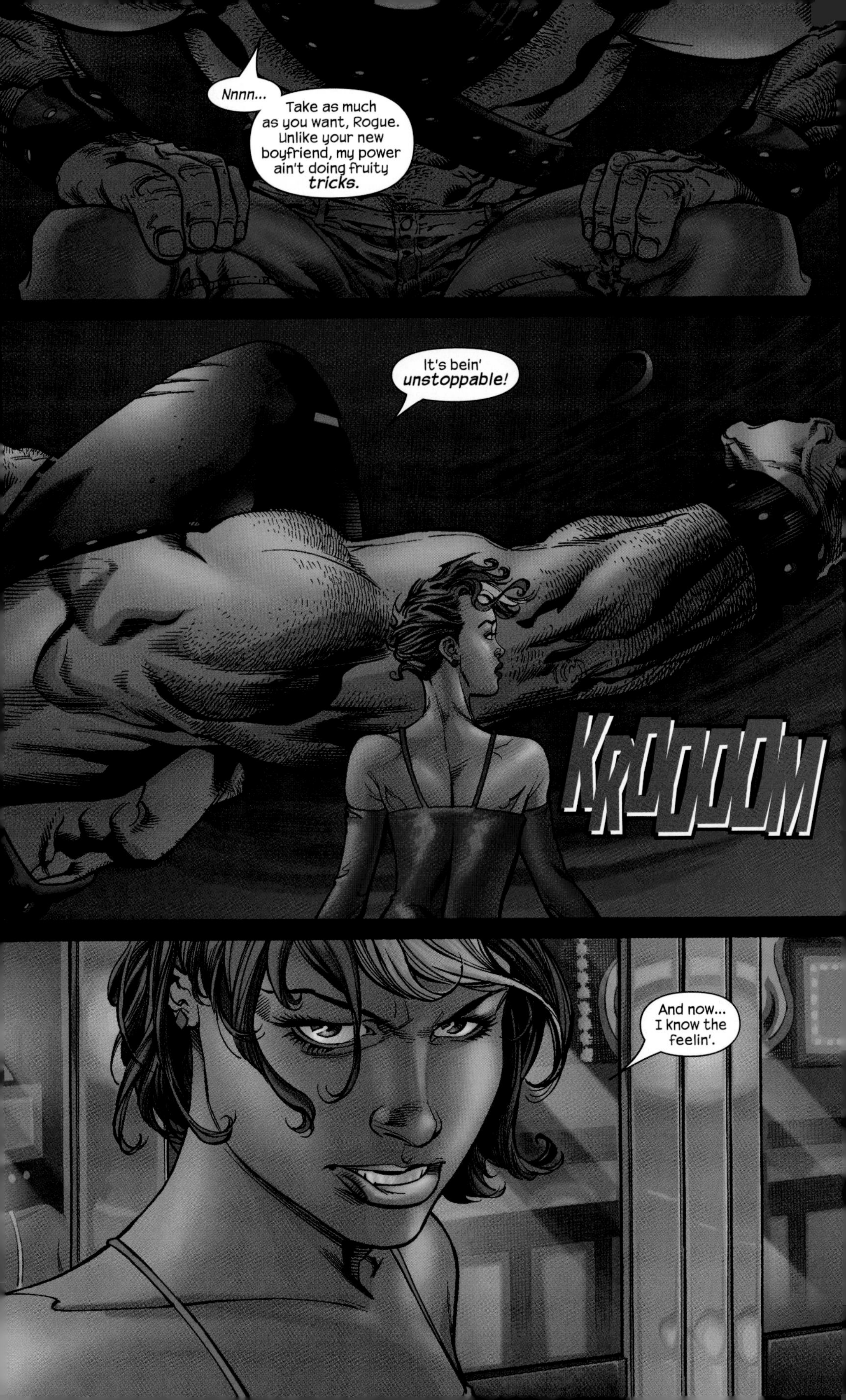
Nnnn... Take as much as you want, Rogue. Unlike your new boyfriend, my power ain't doing fruity tricks.
It's bein' unstoppable!
KROOOOM
And now... I know the feelin'.

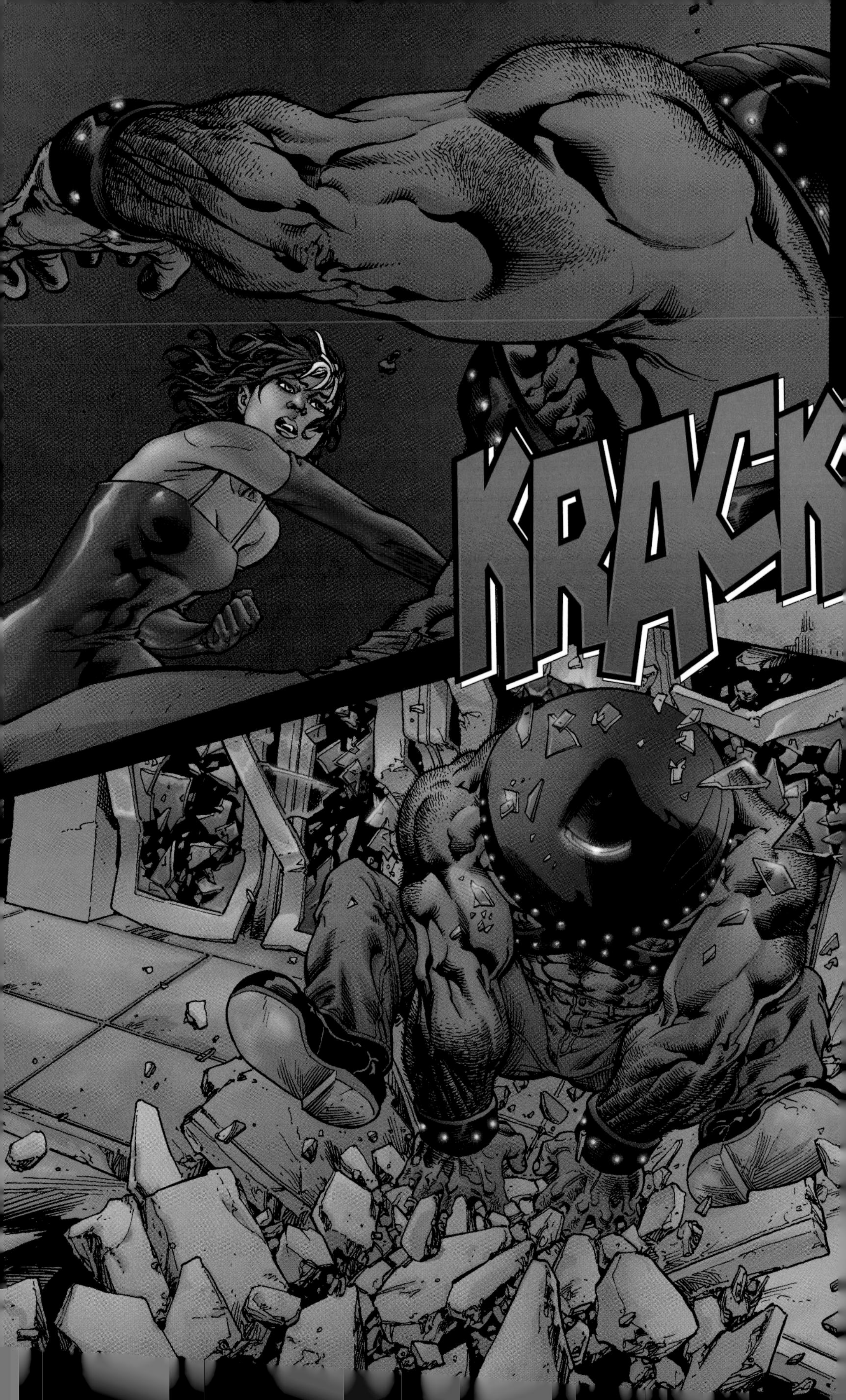
KRACK

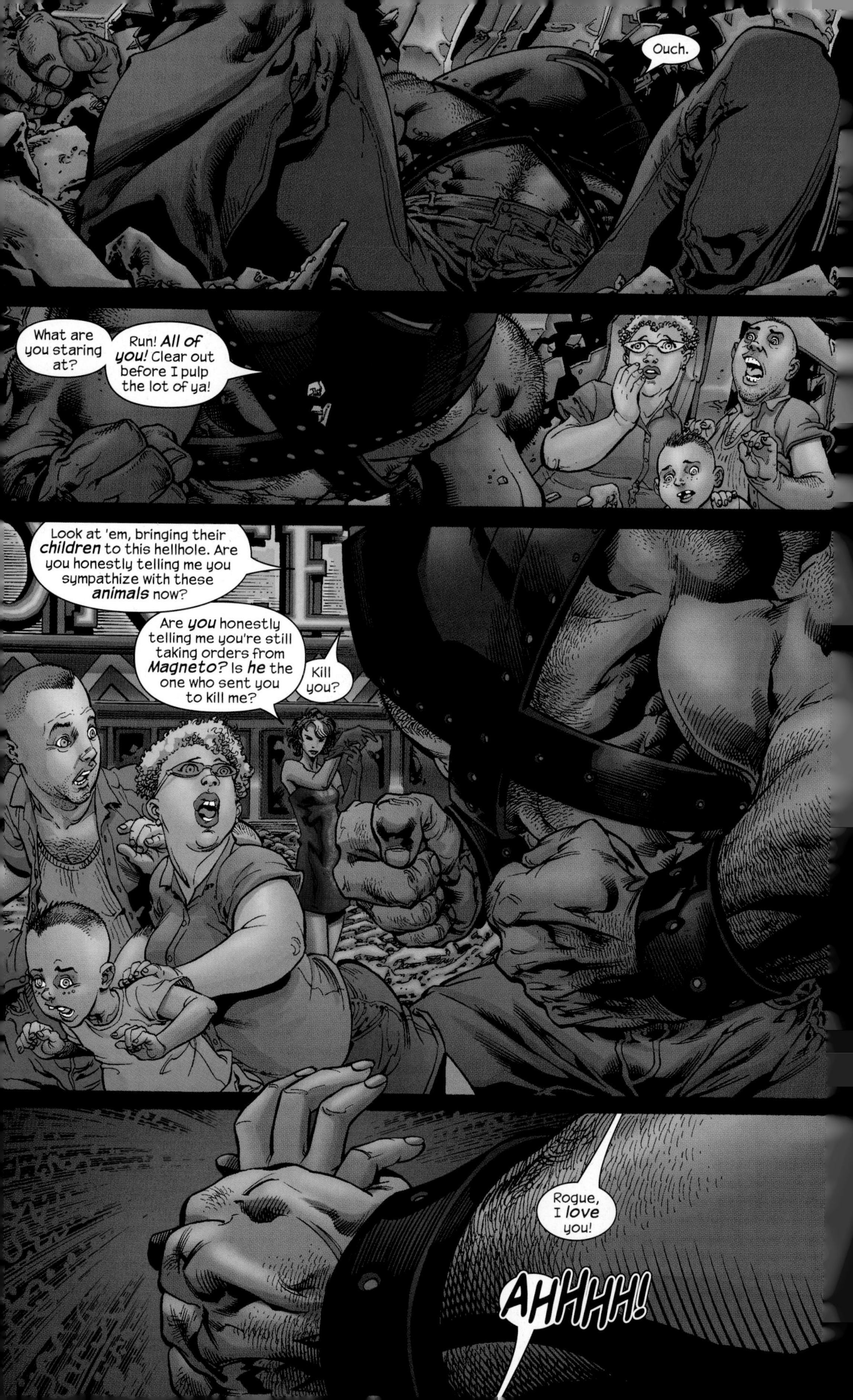
Ouch.
What are you staring at?
Run! All of you! Clear out before I pulp the lot of ya!
Look at 'em, bringing their children to this hellhole. Are you honestly telling me you sympathize with these animals now?
Are you honestly telling me you're still taking orders from Magneto? Is he the one who sent you to kill me?
Kill you?
Rogue, I love you!
AHHHH!

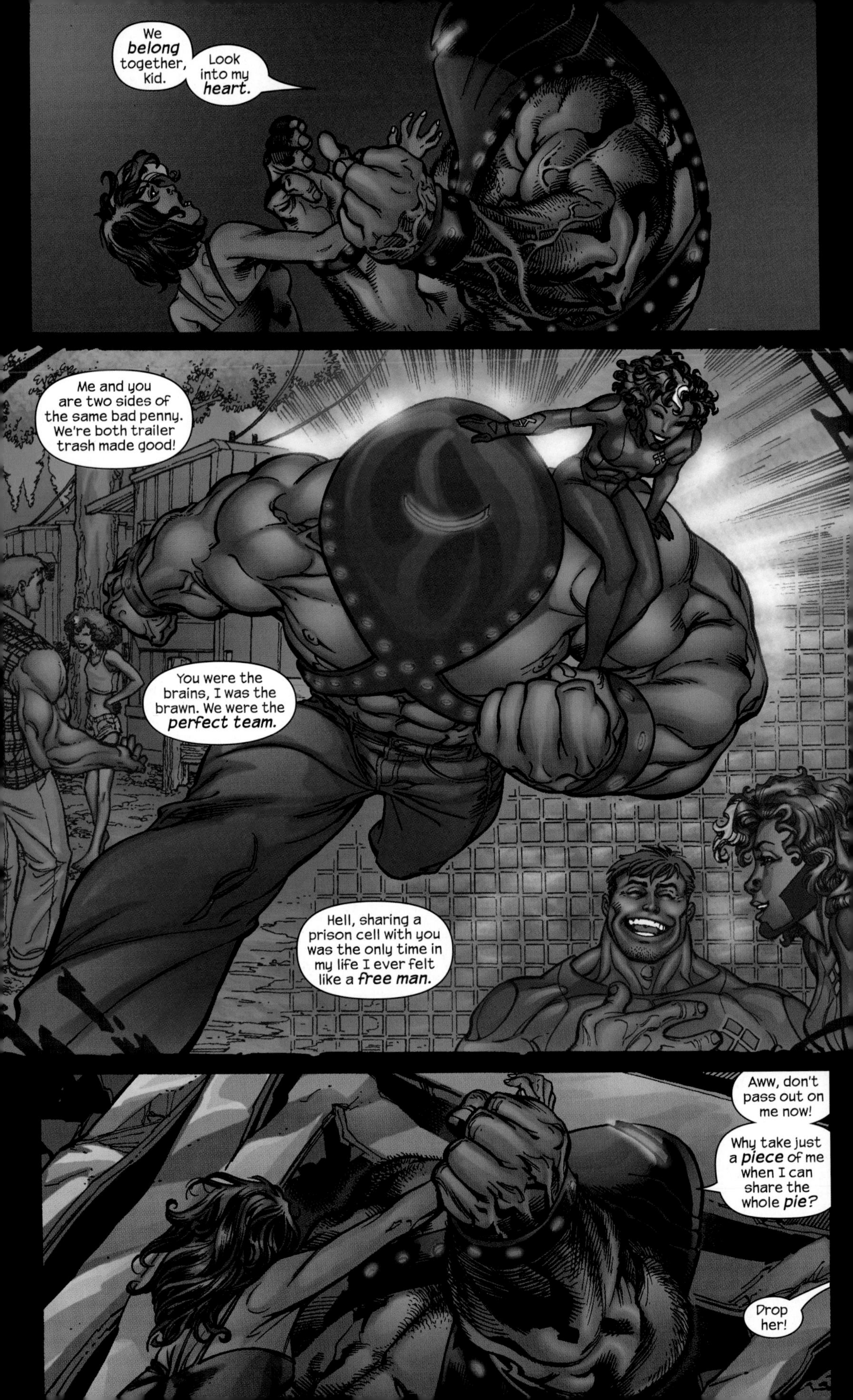

We belong together, kid.
Look into my heart.
Me and you are two sides of the same bad penny. We're both trailer trash made good!
You were the brains, I was the brawn. We were the perfect team.
Hell, sharing a prison cell with you was the only time in my life I ever felt like a free man.
Aww, don't pass out on me now!
Why take just a piece of me when I can share the whole pie?
Drop her!

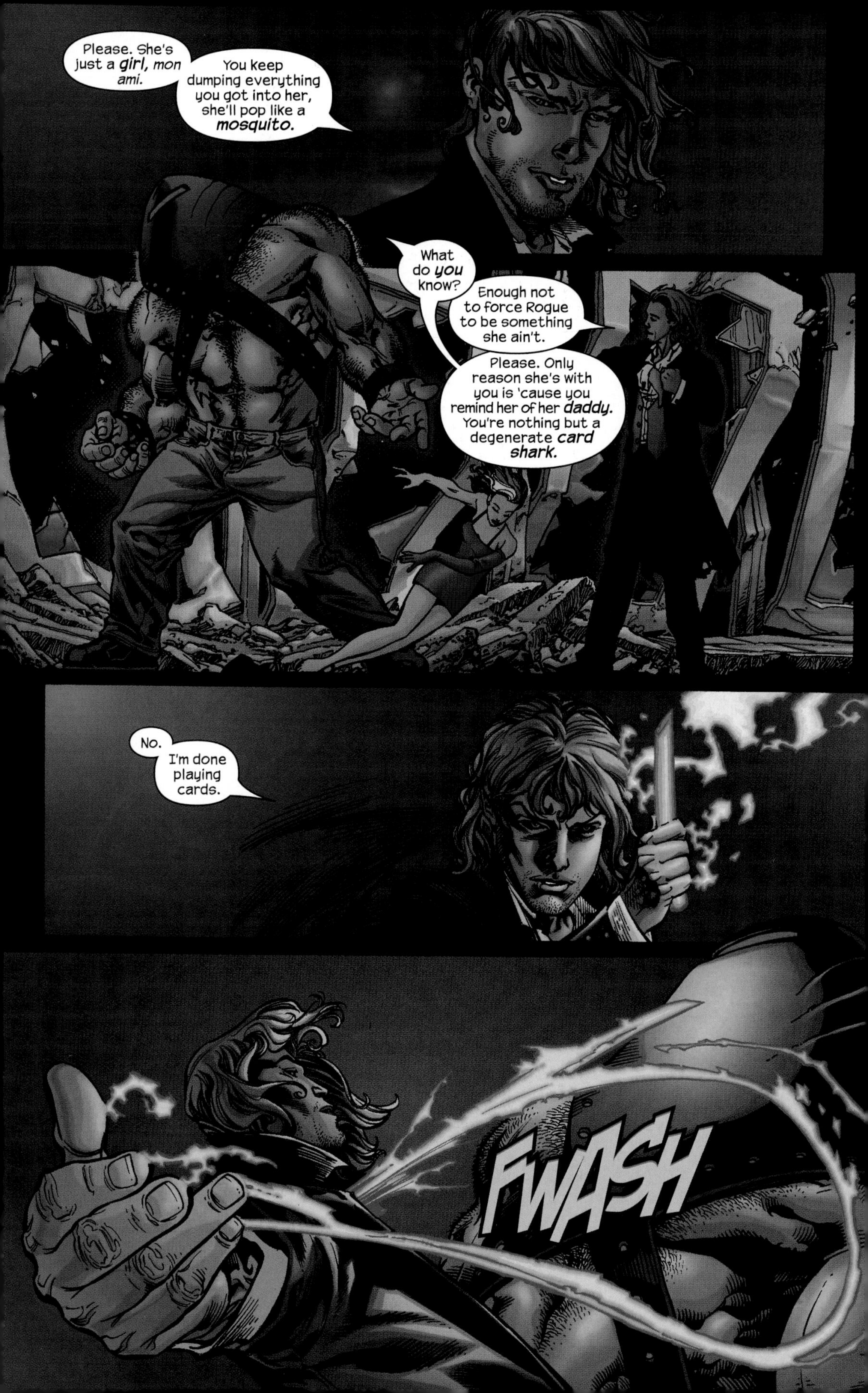
Please. She's just a girl, mon ami.
You keep dumping everything you got into her, she'll pop like a mosquito.
What do you know?
Enough not to force Rogue to be something she ain't.
Please. Only reason she's with you is 'cause you remind her of her daddy. You're nothing but a degenerate card shark.
No. I'm done playing cards.
FWASH

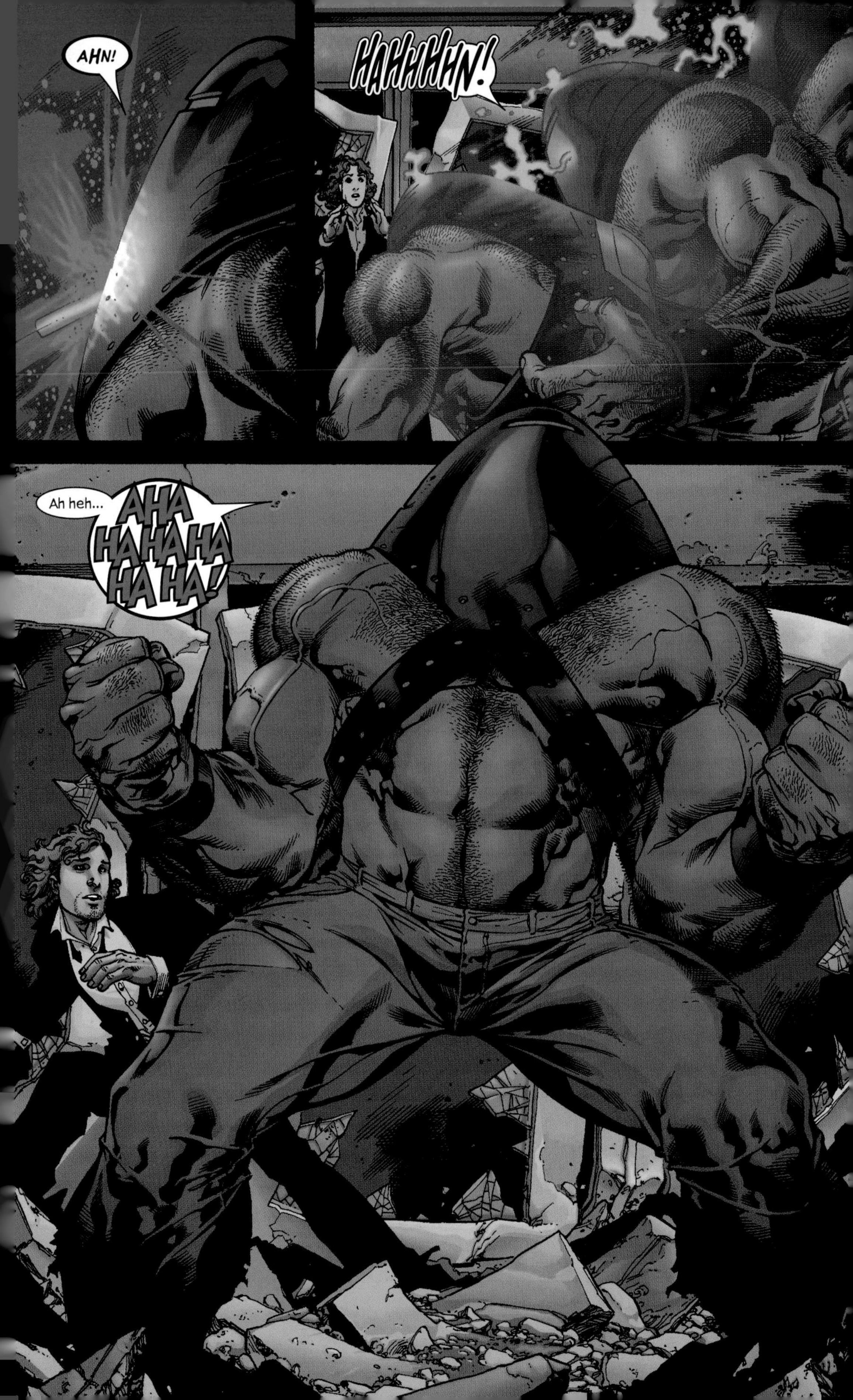
AHN!
HAHHHHHN!
Ah heh...
AHA HA HA HA HA HA HA!

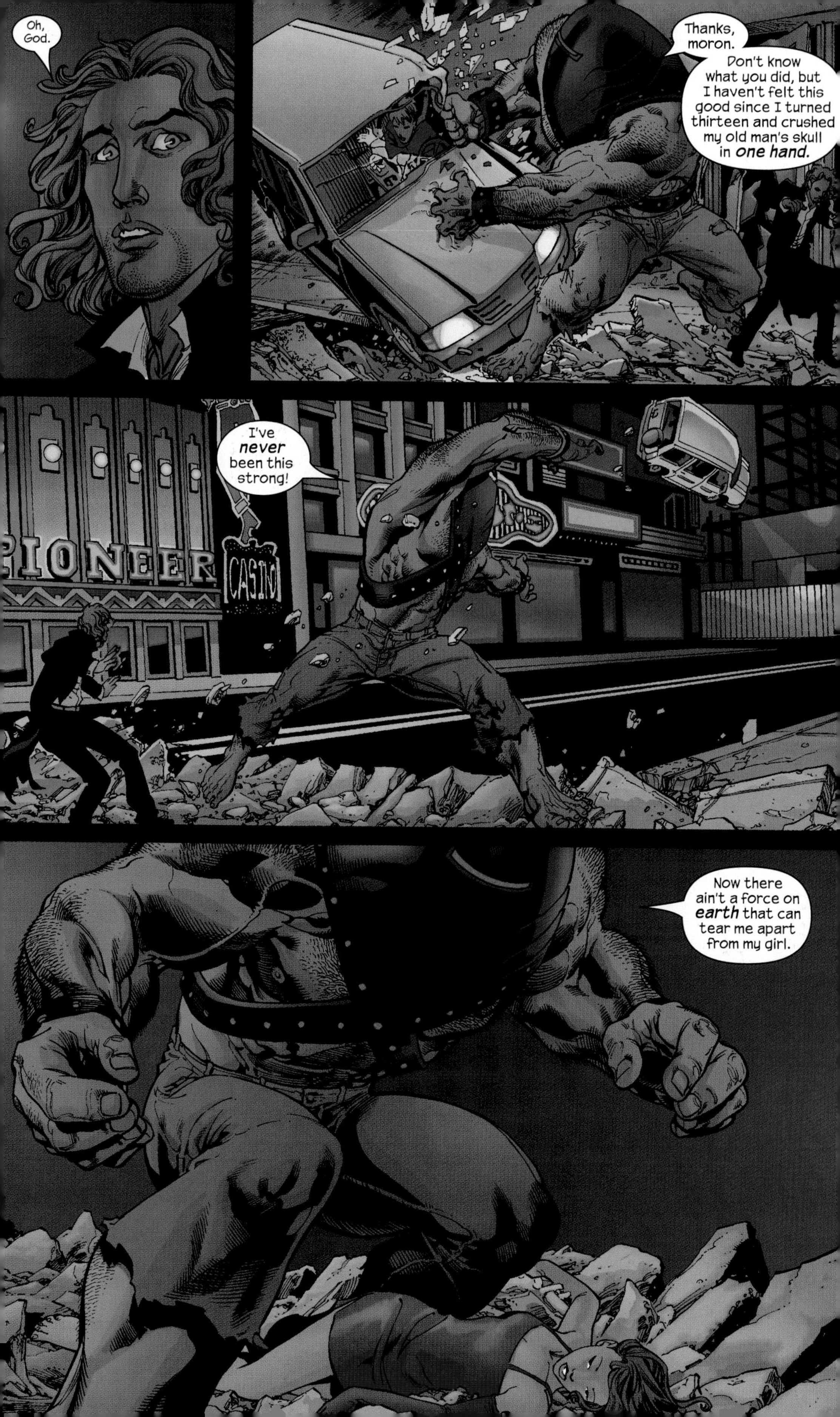
Oh, God.
Thanks, moron.
Don't know what you did, but I haven't felt this good since I turned thirteen and crushed my old man's skull in **one hand.**
I've **never** been this strong!
PIONEER
CASINO
Now there ain't a force on **earth** that can tear me apart from my girl.

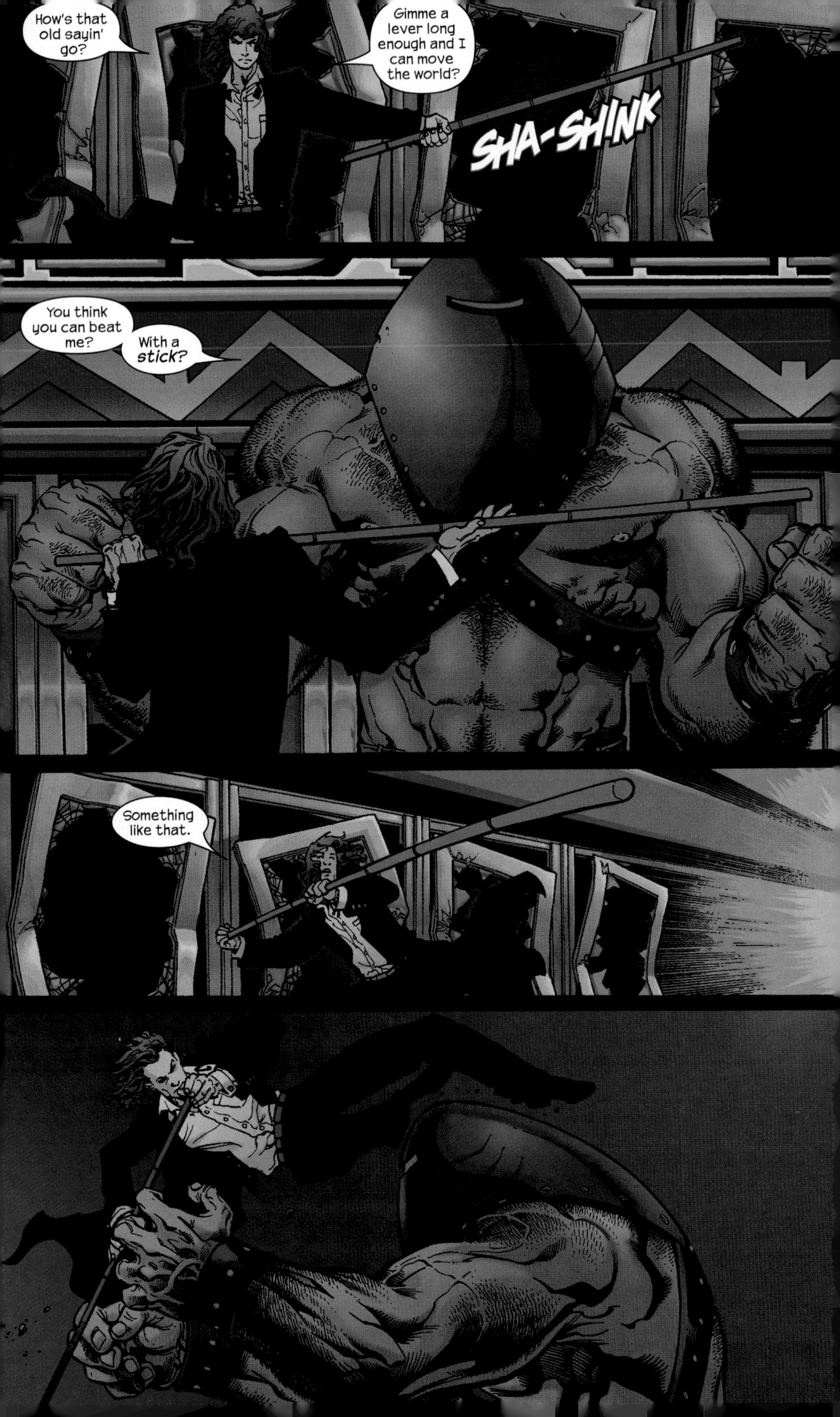
How's that old sayin' go?
Gimme a lever long enough and I can move the world?
SHA-SHINK
You think you can beat me?
With a *stick?*
Something like that.

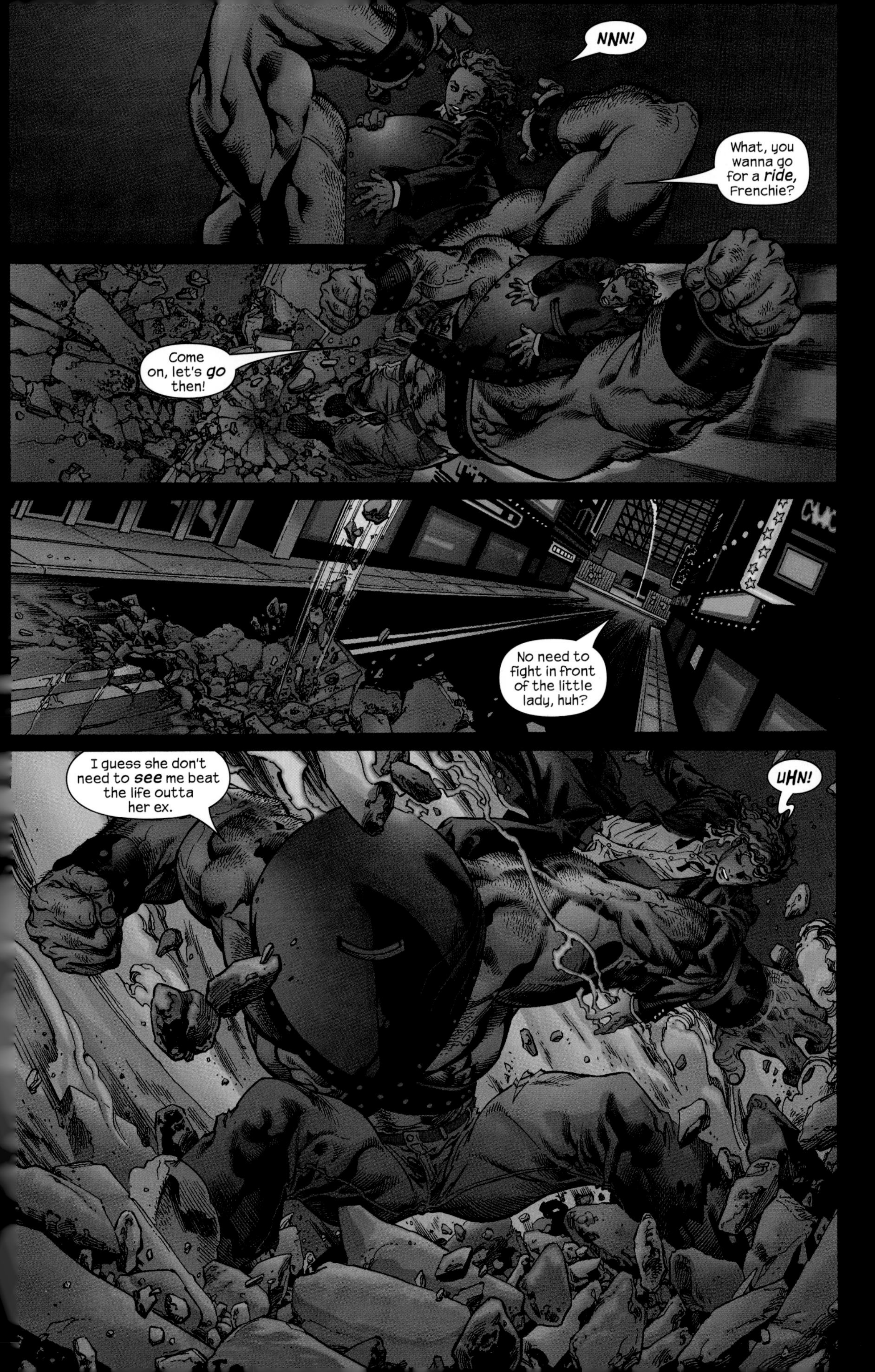
NNN!
What, you wanna go for a ride, Frenchie?
Come on, let's go then!
No need to fight in front of the little lady, huh?
I guess she don't need to see me beat the life outta her ex.
UHN!

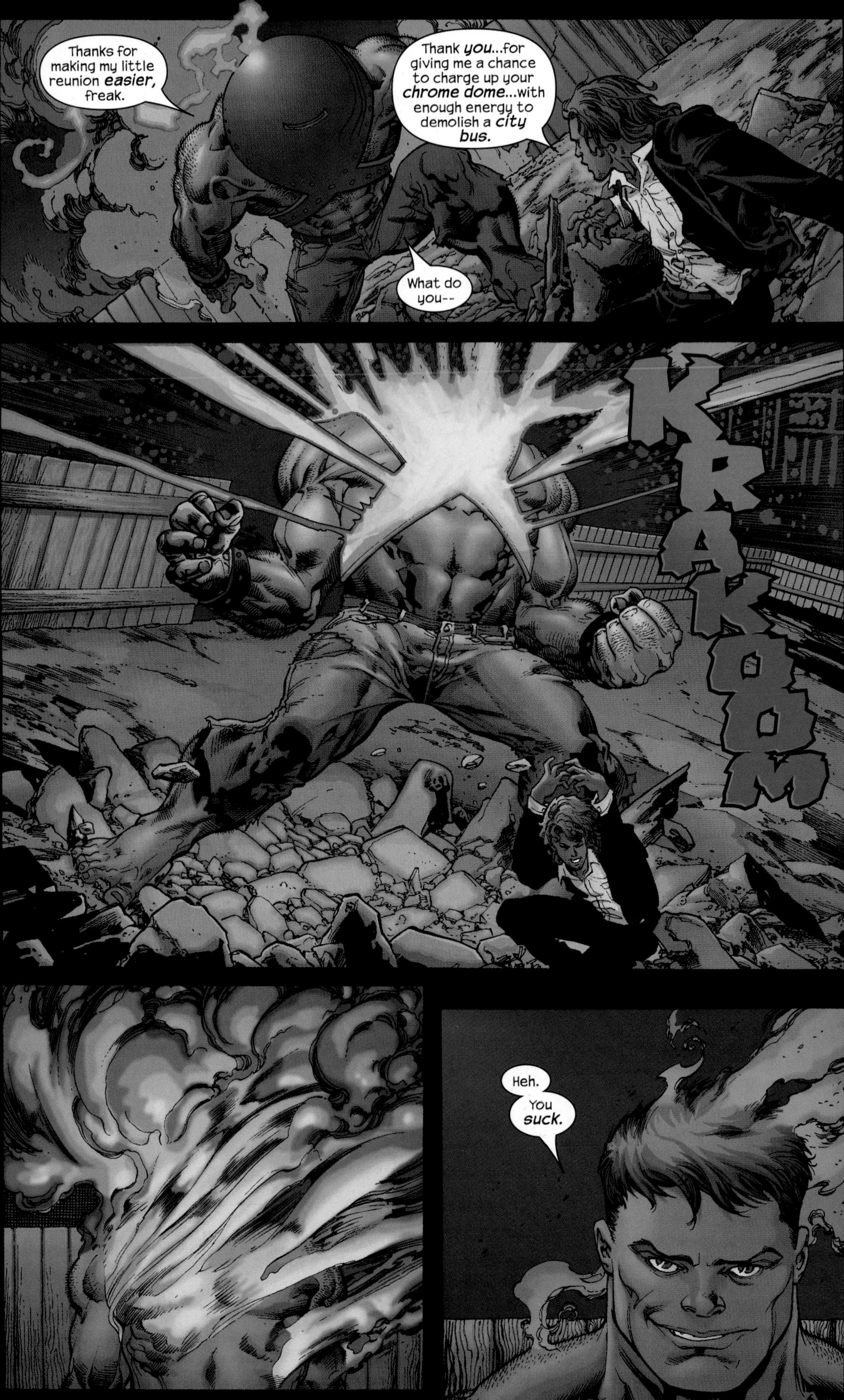
Thanks for making my little reunion *easier,* freak.
Thank *you*...for giving me a chance to charge up your *chrome dome*...with enough energy to demolish a *city bus.*
What do you--
KRAKOOM
Heh.
You *suck.*

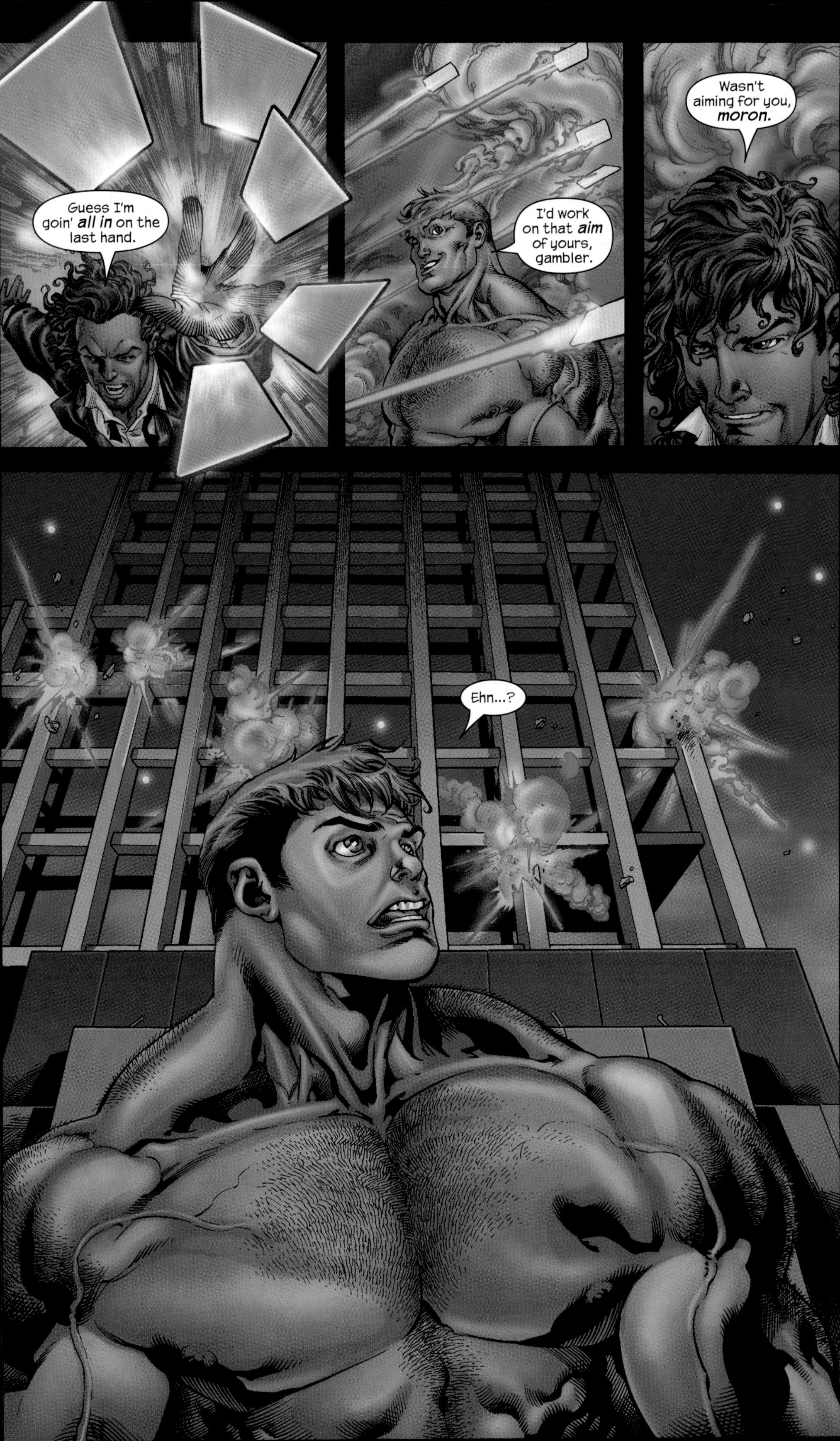

Guess I'm goin' **all in** on the last hand.
I'd work on that **aim** of yours, gambler.
Wasn't aiming for you, **moron.**
Ehn...?

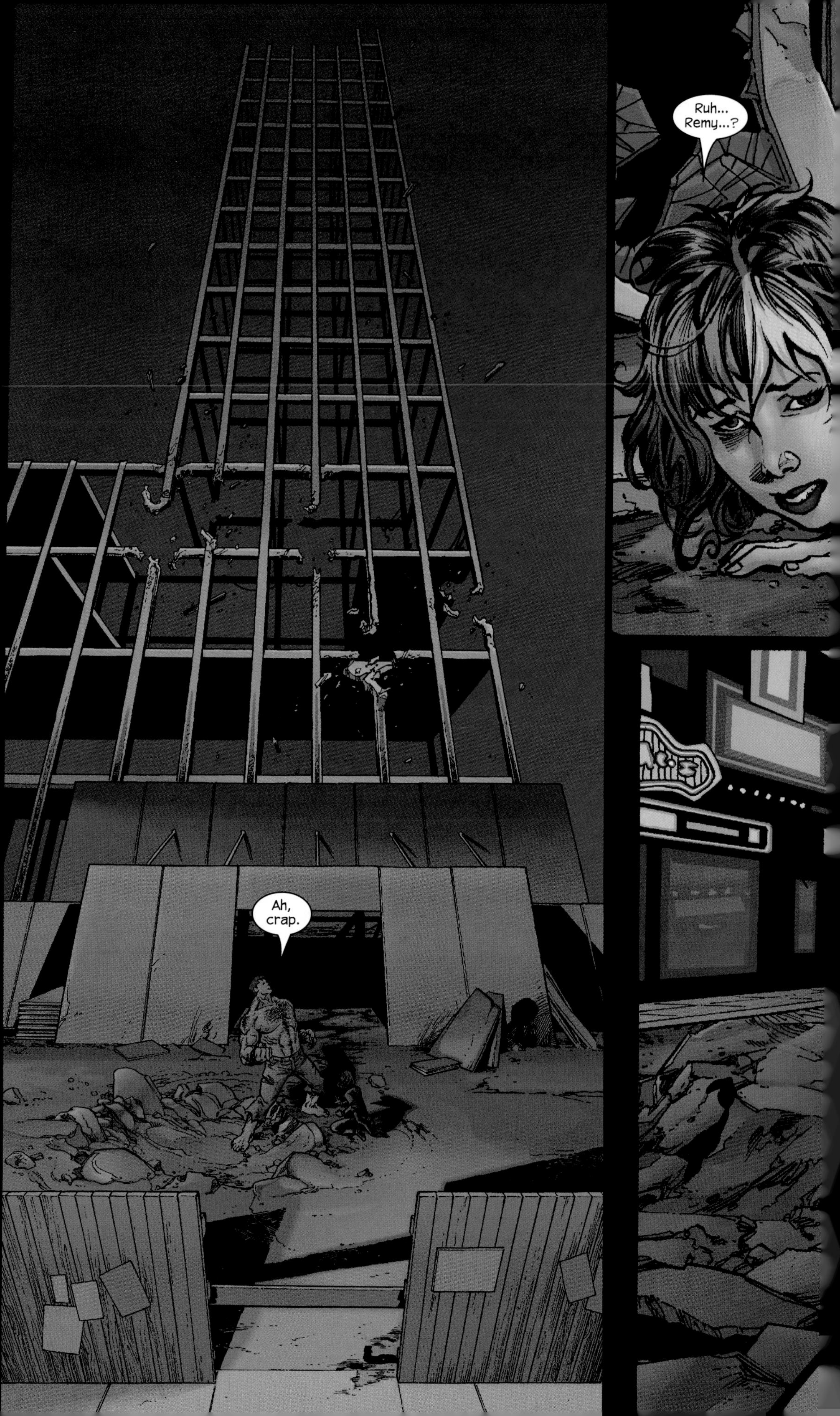
Ruh...
Remy...?
Ah, crap.

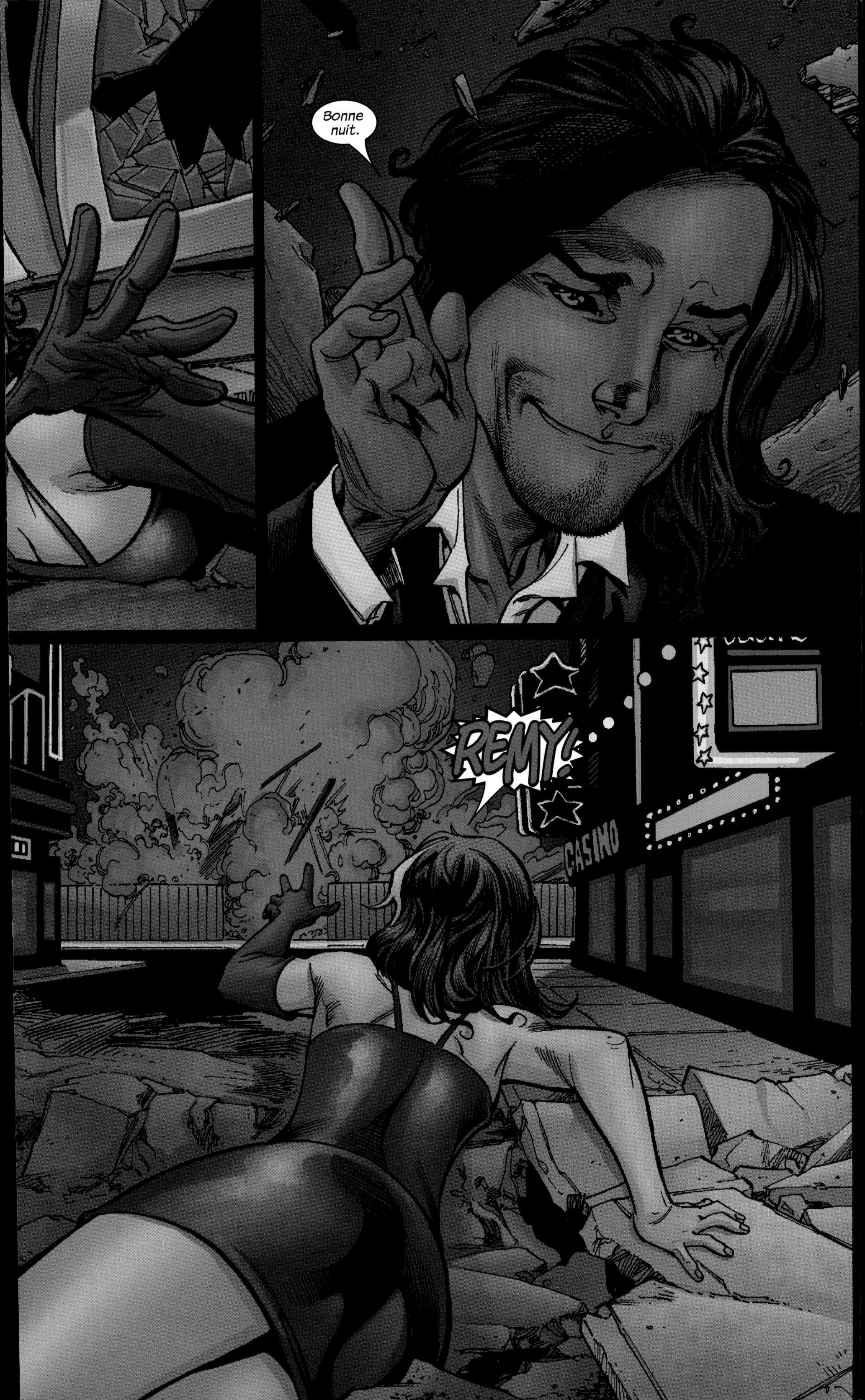
Bonne nuit.
REMY!
CASINO

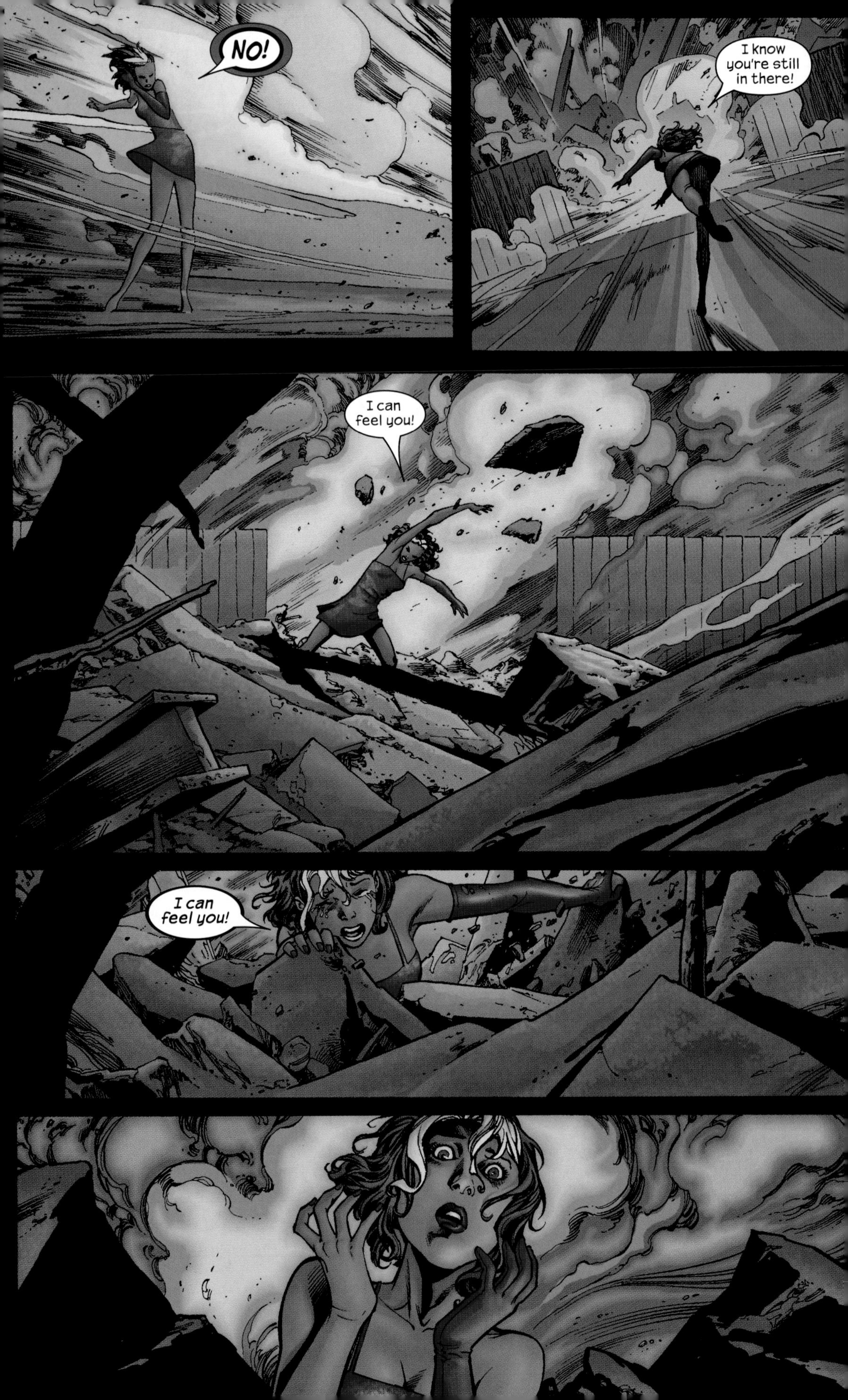
NO!
I know you're still in there!
I can feel you!
I can feel you!

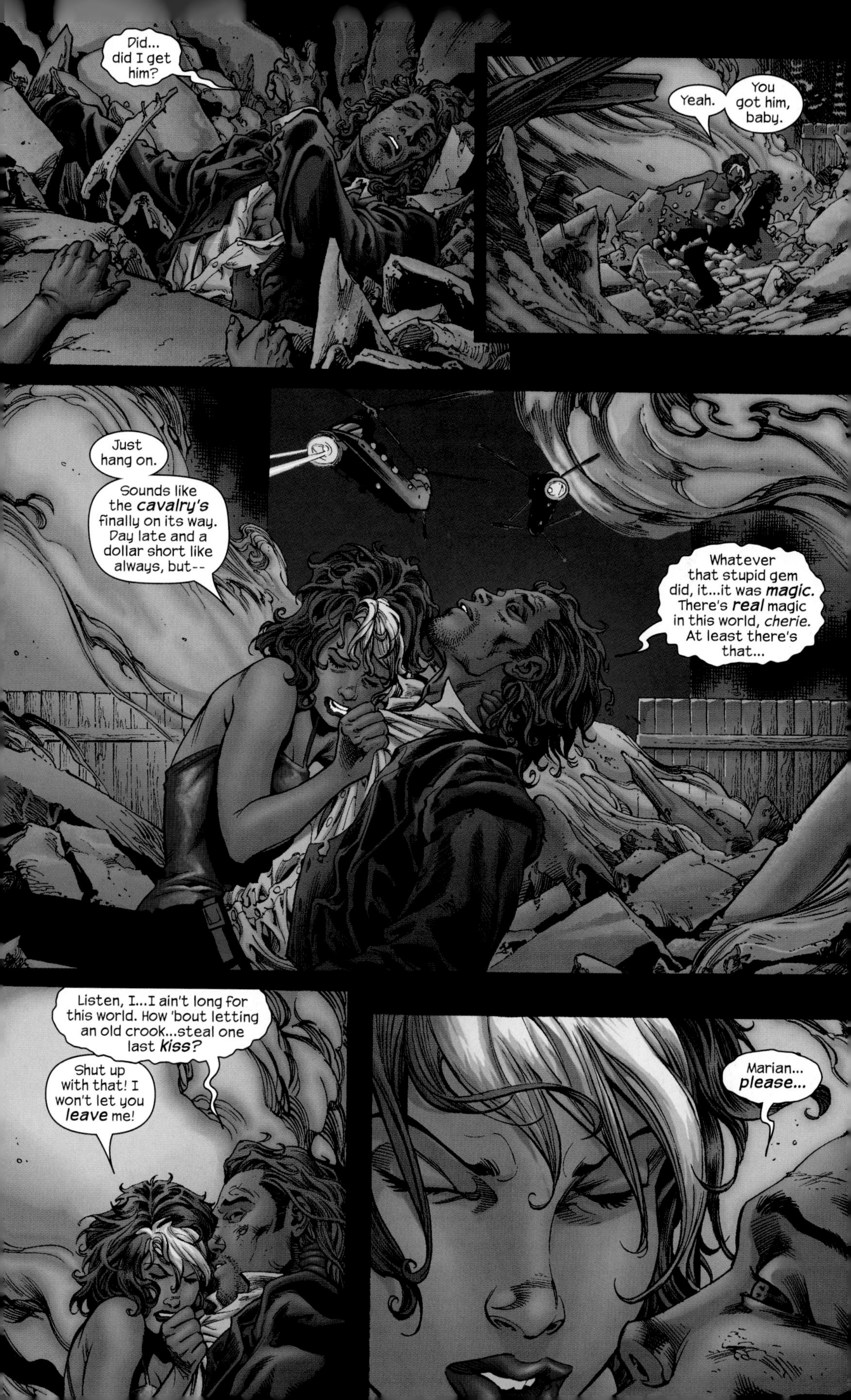
Did... did I get him?
Yeah.
You got him, baby.
Just hang on.
Sounds like the *cavalry's* finally on its way. Day late and a dollar short like always, but--
Whatever that stupid gem did, it...it was *magic.* There's *real* magic in this world, *cherie.* At least there's that...
Listen, I...I ain't long for this world. How 'bout letting an old crook...steal one last *kiss?*
Shut up with that! I won't let you *leave* me!
Marian... *please...*

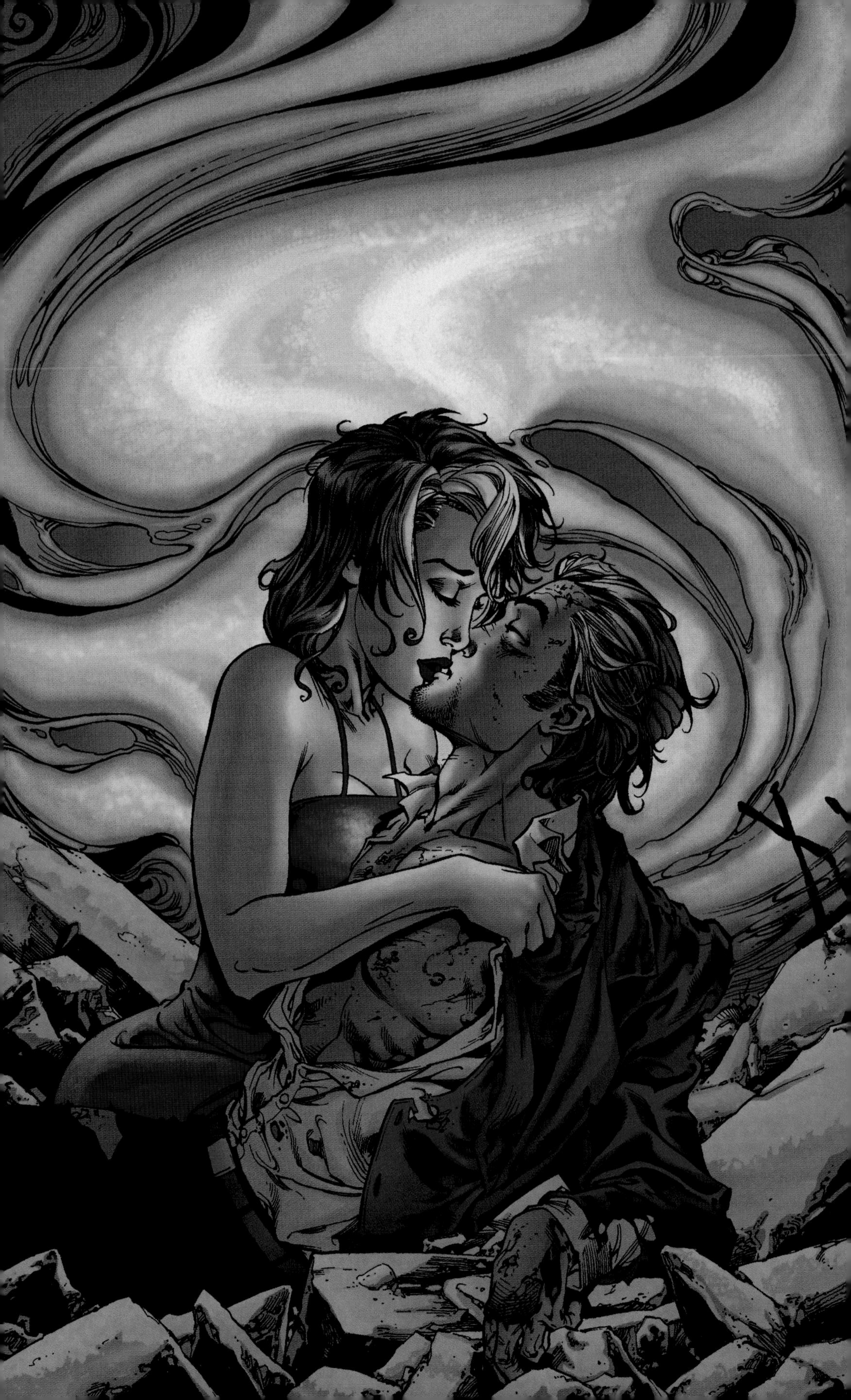

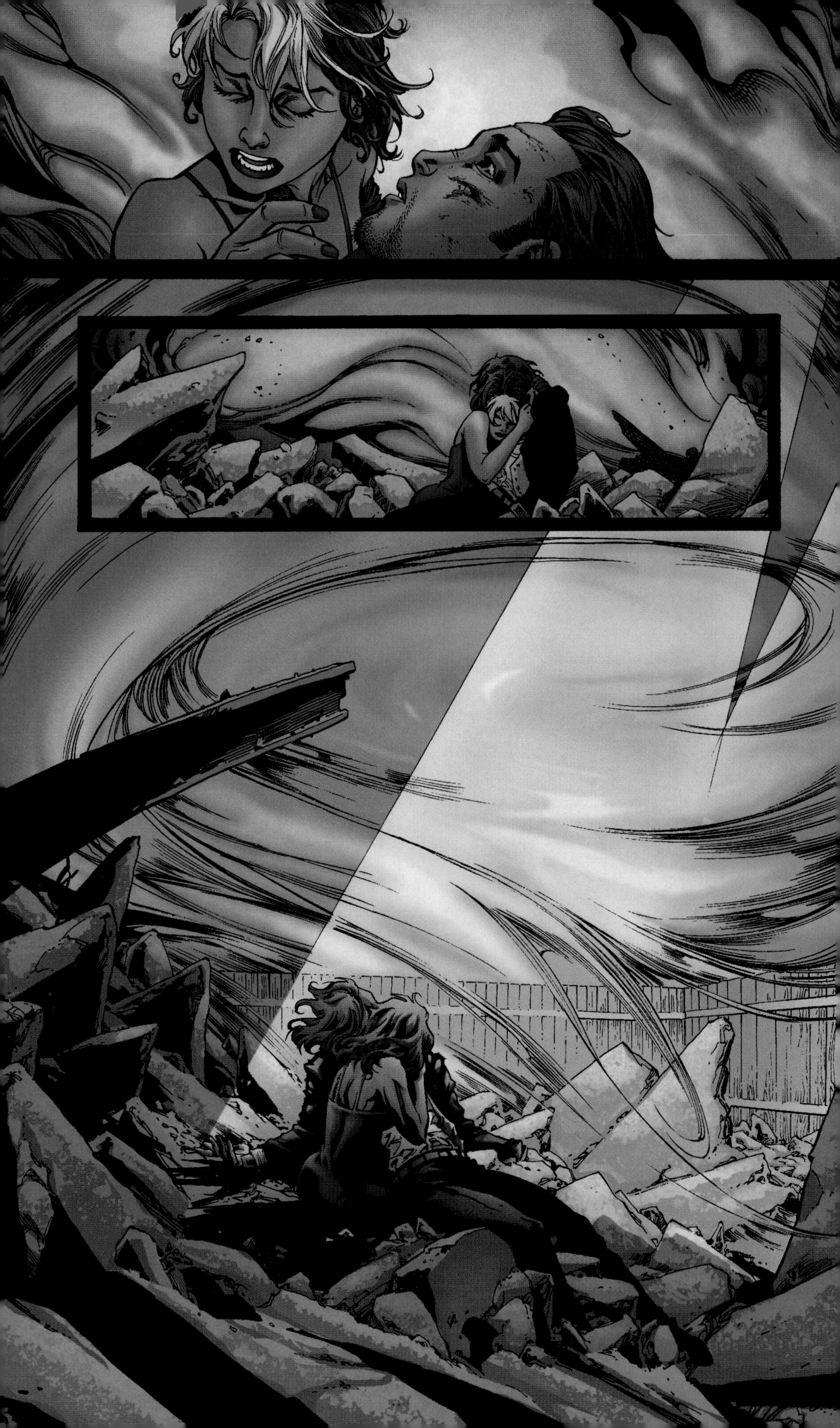

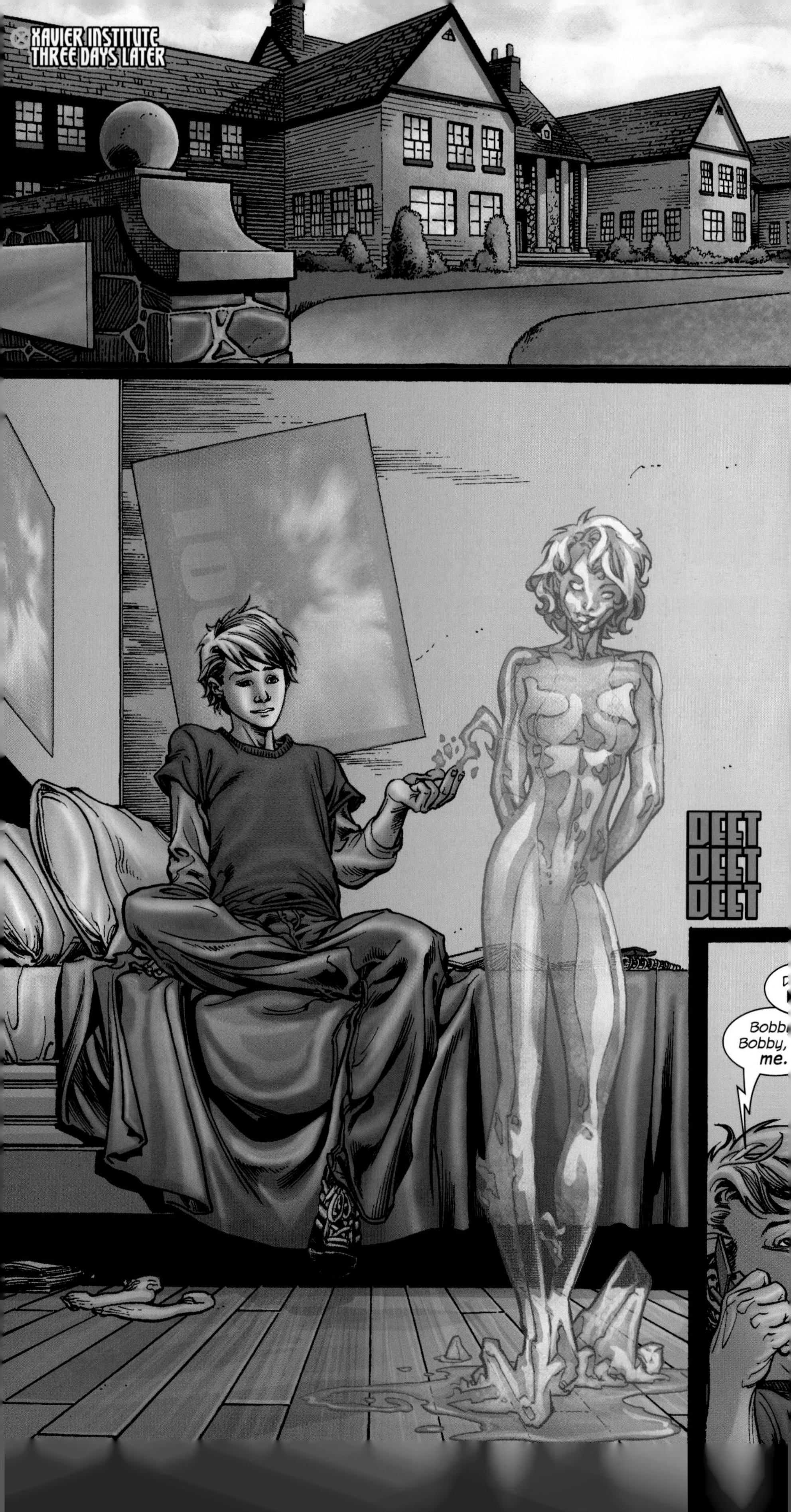
XAVIER INSTITUTE
THREE DAYS LATER
DEET
DEET
DEET
Bobby,
me.

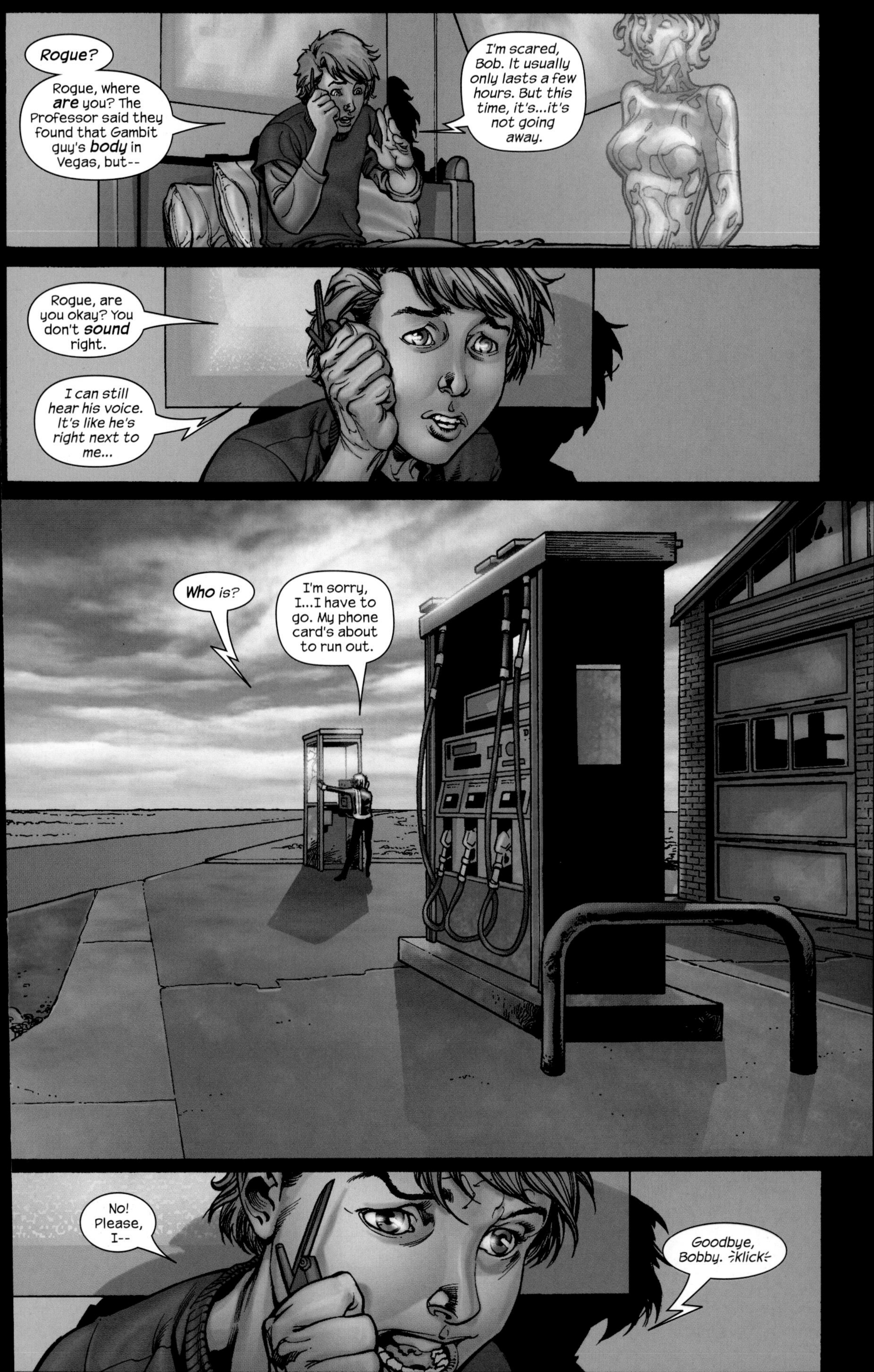
Rogue?
Rogue, where are you? The Professor said they found that Gambit guy's body in Vegas, but--
I'm scared, Bob. It usually only lasts a few hours. But this time, it's...it's not going away.
Rogue, are you okay? You don't sound right.
I can still hear his voice. It's like he's right next to me...
Who is?
I'm sorry, I...I have to go. My phone card's about to run out.
No! Please, I--
Goodbye, Bobby. klick

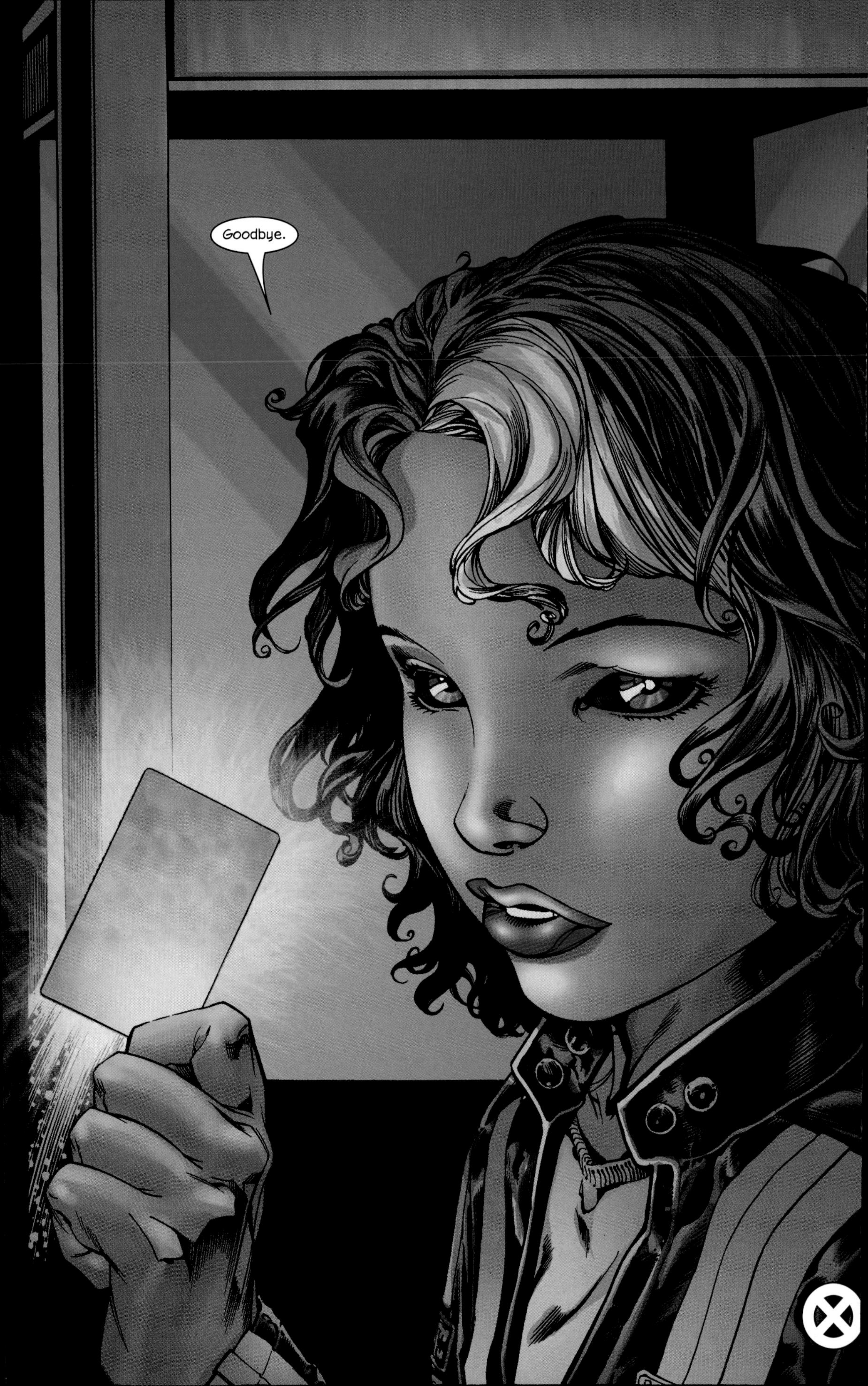
Goodbye.

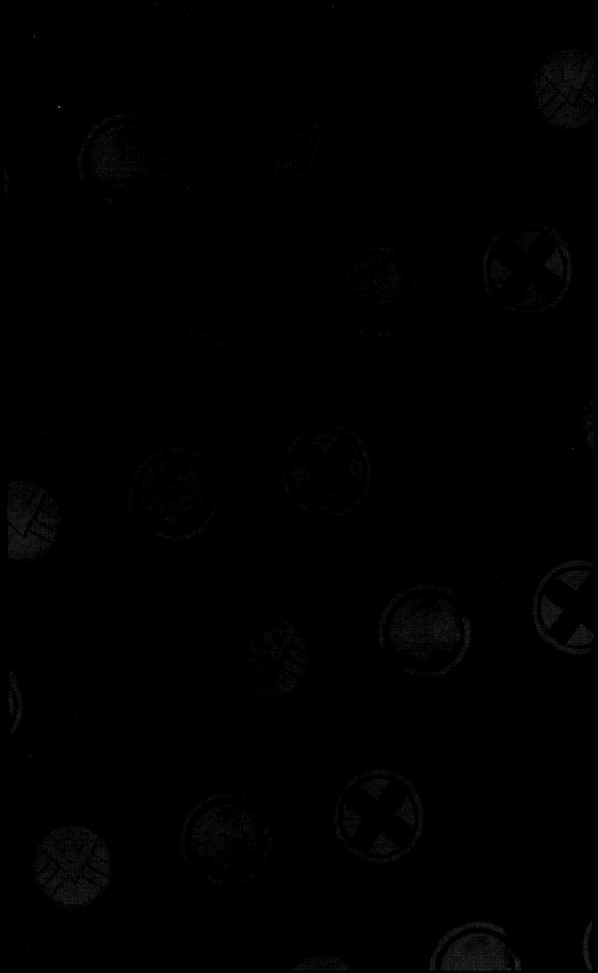

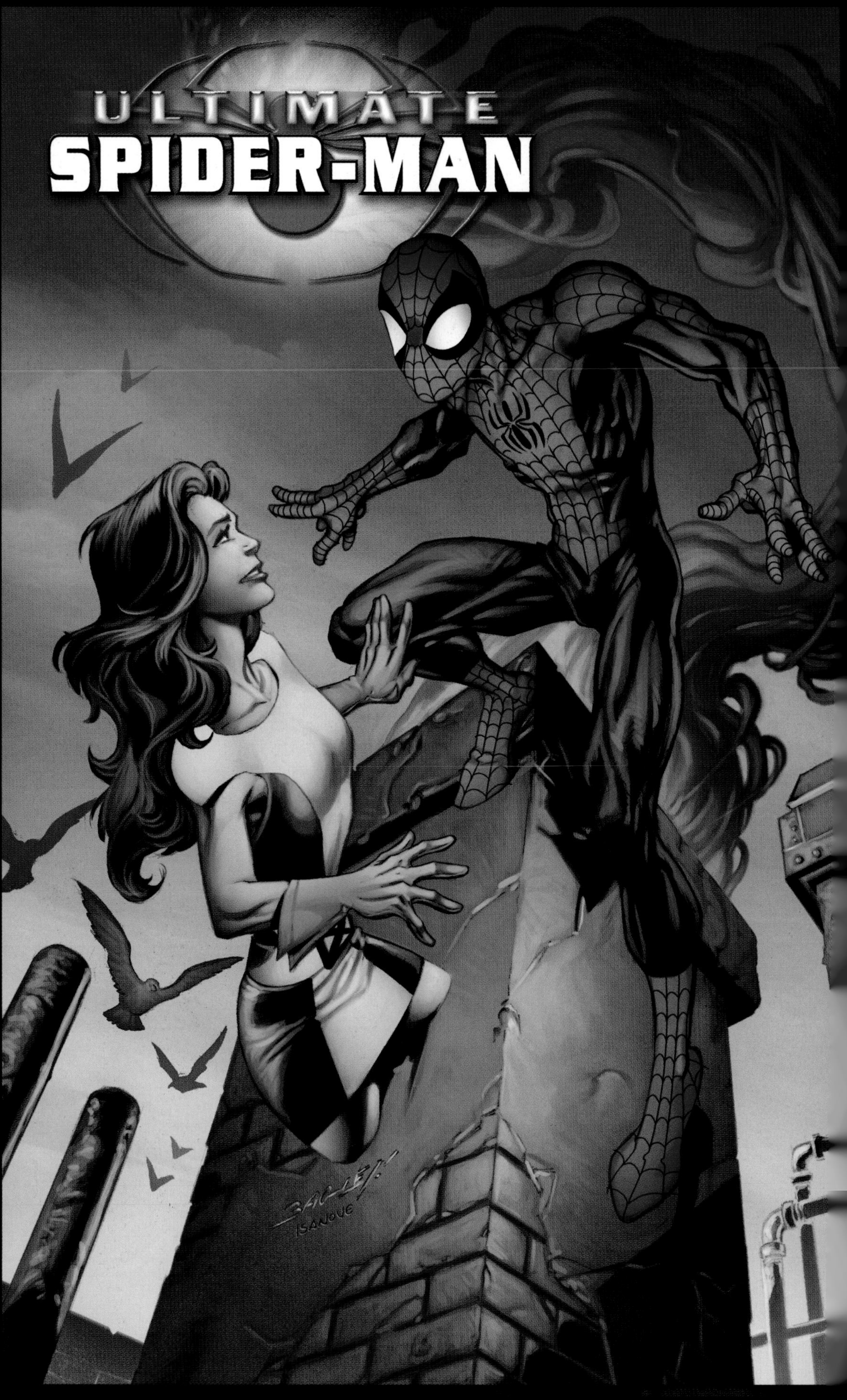
ULTIMATE
SPIDER-MAN

ULTIMATE
SPIDER-MAN

The bite of a genetically altered spider granted high school student Peter Parker incredible, arachnid-like powers! When a burglar killed his beloved Uncle Ben, a grief-stricken Peter vowed to use his amazing abilities to protect his fellow man. He learned the invaluable lesson that with great power there must also come great responsibility. Peter's life has been turned upside-down in recent months, thanks in no small part to his breakup with girlfriend Mary Jane Watson...

Born with strange and amazing abilities, the X-Men are young mutant heroes, sworn to protect a world that hates and fears them. Kitty Pride's ability to "phase" through solid objects has made her a valued member of the X-Men, even though she is the youngest person on the team. Kitty's also been having problems with her love life, and has just recently broken off her relationship with fellow teammate Bobby Drake (a.k.a Iceman)...

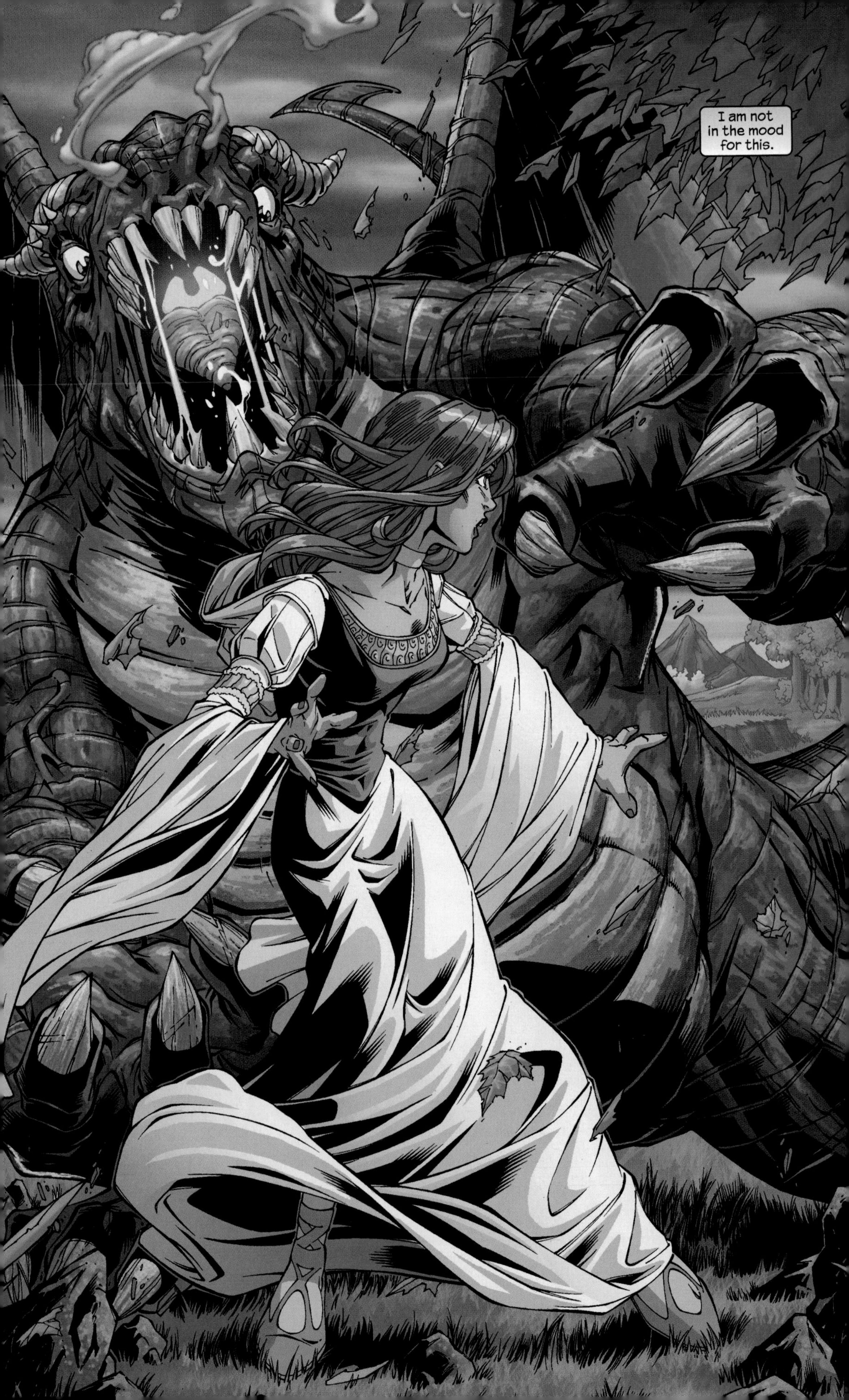
I am not in the mood for this.

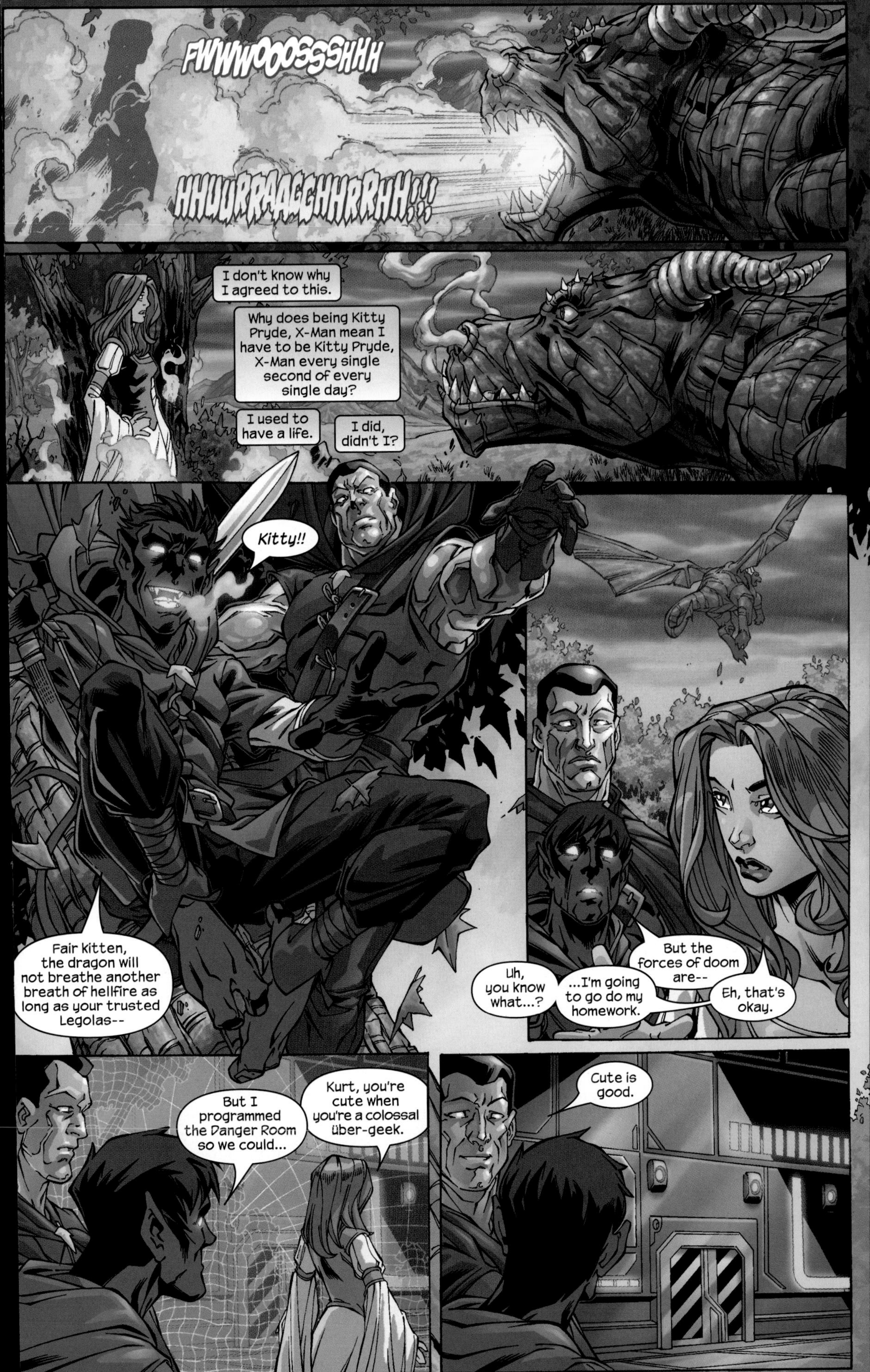
FWWWOOOSSSHHH
HHUURRAAGGHHRRHH!!!
I don't know why I agreed to this.
Why does being Kitty Pryde, X-Man mean I have to be Kitty Pryde, X-Man every single second of every single day?
I used to have a life.
I did, didn't I?
Kitty!!
Fair kitten, the dragon will not breathe another breath of hellfire as long as your trusted Legolas--
Uh, you know what...?
...I'm going to go do my homework.
But the forces of doom are--
Eh, that's okay.
But I programmed the Danger Room so we could...
Kurt, you're cute when you're a colossal über-geek.
Cute is good.

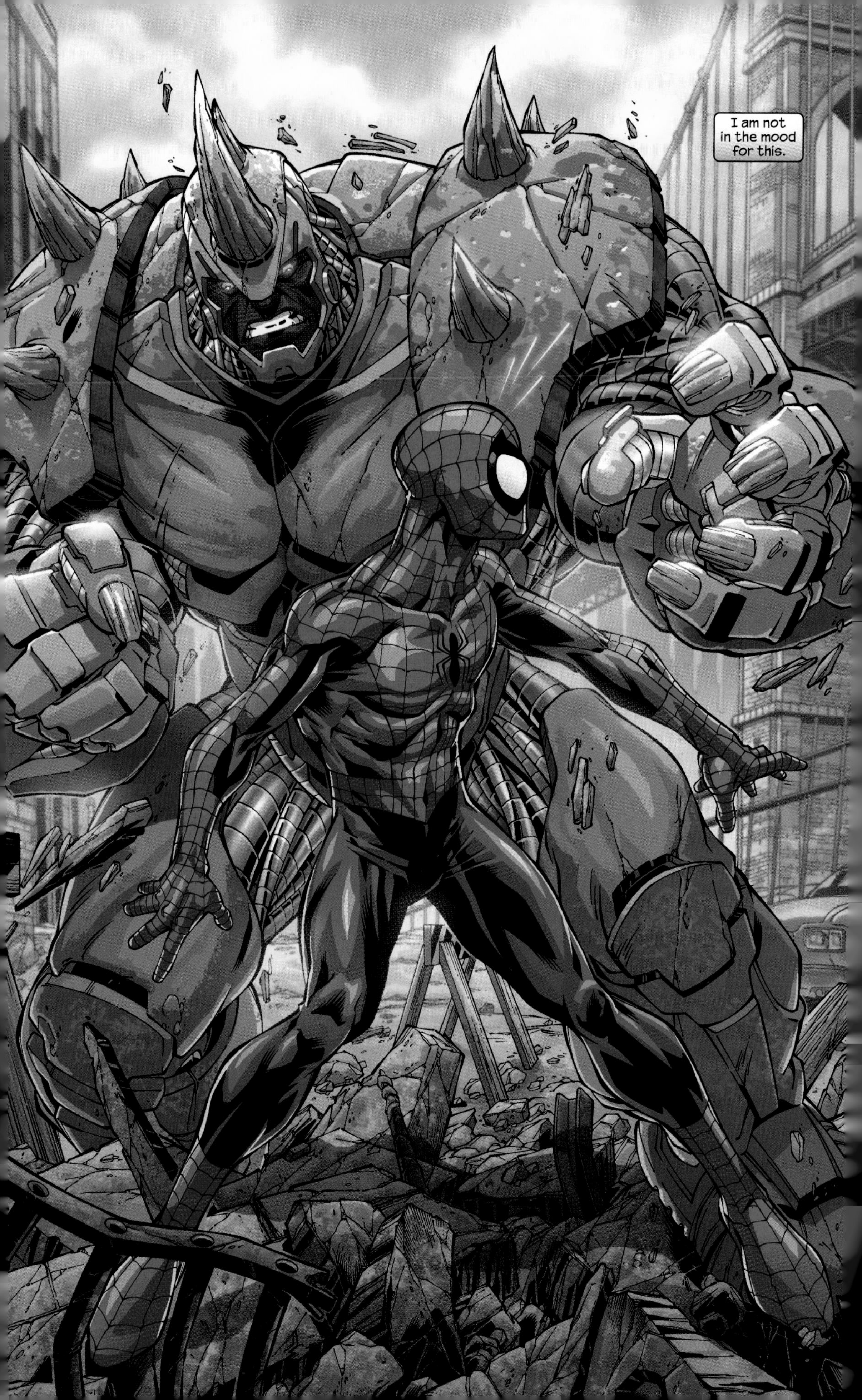
I am not in the mood for this.

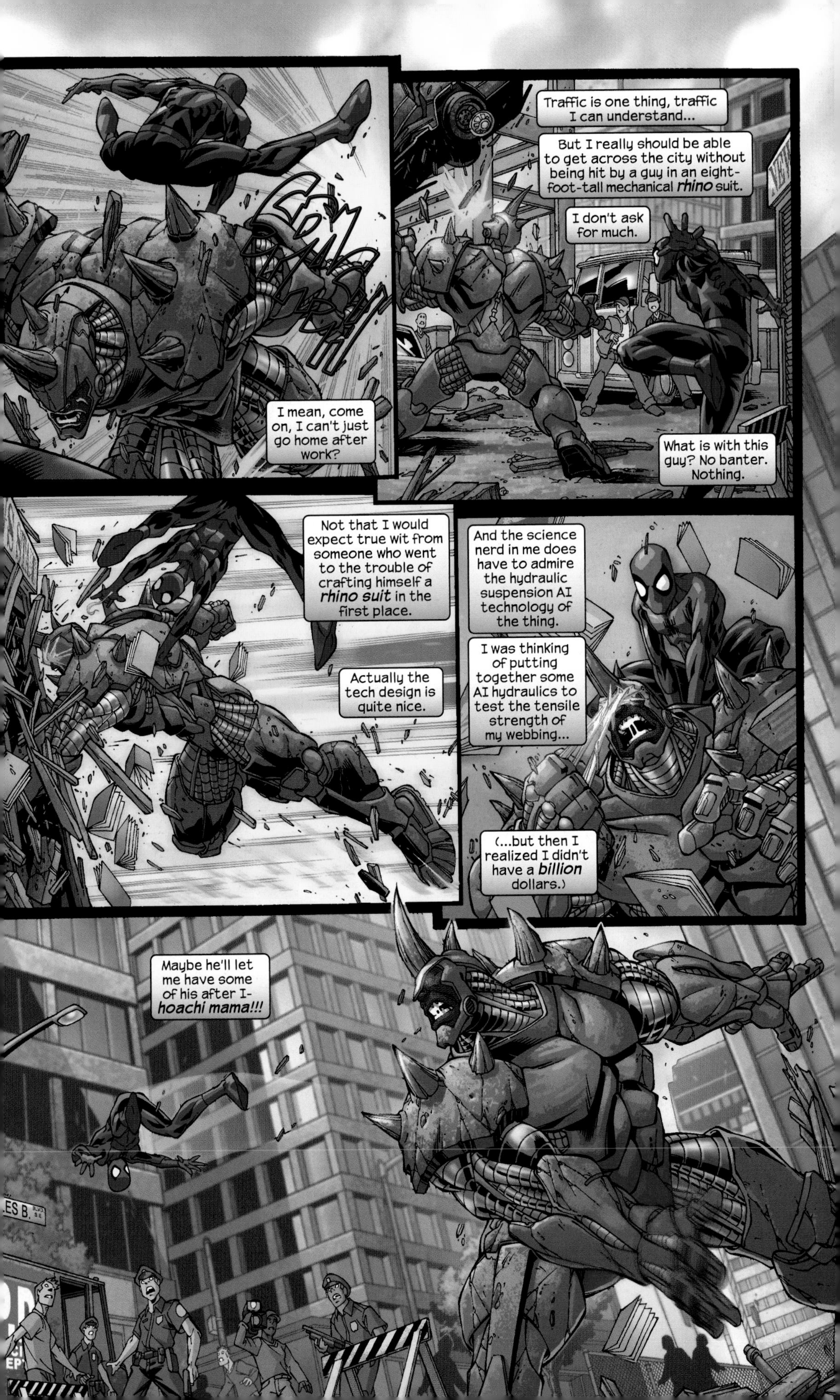

I mean, come on, I can't just go home after work?
Traffic is one thing, traffic I can understand...
But I really should be able to get across the city without being hit by a guy in an eight-foot-tall mechanical *rhino* suit.
I don't ask for much.
What is with this guy? No banter. Nothing.
Not that I would expect true wit from someone who went to the trouble of crafting himself a *rhino suit* in the first place.
Actually the tech design is quite nice.
And the science nerd in me does have to admire the hydraulic suspension AI technology of the thing.
I was thinking of putting together some AI hydraulics to test the tensile strength of my webbing...
(...but then I realized I didn't have a *billion* dollars.)
Maybe he'll let me have some of his after I-*hoachi mama!!!*

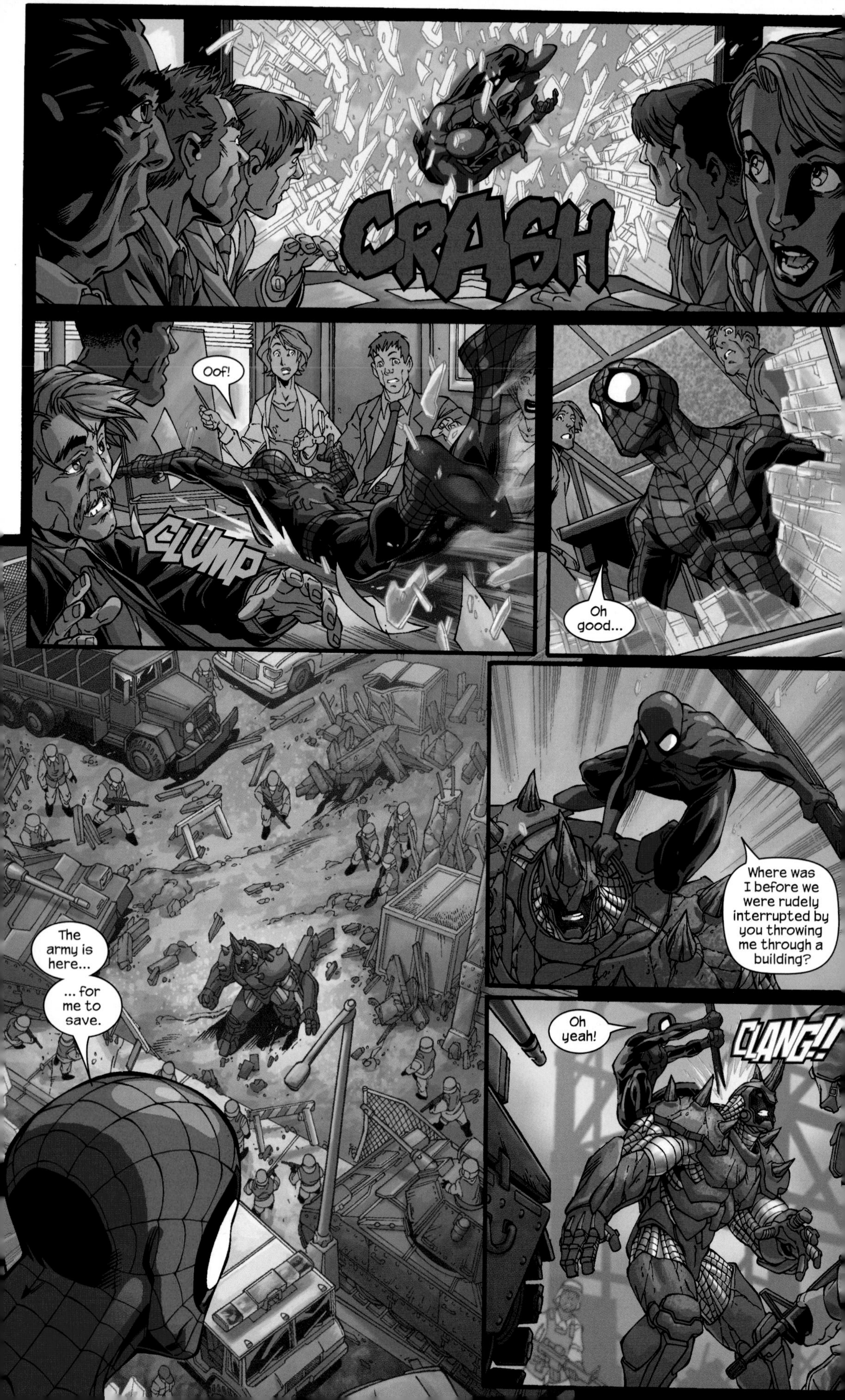
CRASH
Oof!
CLUMP
Oh good...
The army is here...
... for me to save.
Where was I before we were rudely interrupted by you throwing me through a building?
Oh yeah!
CLANG!!

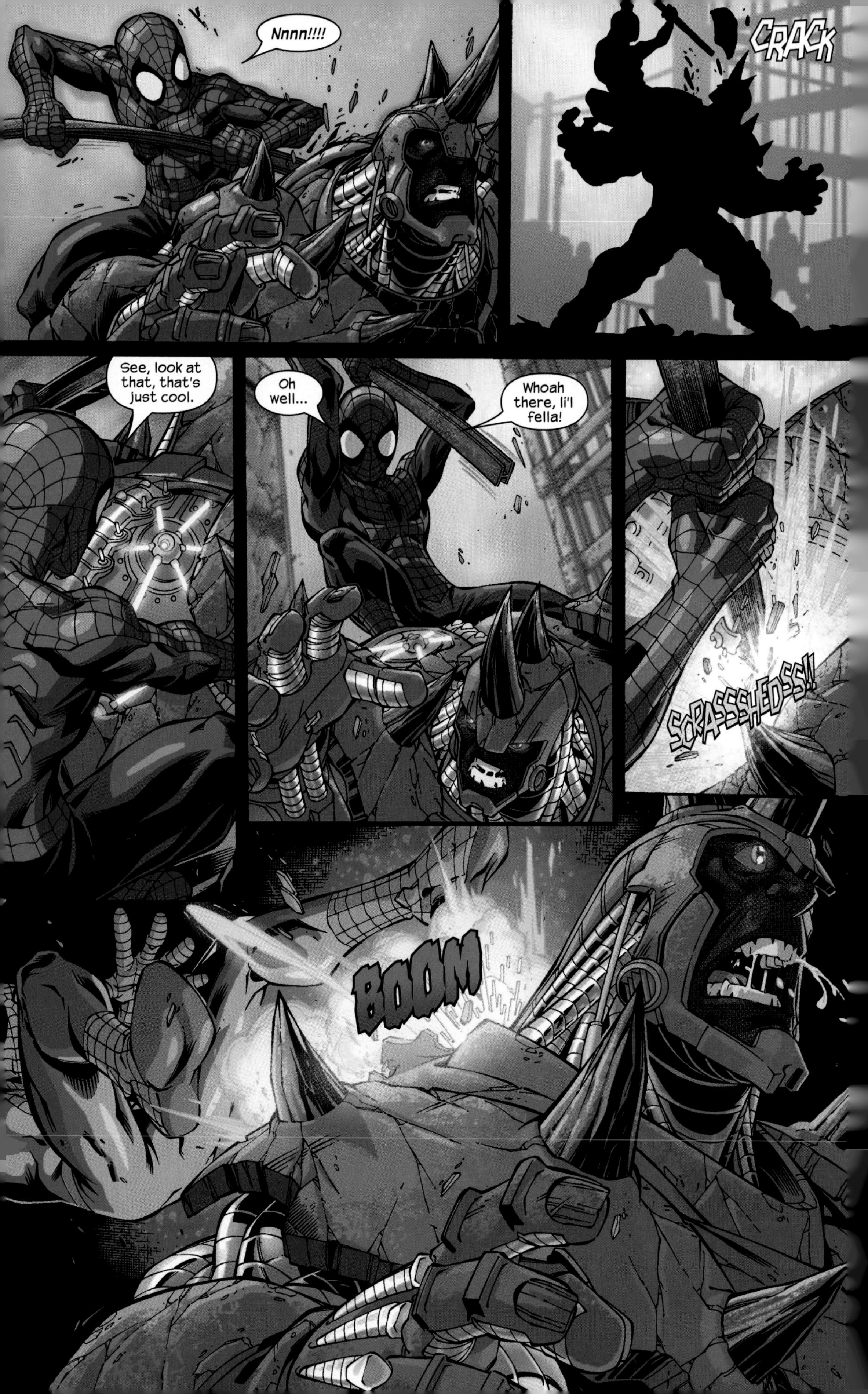
Nnnn!!!!
CRACK
See, look at that, that's just cool.
Oh well...
Whoah there, li'l fella!
SCRASSSHED-SS!!
BOOM

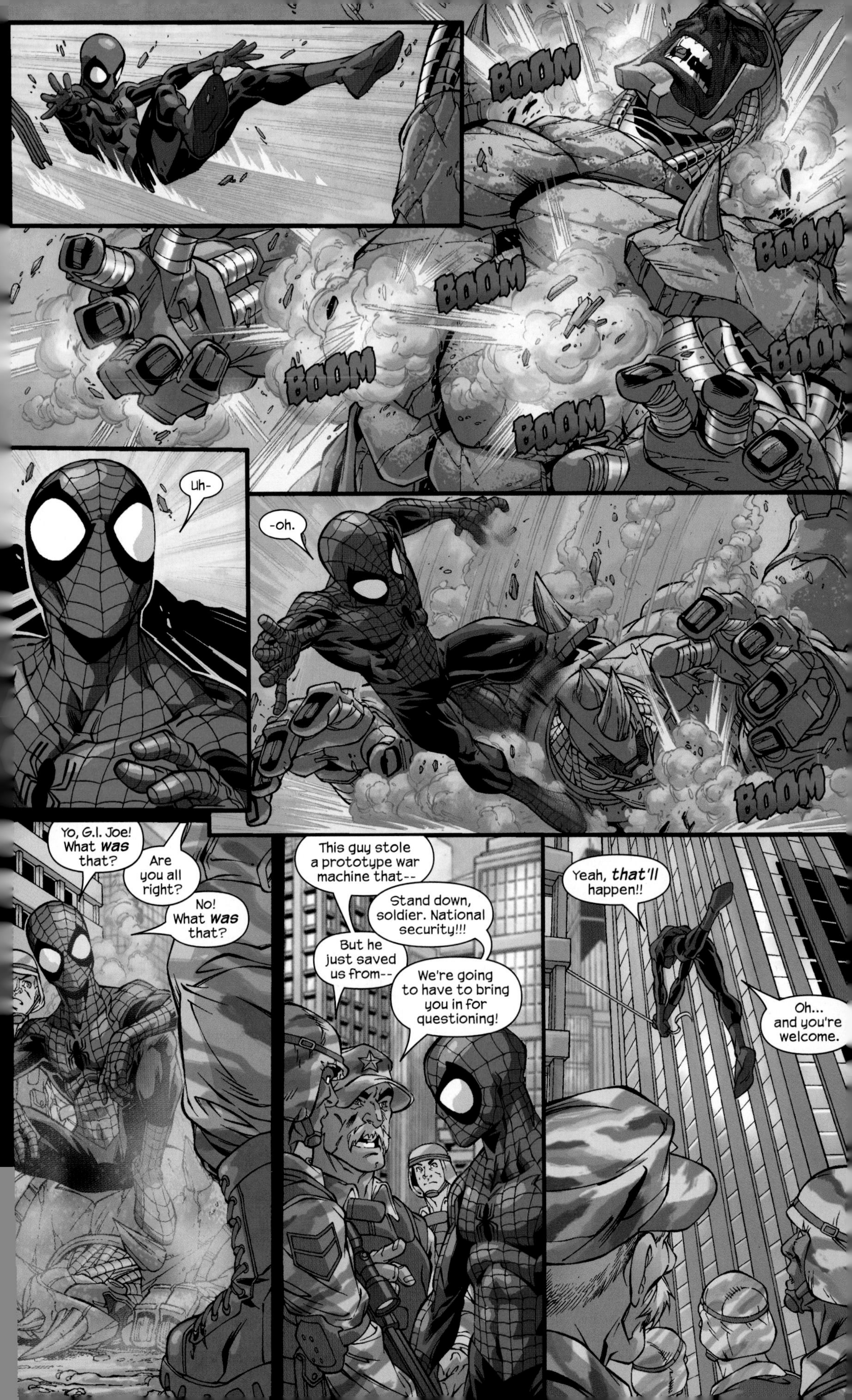
BOOM
BOOM
BOOM
BOOM
BOOM
BOOM
Uh-
-oh.
BOOM
Yo, G.I. Joe! What *was* that?
Are you all right?
No! What *was* that?
This guy stole a prototype war machine that--
Stand down, soldier. National security!!!
But he just saved us from--
We're going to have to bring you in for questioning!
Yeah, *that'll* happen!!
Oh... and you're welcome.

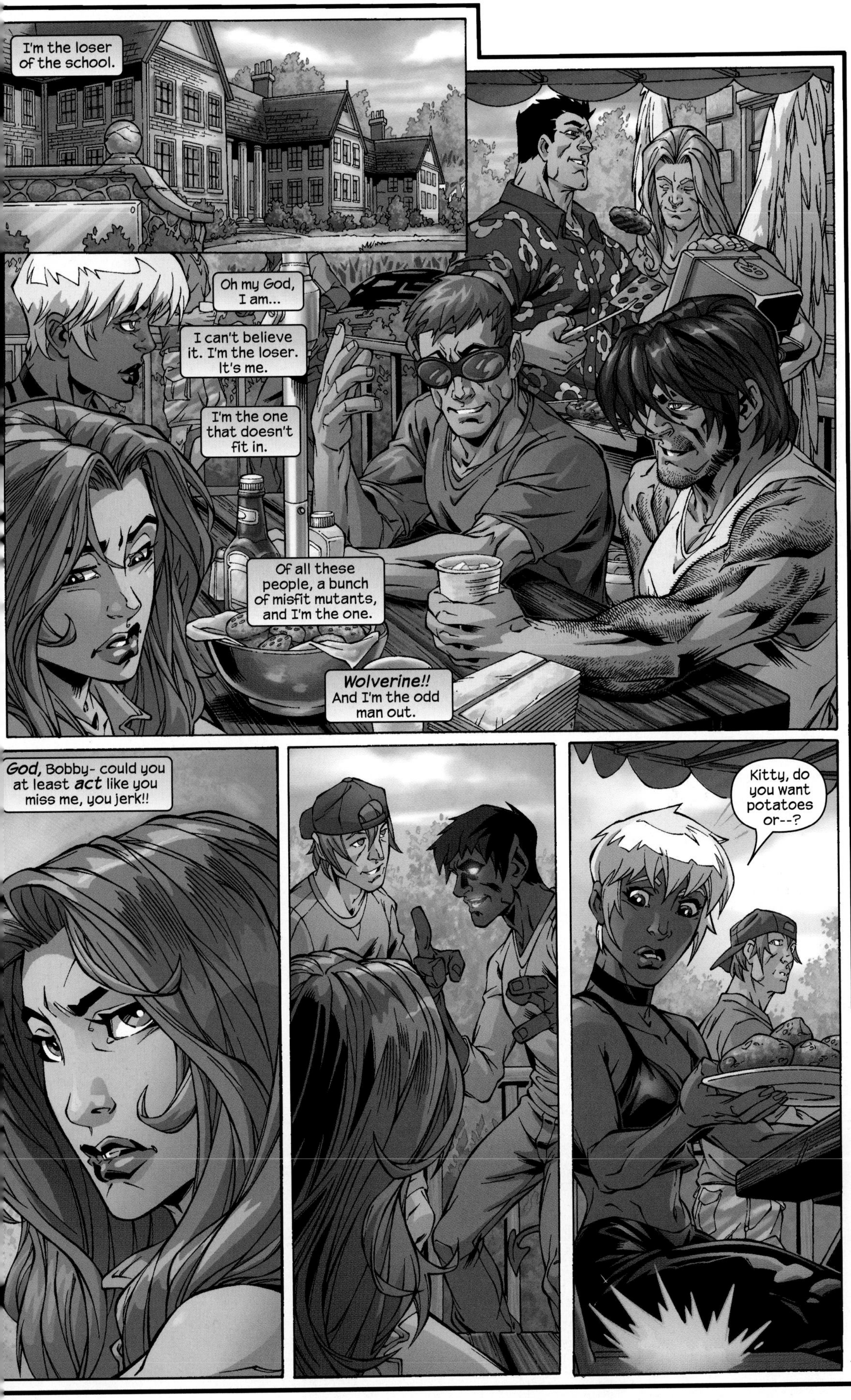
I'm the loser of the school.
Oh my God, I am...
I can't believe it. I'm the loser. It's me.
I'm the one that doesn't fit in.
Of all these people, a bunch of misfit mutants, and I'm the one.
Wolverine!! And I'm the odd man out.
God, Bobby- could you at least act like you miss me, you jerk!!
Kitty, do you want potatoes or--?

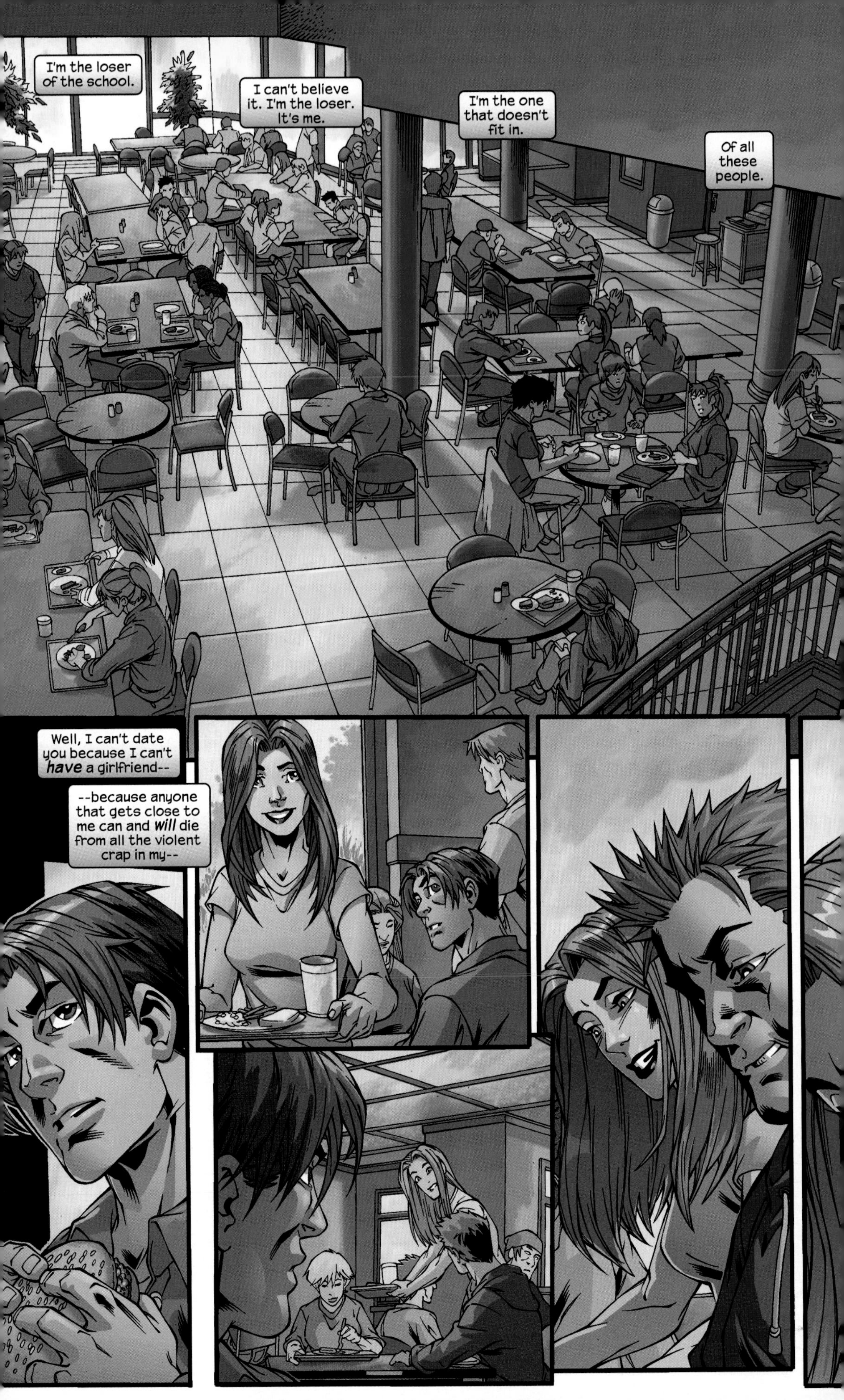

I'm the loser of the school.
I can't believe it. I'm the loser. It's me.
I'm the one that doesn't fit in.
Of all these people.
Well, I can't date you because I can't *have* a girlfriend--
--because anyone that gets close to me can and *will* die from all the violent crap in my--

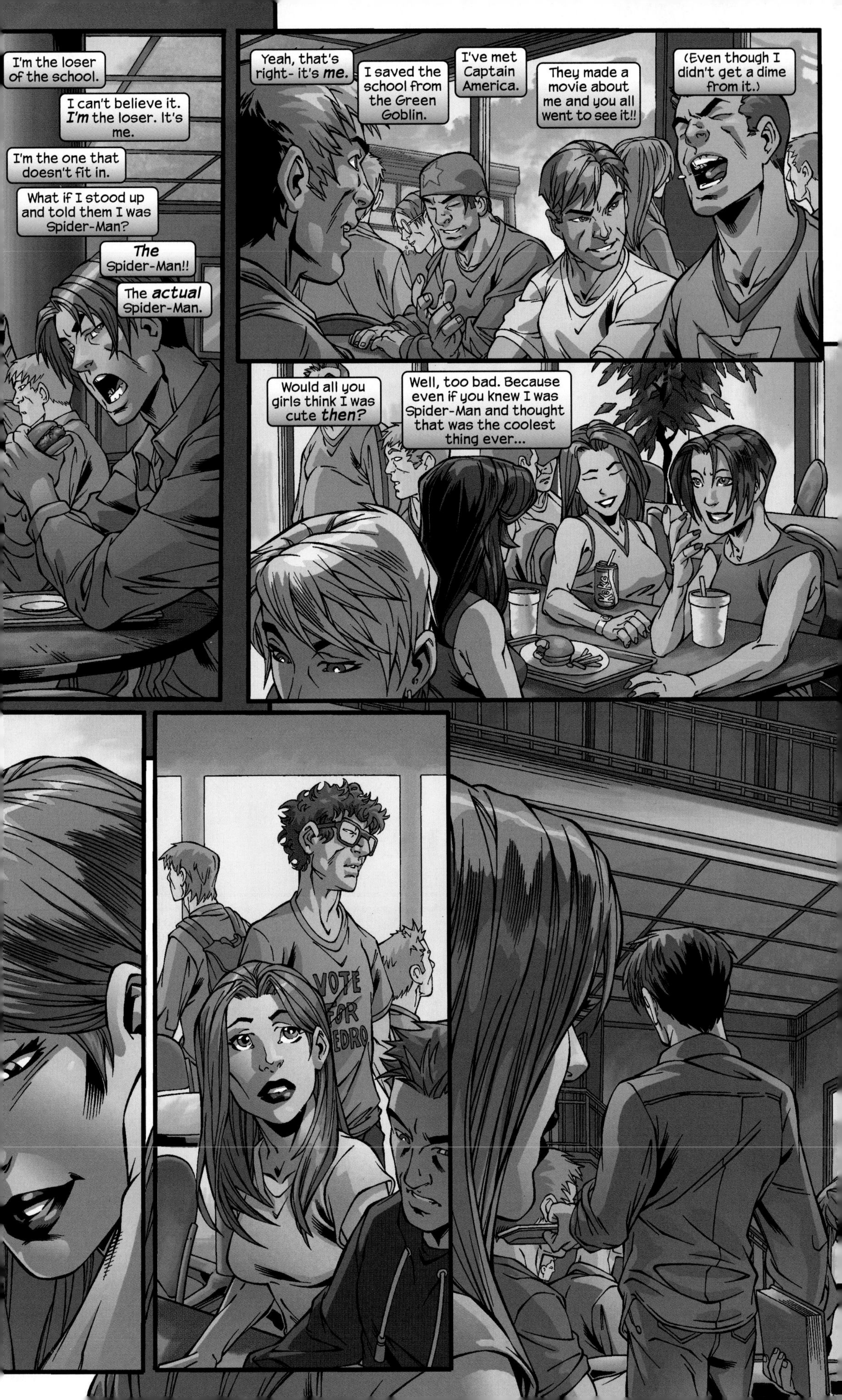
I'm the loser of the school.
I can't believe it. *I'm* the loser. It's me.
I'm the one that doesn't fit in.
What if I stood up and told them I was Spider-Man?
The Spider-Man!!
The *actual* Spider-Man.
Yeah, that's right- it's *me.*
I saved the school from the Green Goblin.
I've met Captain America.
They made a movie about me and you all went to see it!!
(Even though I didn't get a dime from it.)
Would all you girls think I was cute *then?*
Well, too bad. Because even if you knew I was Spider-Man and thought that was the coolest thing ever...
VOTE FOR PEDRO

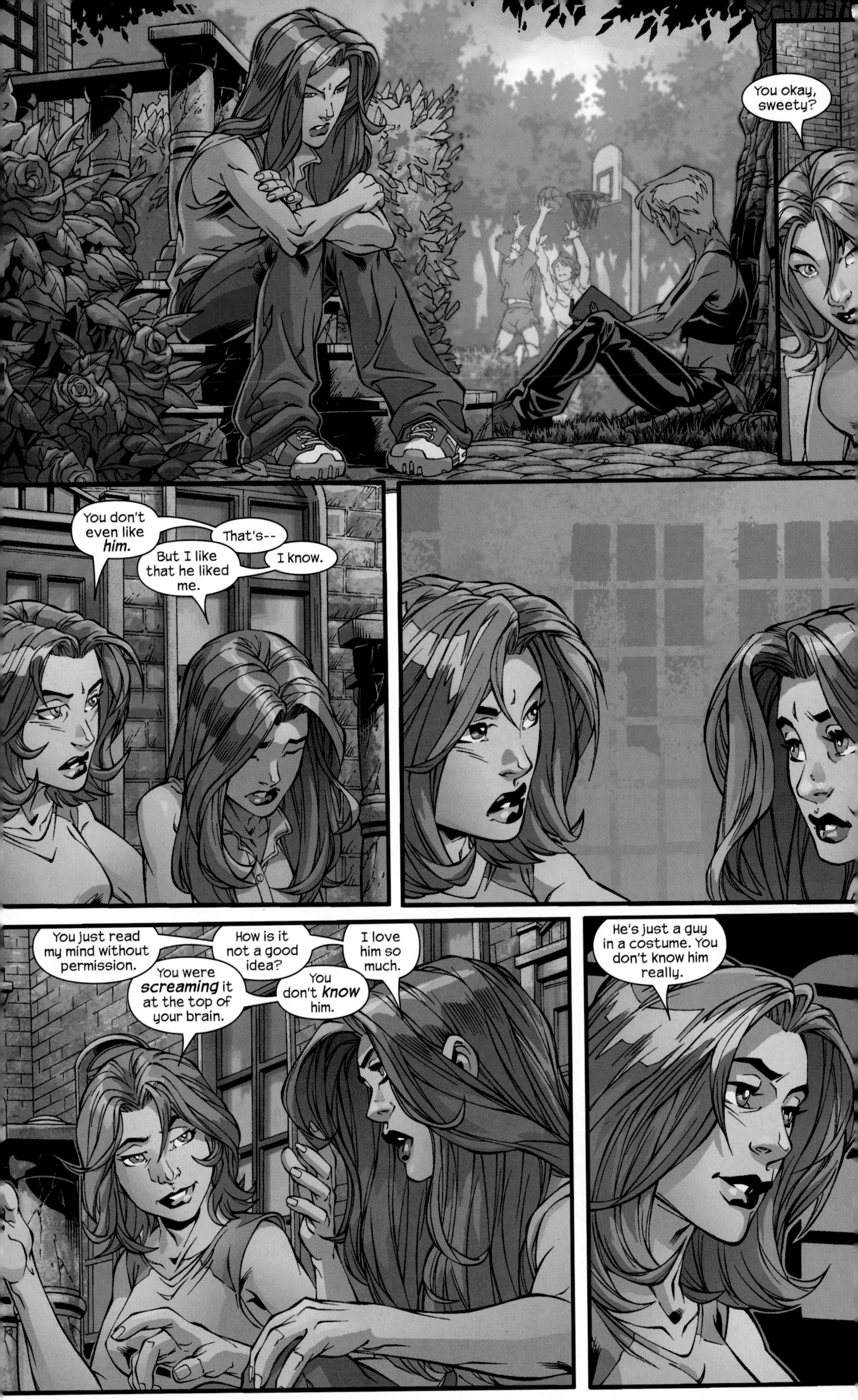
You okay, sweety?
You don't even like *him.*
That's--
But I like that he liked me.
I know.
You just read my mind without permission.
How is it not a good idea?
I love him so much.
You were *screaming* it at the top of your brain.
You don't *know* him.
He's just a guy in a costume. You don't know him really.

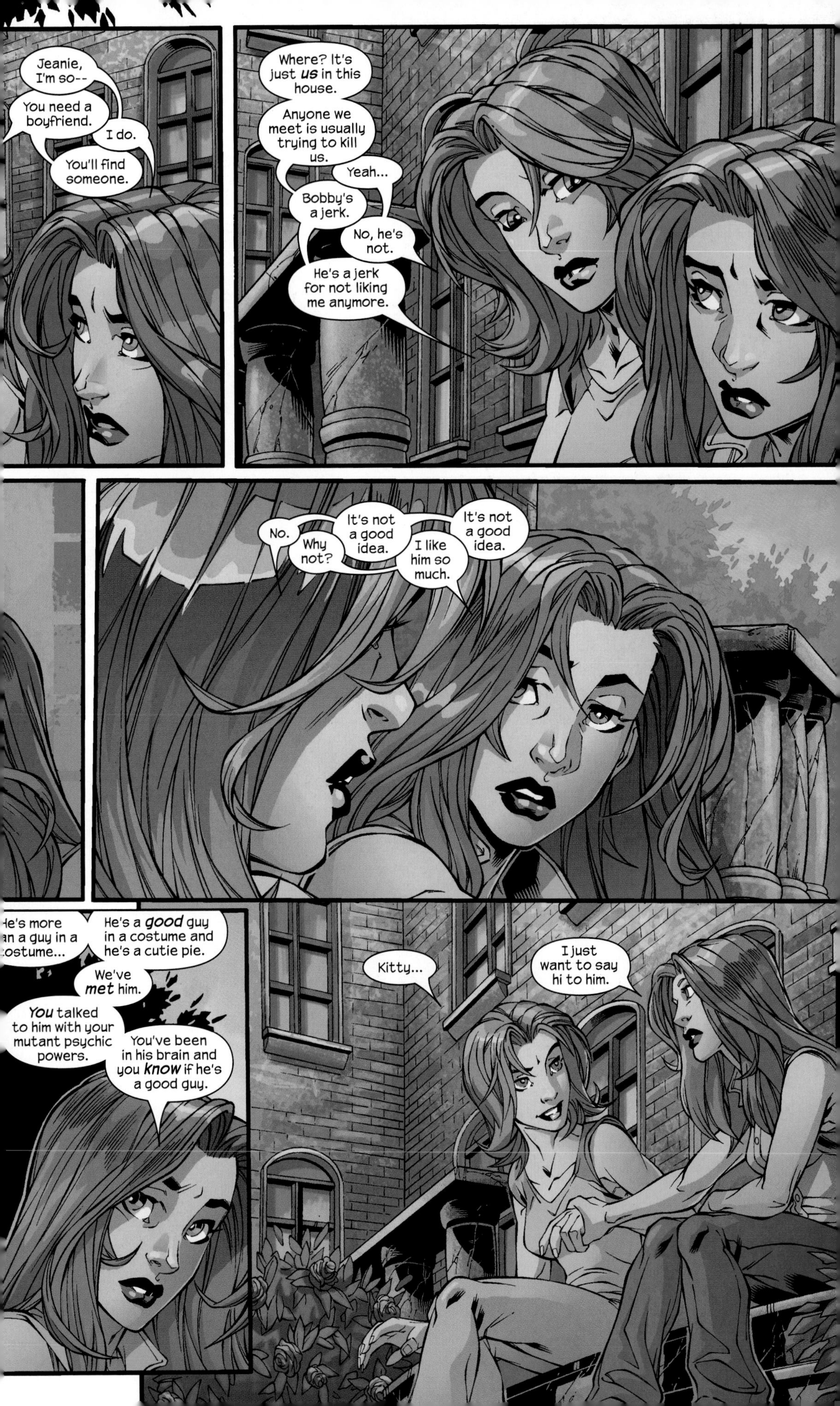

Jeanie, I'm so--
You need a boyfriend.
I do.
You'll find someone.
Where? It's just *us* in this house.
Anyone we meet is usually trying to kill us.
Yeah...
Bobby's a jerk.
No, he's not.
He's a jerk for not liking me anymore.
No.
Why not?
It's not a good idea.
I like him so much.
It's not a good idea.
He's more an a guy in a costume...
He's a *good* guy in a costume and he's a cutie pie.
We've *met* him.
You talked to him with your mutant psychic powers.
You've been in his brain and you *know* if he's a good guy.
Kitty...
I just want to say hi to him.

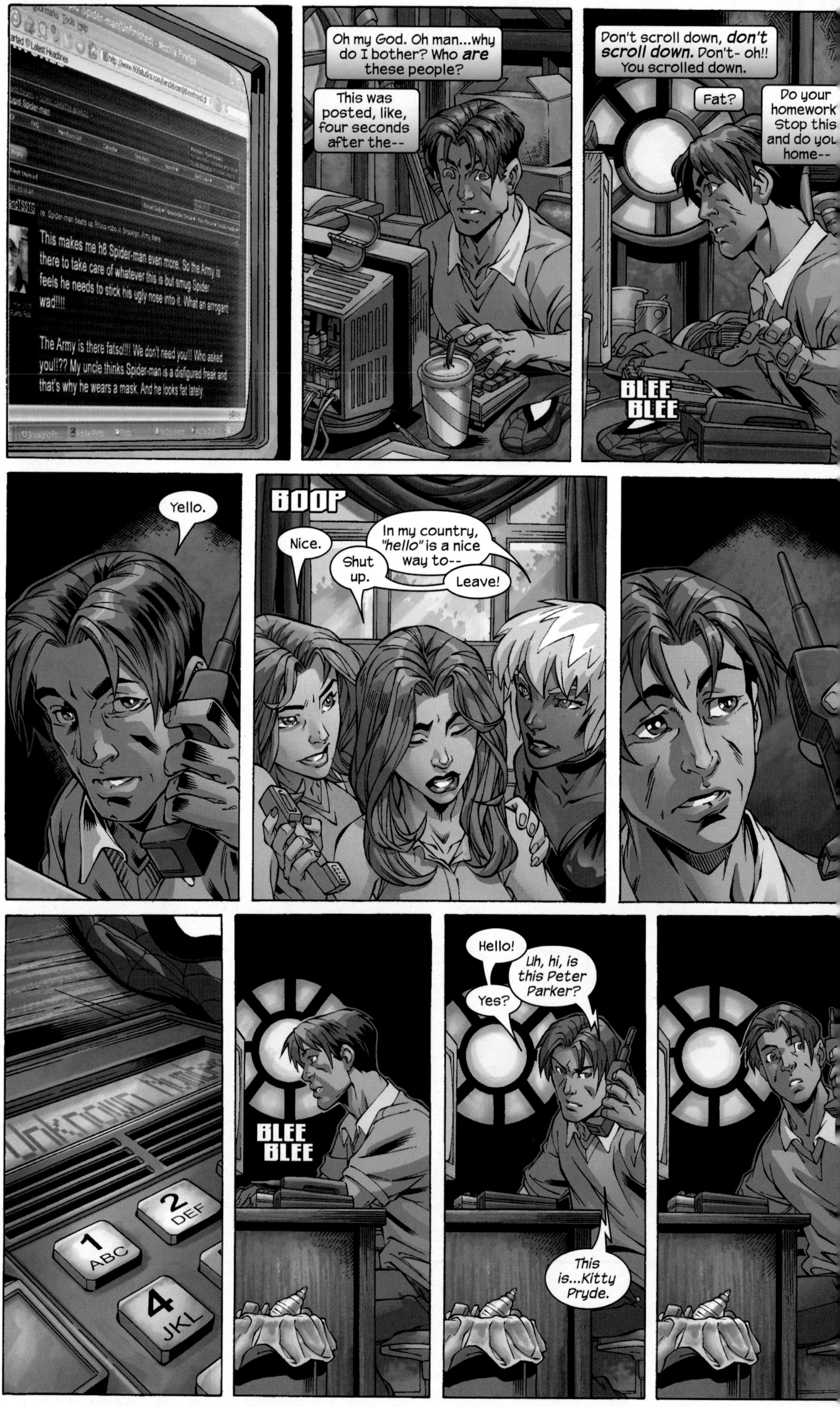
This makes me h8 Spider-man even more. So the Army is there to take care of whatever this is but smug Spider feels he needs to stick his ugly nose into it. What an arrogant wad!!!!
The Army is there fatso!!!! We don't need you!! Who asked you!!?? My uncle thinks Spider-man is a disfigured freak and that's why he wears a mask. And he looks fat lately.
Oh my God. Oh man...why do I bother? Who *are* these people?
This was posted, like, four seconds after the--
Don't scroll down, ***don't scroll down.*** Don't- oh!! You scrolled down.
Fat?
Do your homework Stop this and do you home--
BLEE BLEE
Yello.
BOOP
Nice.
In my country, *"hello"* is a nice way to--
Shut up.
Leave!
BLEE BLEE
Hello!
Yes?
Uh, hi, is this Peter Parker?
This is...Kitty Pryde.

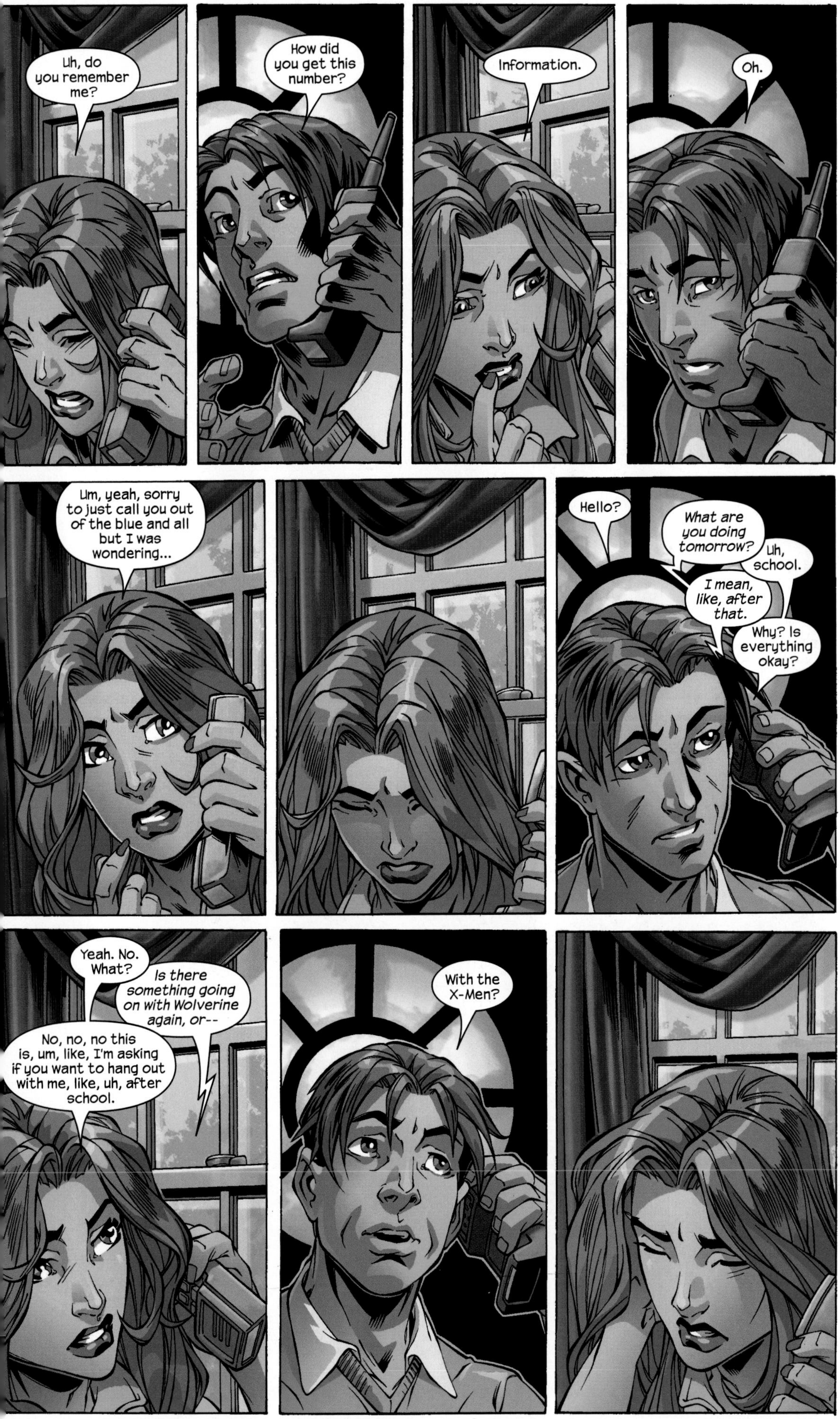
Uh, do you remember me?
How did you get this number?
Information.
Oh.
Um, yeah, sorry to just call you out of the blue and all but I was wondering...
Hello?
What are you doing tomorrow?
Uh, school.
I mean, like, after that.
Why? Is everything okay?
Yeah. No. What?
Is there something going on with Wolverine again, or--
No, no, no this is, um, like, I'm asking if you want to hang out with me, like, uh, after school.
With the X-Men?

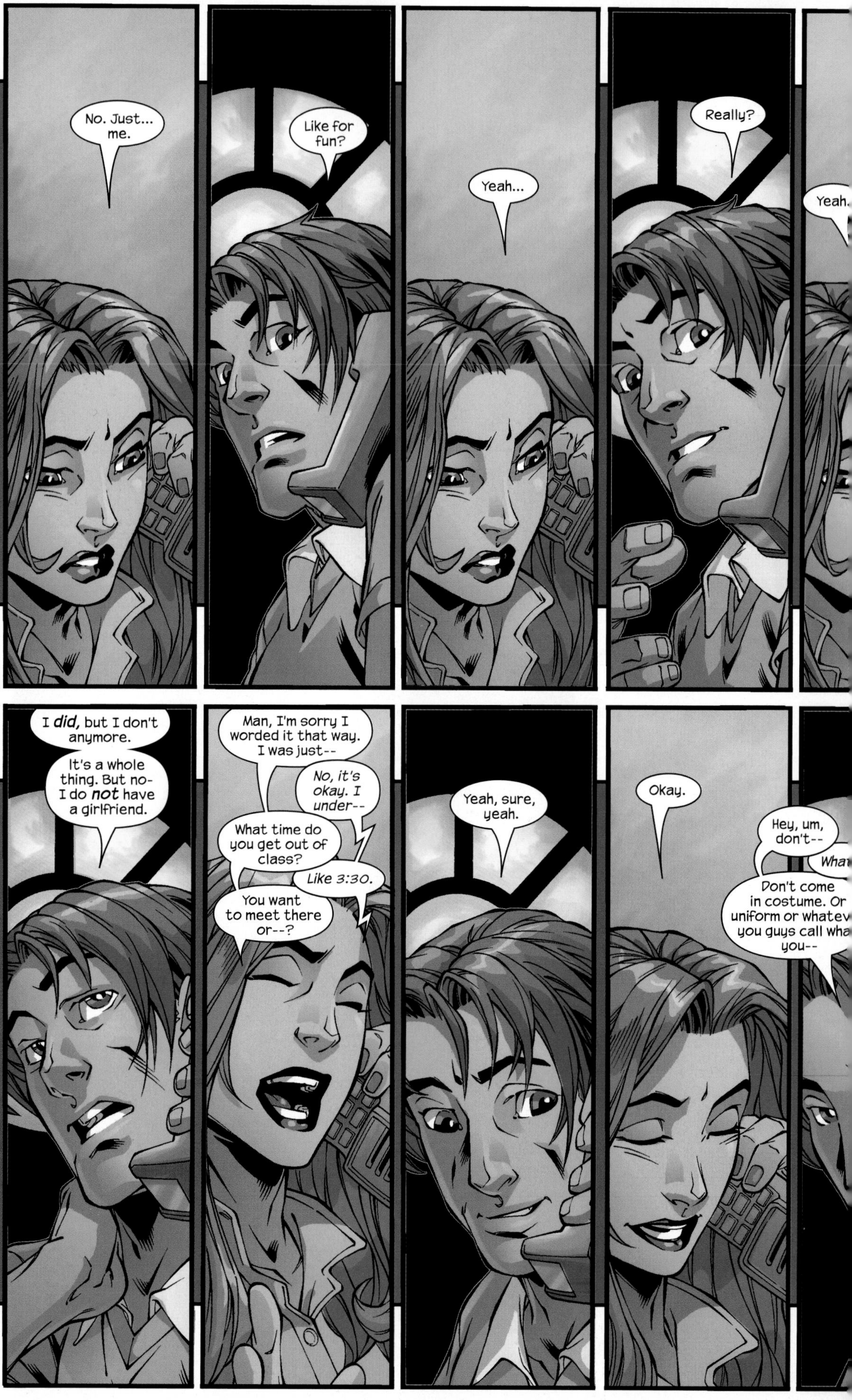
No. Just... me.
Like for fun?
Yeah...
Really?
Yeah.
I did, but I don't anymore.
It's a whole thing. But no- I do not have a girlfriend.
Man, I'm sorry I worded it that way. I was just--
No, it's okay. I under--
What time do you get out of class?
Like 3:30.
You want to meet there or--?
Yeah, sure, yeah.
Okay.
Hey, um, don't--
Don't come in costume. Or uniform or whatev you guys call wha you--

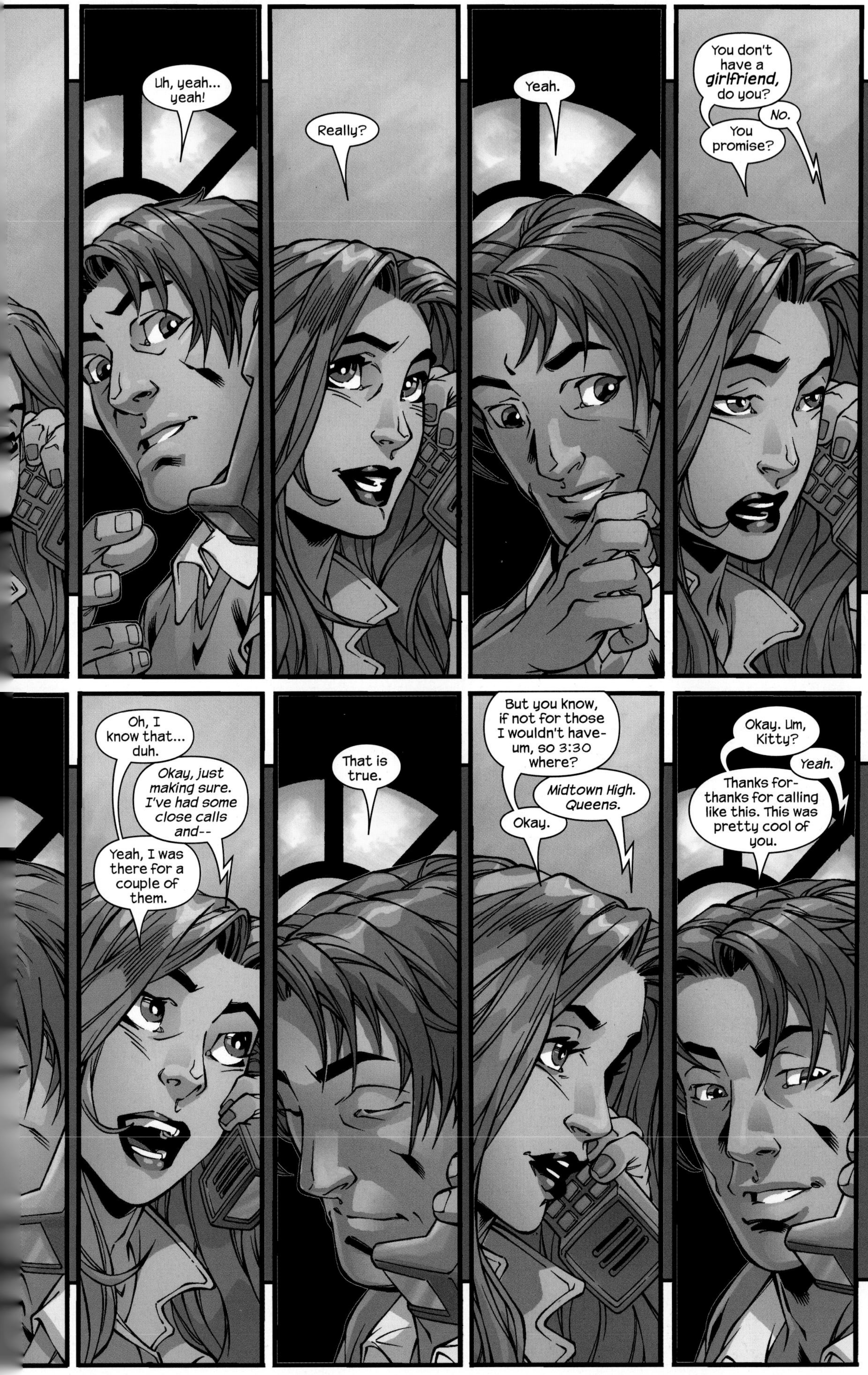
Uh, yeah... yeah!
Really?
Yeah.
You don't have a *girlfriend,* do you?
No.
You promise?
Oh, I know that... duh.
Okay, just making sure. I've had some close calls and--
Yeah, I was there for a couple of them.
That is true.
But you know, if not for those I wouldn't have- um, so 3:30 where?
Midtown High. Queens.
Okay.
Okay. Um, Kitty?
Yeah.
Thanks for- thanks for calling like this. This was pretty cool of you.

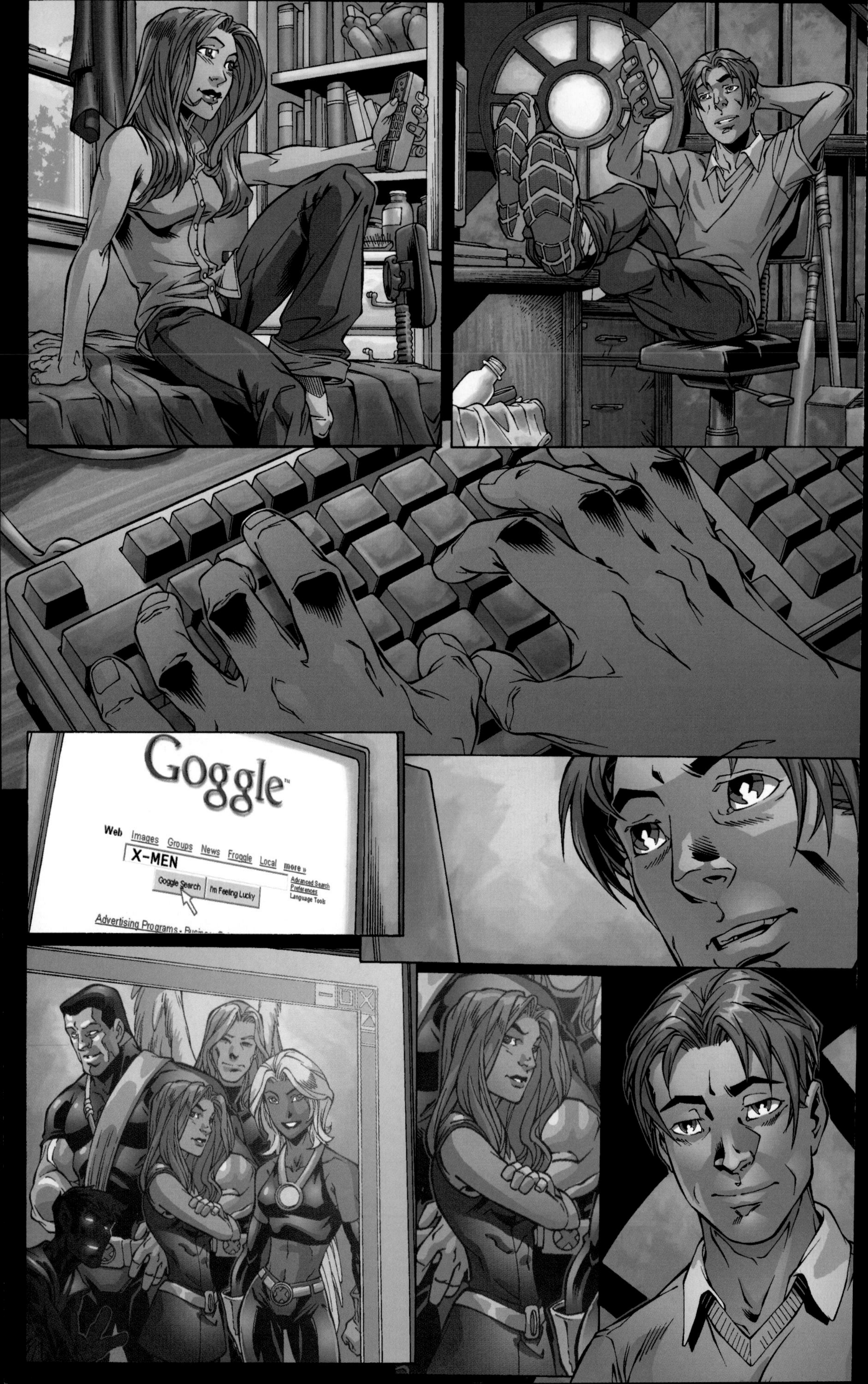

Goggle™
Web Images Groups News Froggle Local more »
X-MEN
Goggle Search
I'm Feeling Lucky
Advanced Search
Preferences
Language Tools

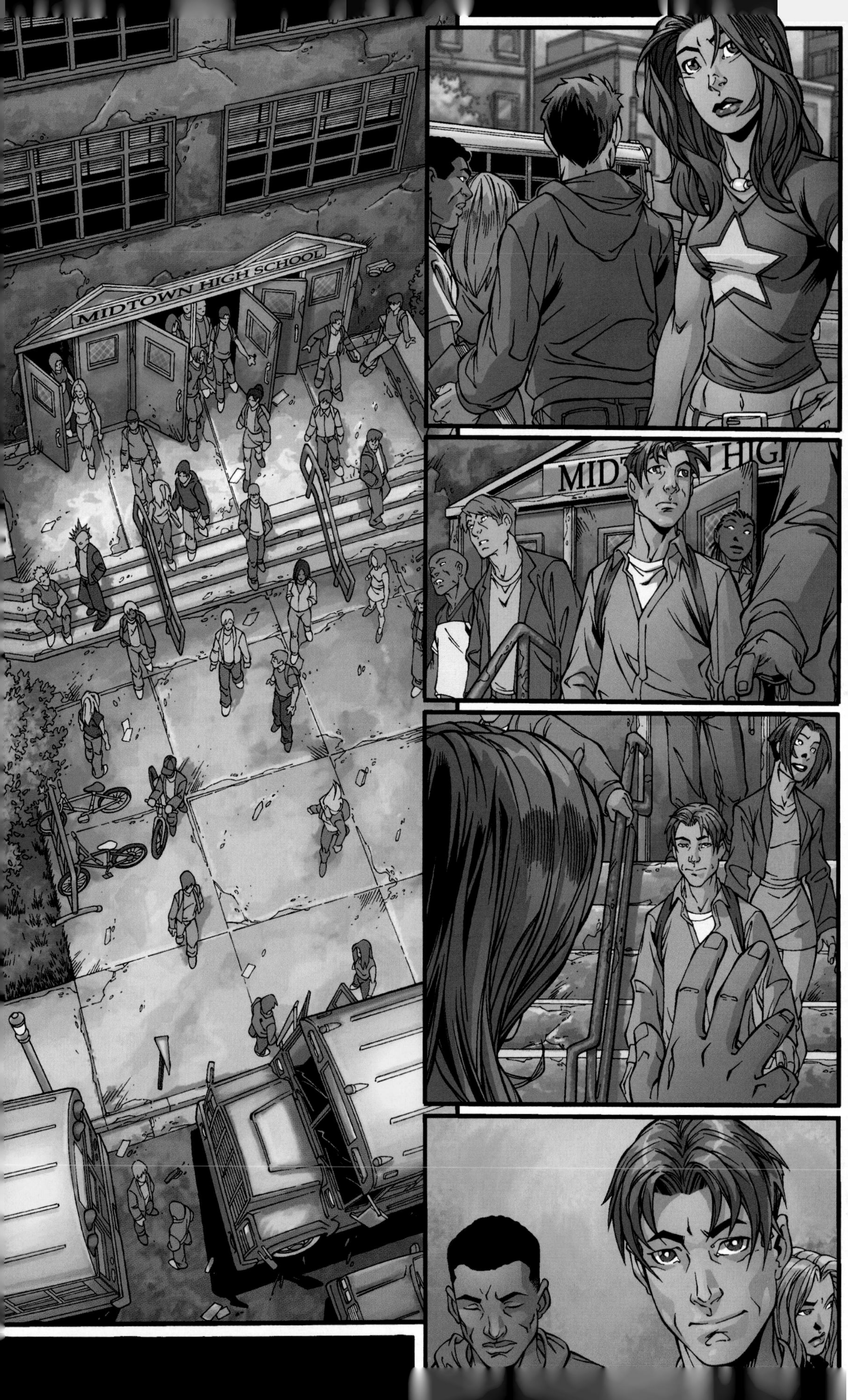
MIDTOWN HIGH SCHOOL

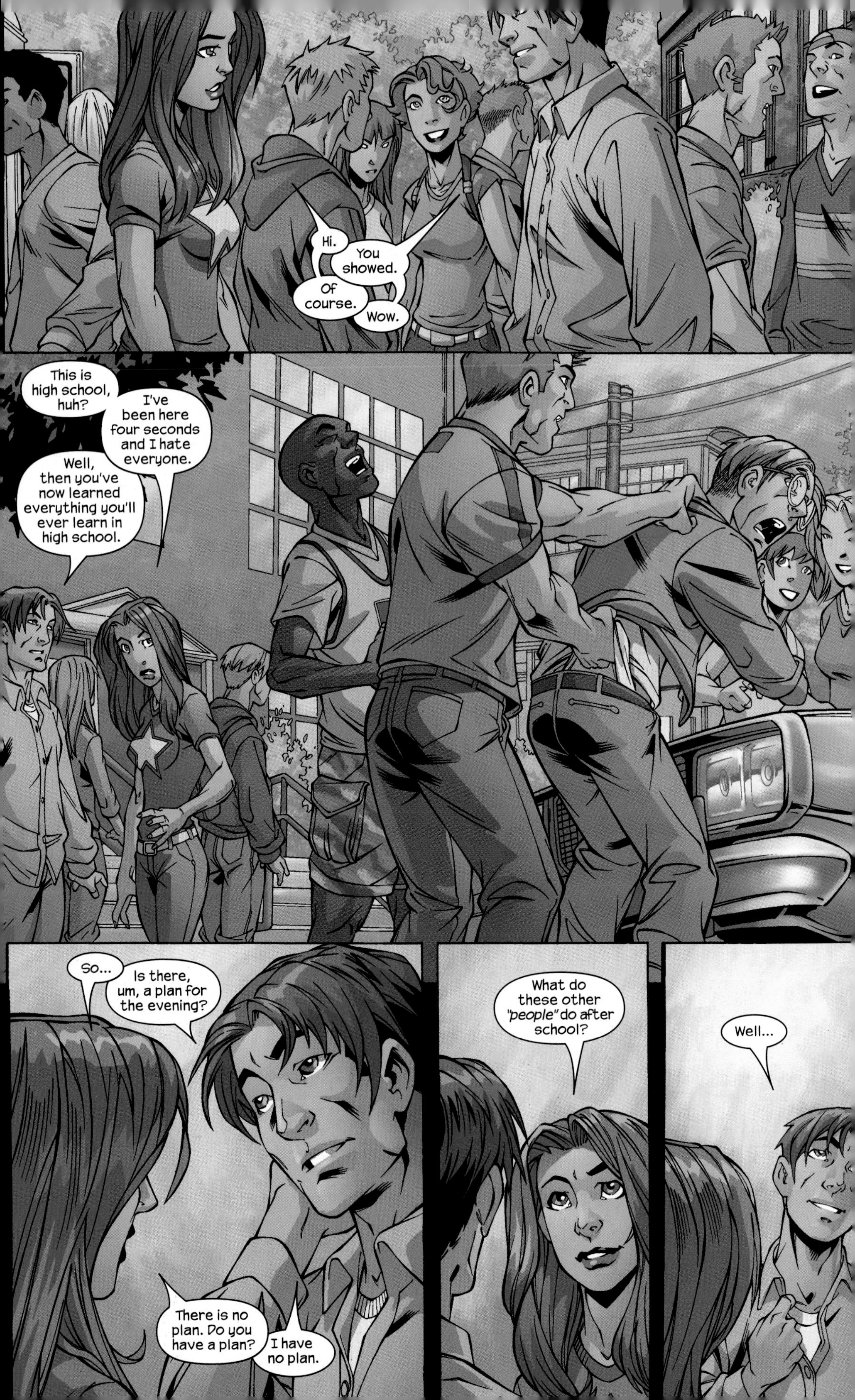

Hi.
You showed.
Of course.
Wow.
This is high school, huh?
I've been here four seconds and I hate everyone.
Well, then you've now learned everything you'll ever learn in high school.
So...
Is there, um, a plan for the evening?
There is no plan. Do you have a plan?
I have no plan.
What do these other *"people"* do after school?
Well...

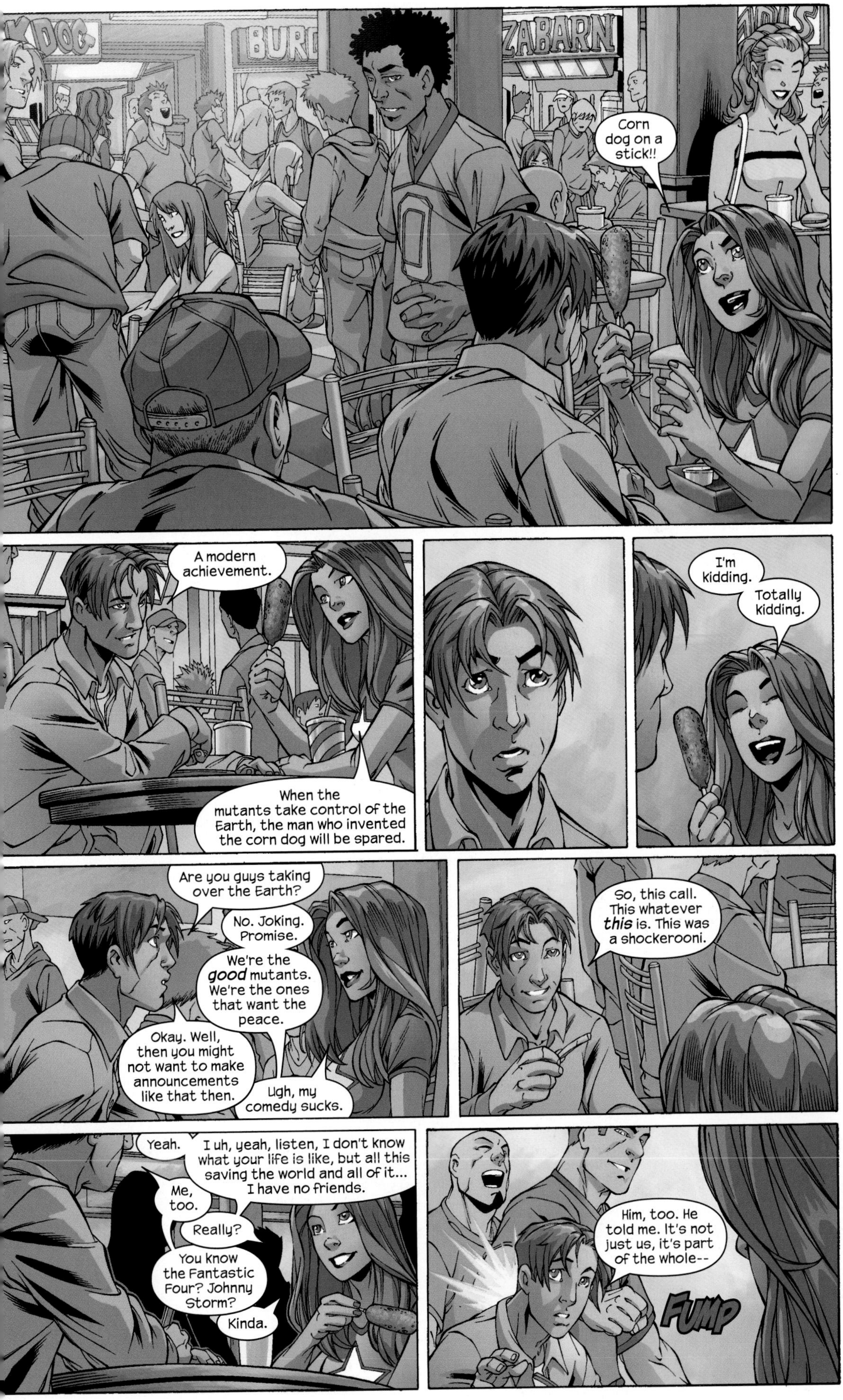
Corn dog on a stick!!
A modern achievement.
When the mutants take control of the Earth, the man who invented the corn dog will be spared.
I'm kidding.
Totally kidding.
Are you guys taking over the Earth?
No. Joking. Promise.
We're the *good* mutants. We're the ones that want the peace.
Okay. Well, then you might not want to make announcements like that then.
Ugh, my comedy sucks.
So, this call. This whatever *this* is. This was a shockerooni.
Yeah.
I uh, yeah, listen, I don't know what your life is like, but all this saving the world and all of it... I have no friends.
Me, too.
Really?
You know the Fantastic Four? Johnny Storm?
Kinda.
Him, too. He told me. It's not just us, it's part of the whole--
FUMP

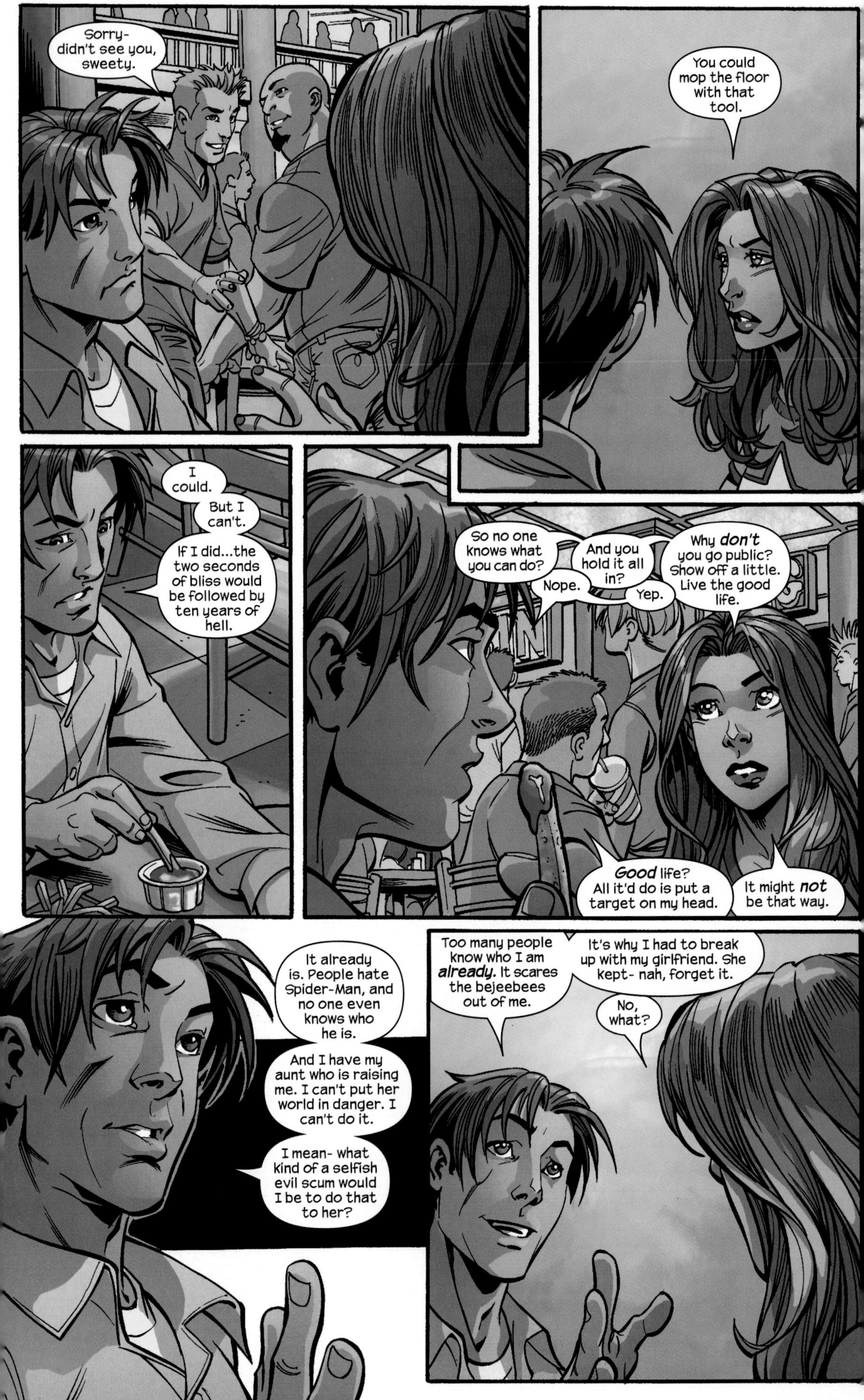
Sorry- didn't see you, sweety.
You could mop the floor with that tool.
I could.
But I can't.
If I did...the two seconds of bliss would be followed by ten years of hell.
So no one knows what you can do?
Nope.
And you hold it all in?
Yep.
Why *don't* you go public? Show off a little. Live the good life.
Good life? All it'd do is put a target on my head.
It might *not* be that way.
It already is. People hate Spider-Man, and no one even knows who he is.
And I have my aunt who is raising me. I can't put her world in danger. I can't do it.
I mean- what kind of a selfish evil scum would I be to do that to her?
Too many people know who I am *already.* It scares the bejeebees out of me.
It's why I had to break up with my girlfriend. She kept- nah, forget it.
No, what?

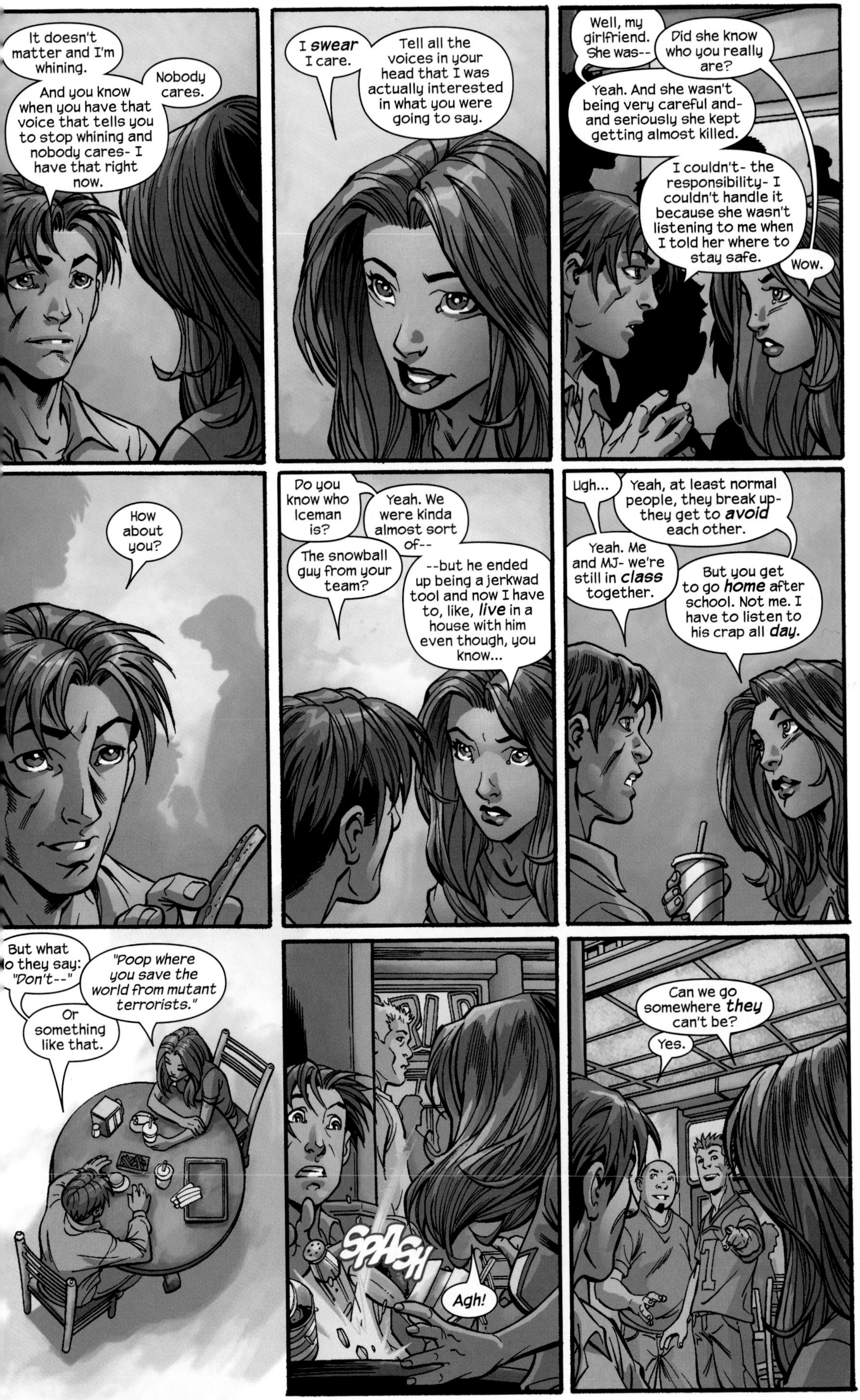
It doesn't matter and I'm whining.
Nobody cares.
And you know when you have that voice that tells you to stop whining and nobody cares- I have that right now.
I swear I care.
Tell all the voices in your head that I was actually interested in what you were going to say.
Well, my girlfriend. She was--
Did she know who you really are?
Yeah. And she wasn't being very careful and- and seriously she kept getting almost killed.
I couldn't- the responsibility- I couldn't handle it because she wasn't listening to me when I told her where to stay safe.
Wow.
How about you?
Do you know who Iceman is?
Yeah. We were kinda almost sort of--
The snowball guy from your team?
--but he ended up being a jerkwad tool and now I have to, like, live in a house with him even though, you know...
Ugh...
Yeah, at least normal people, they break up- they get to avoid each other.
Yeah. Me and MJ- we're still in class together.
But you get to go home after school. Not me. I have to listen to his crap all day.
But what o they say: "Don't--"
"Poop where you save the world from mutant terrorists."
Or something like that.
SPASH
Agh!
Can we go somewhere they can't be?
Yes.

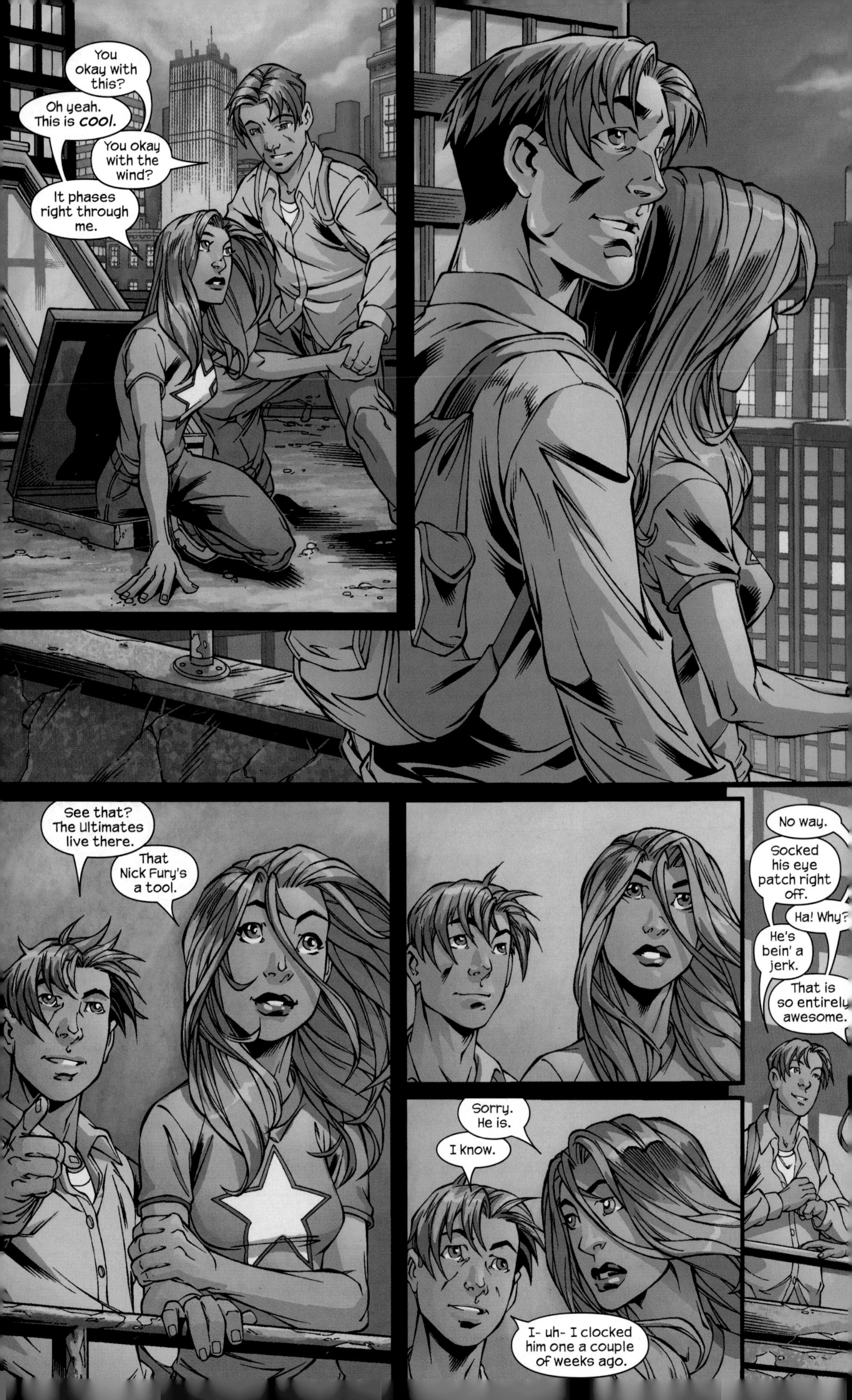

You okay with this?
Oh yeah. This is *cool.*
You okay with the wind?
It phases right through me.
See that? The Ultimates live there.
That Nick Fury's a tool.
Sorry. He is.
I know.
I- uh- I clocked him one a couple of weeks ago.
No way.
Socked his eye patch right off.
Ha! Why?
He's bein' a jerk.
That is so entirely awesome.

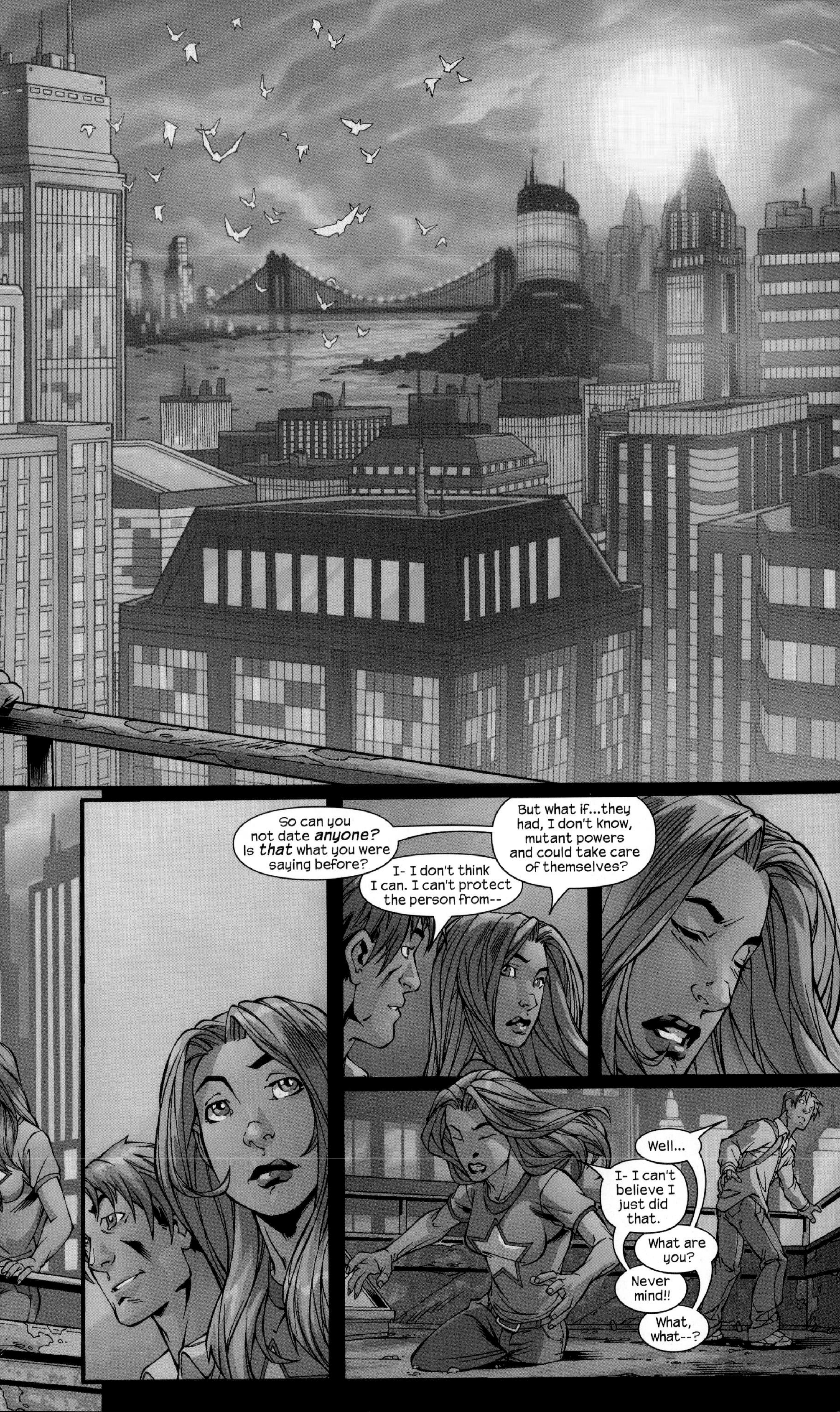
So can you not date *anyone?* Is *that* what you were saying before?
I- I don't think I can. I can't protect the person from--
But what if...they had, I don't know, mutant powers and could take care of themselves?
Well...
I- I can't believe I just did that.
What are you?
Never mind!!
What, what--?

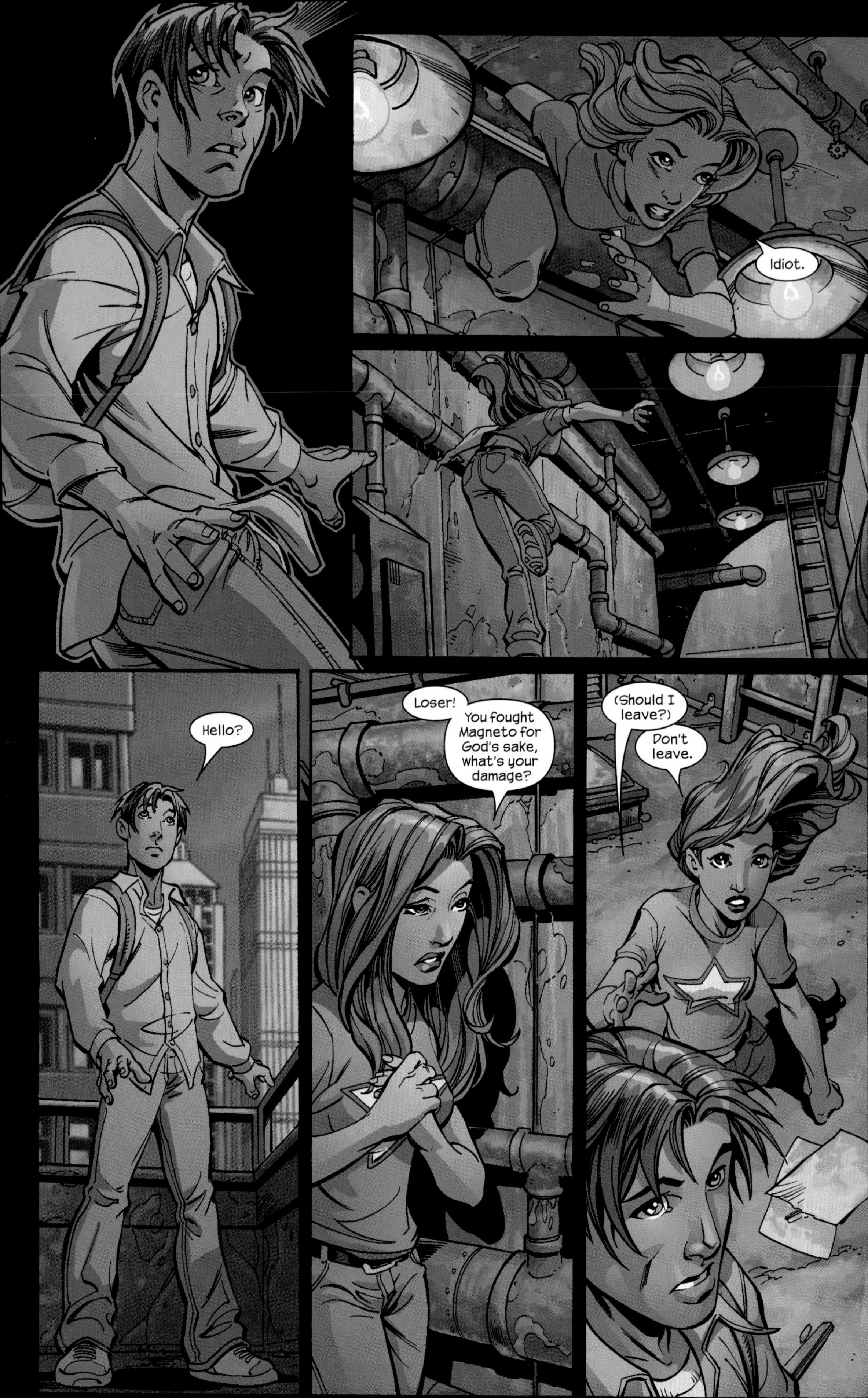

Idiot.
Hello?
Loser!
You fought Magneto for God's sake, what's your damage?
(Should I leave?)
Don't leave.

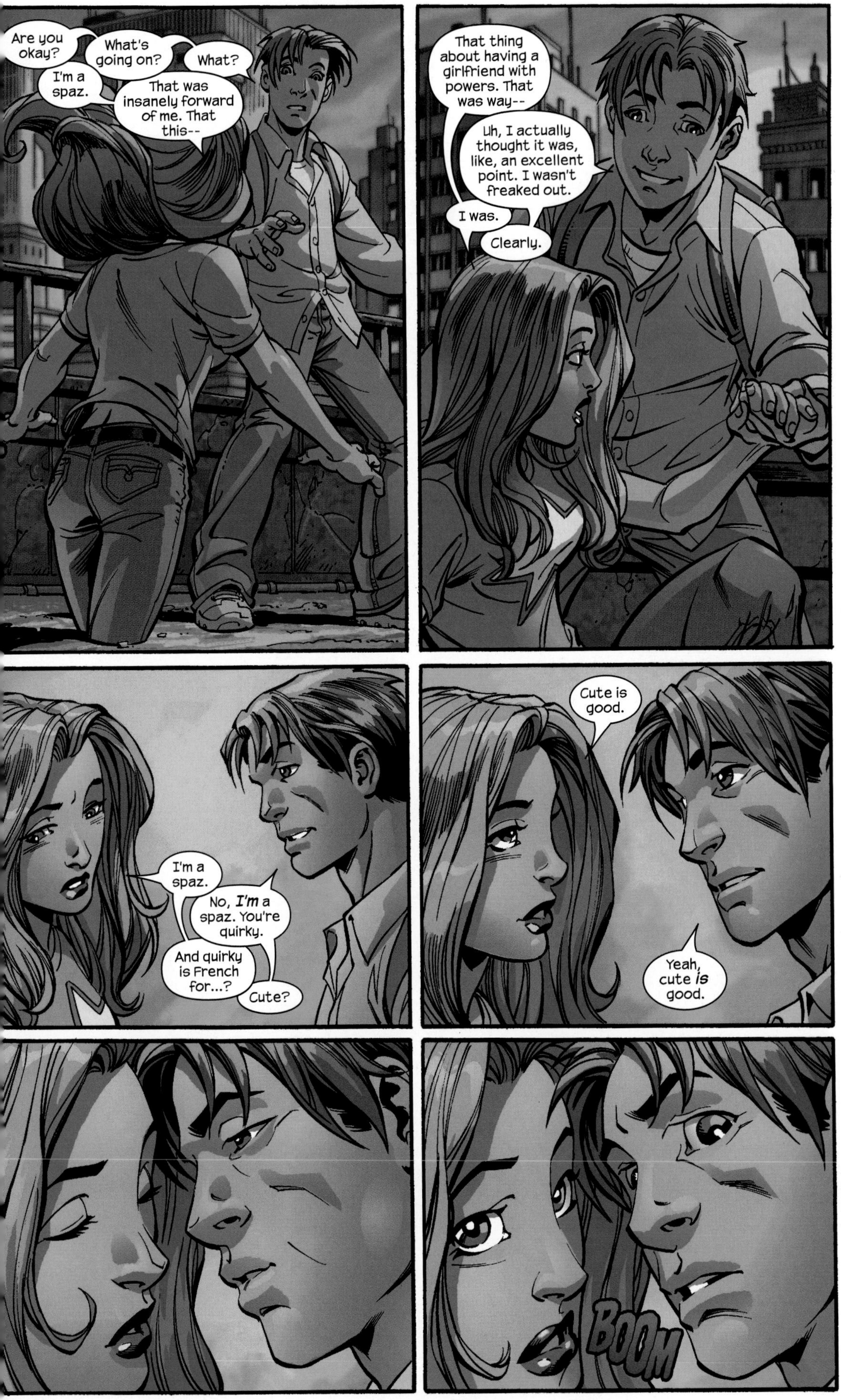
Are you okay?
What's going on?
What?
I'm a spaz.
That was insanely forward of me. That this--
That thing about having a girlfriend with powers. That was way--
Uh, I actually thought it was, like, an excellent point. I wasn't freaked out.
I was.
Clearly.
I'm a spaz.
No, *I'm* a spaz. You're quirky.
And quirky is French for...?
Cute?
Cute is good.
Yeah, cute *is* good.
BOOM

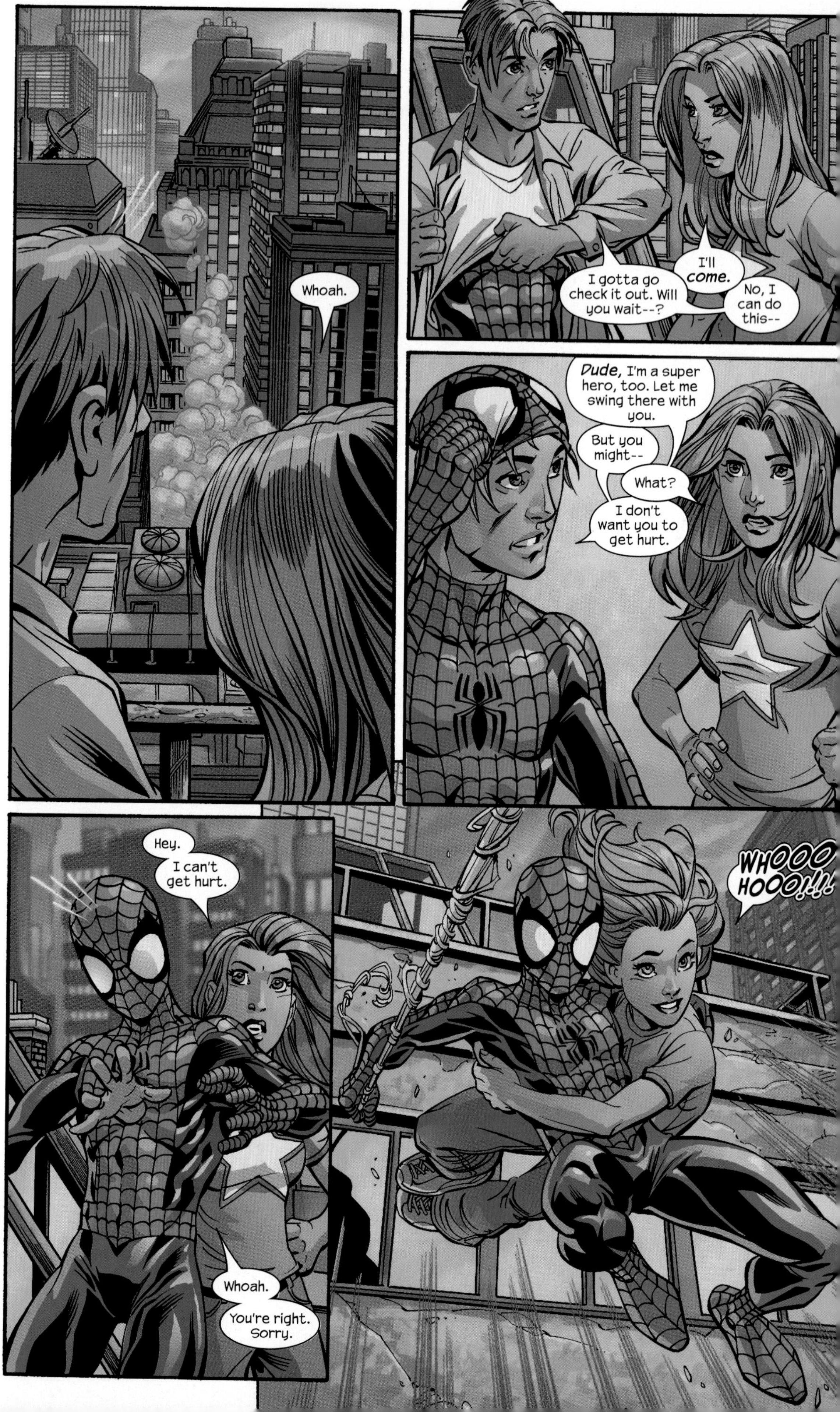

Whoah.
I gotta go check it out. Will you wait--?
I'll *come.*
No, I can do this--
Dude, I'm a super hero, too. Let me swing there with you.
But you might--
What?
I don't want you to get hurt.
Hey.
I can't get hurt.
Whoah.
You're right. Sorry.
WHOOO HOOO!!!

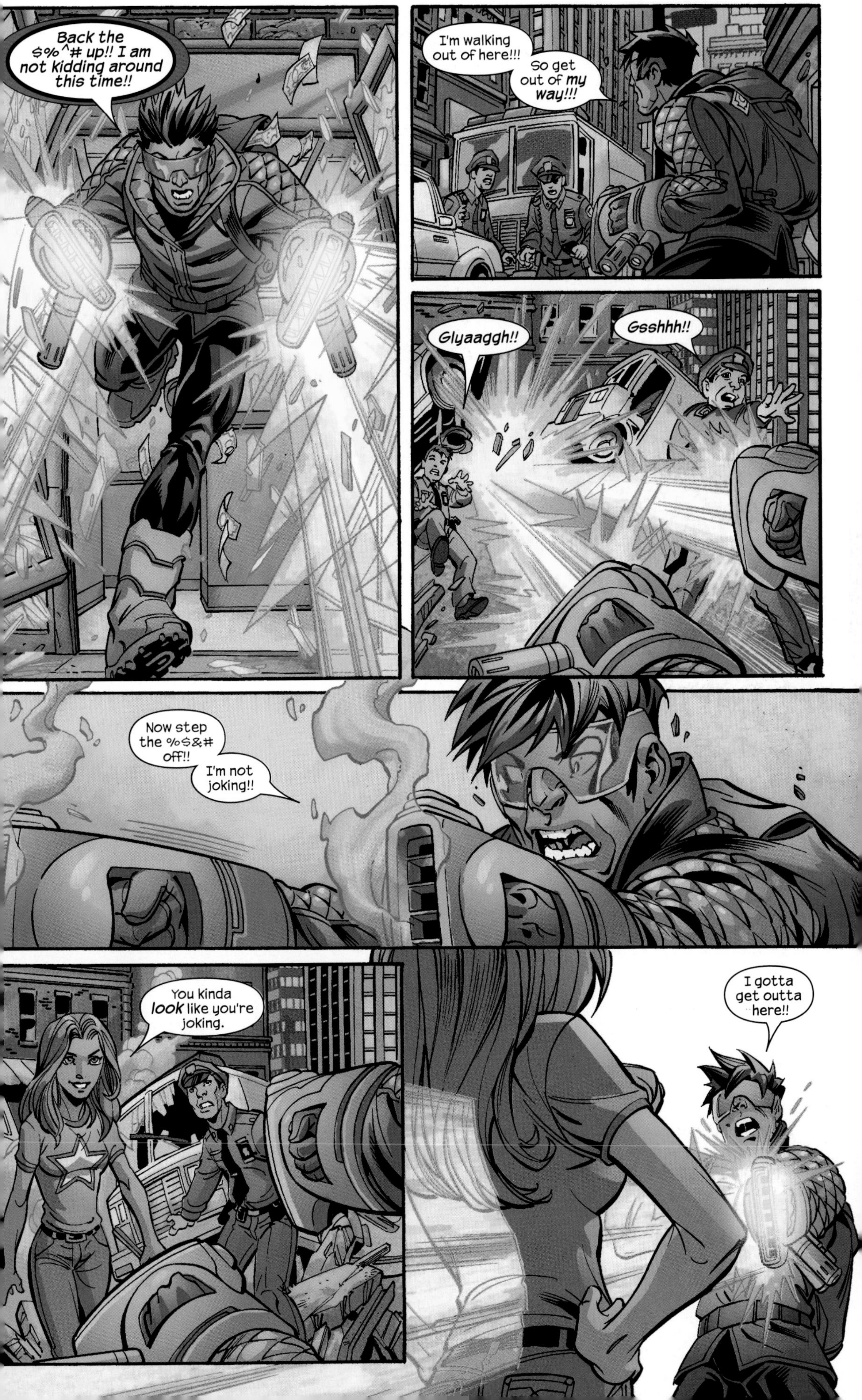
Back the $%^# up!! I am not kidding around this time!!
I'm walking out of here!!!
So get out of *my* way!!!
Glyaaggh!!
Gsshhh!!
Now step the %$&# off!!
I'm not joking!!
You kinda *look* like you're joking.
I gotta get outta here!!

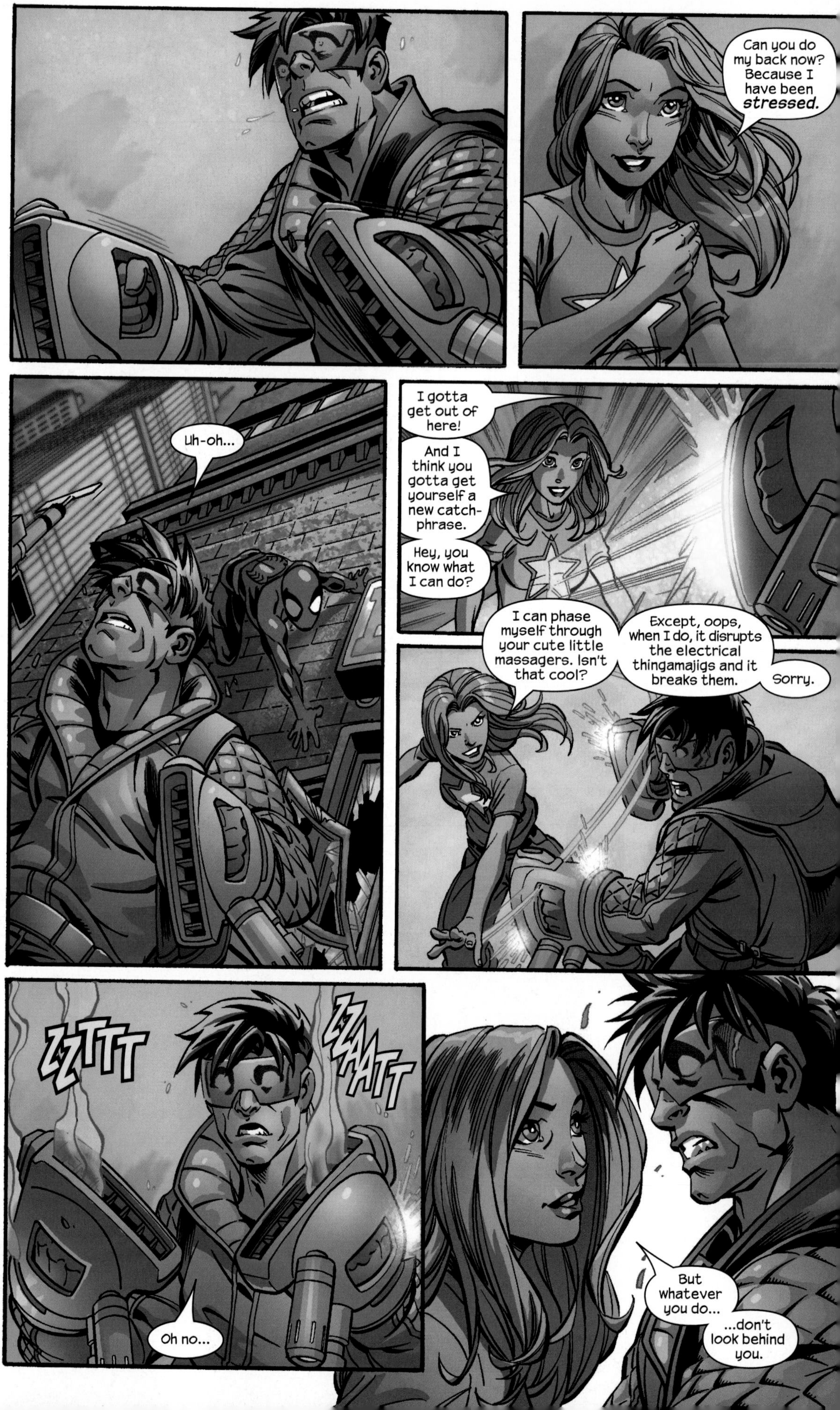
Can you do my back now? Because I have been *stressed.*
Uh-oh...
I gotta get out of here!
And I think you gotta get yourself a new catch-phrase.
Hey, you know what I can do?
I can phase myself through your cute little massagers. Isn't that cool?
Except, oops, when I do, it disrupts the electrical thingamajigs and it breaks them.
Sorry.
ZZTTTT
ZZAATTT
Oh no...
But whatever you do...
...don't look behind you.

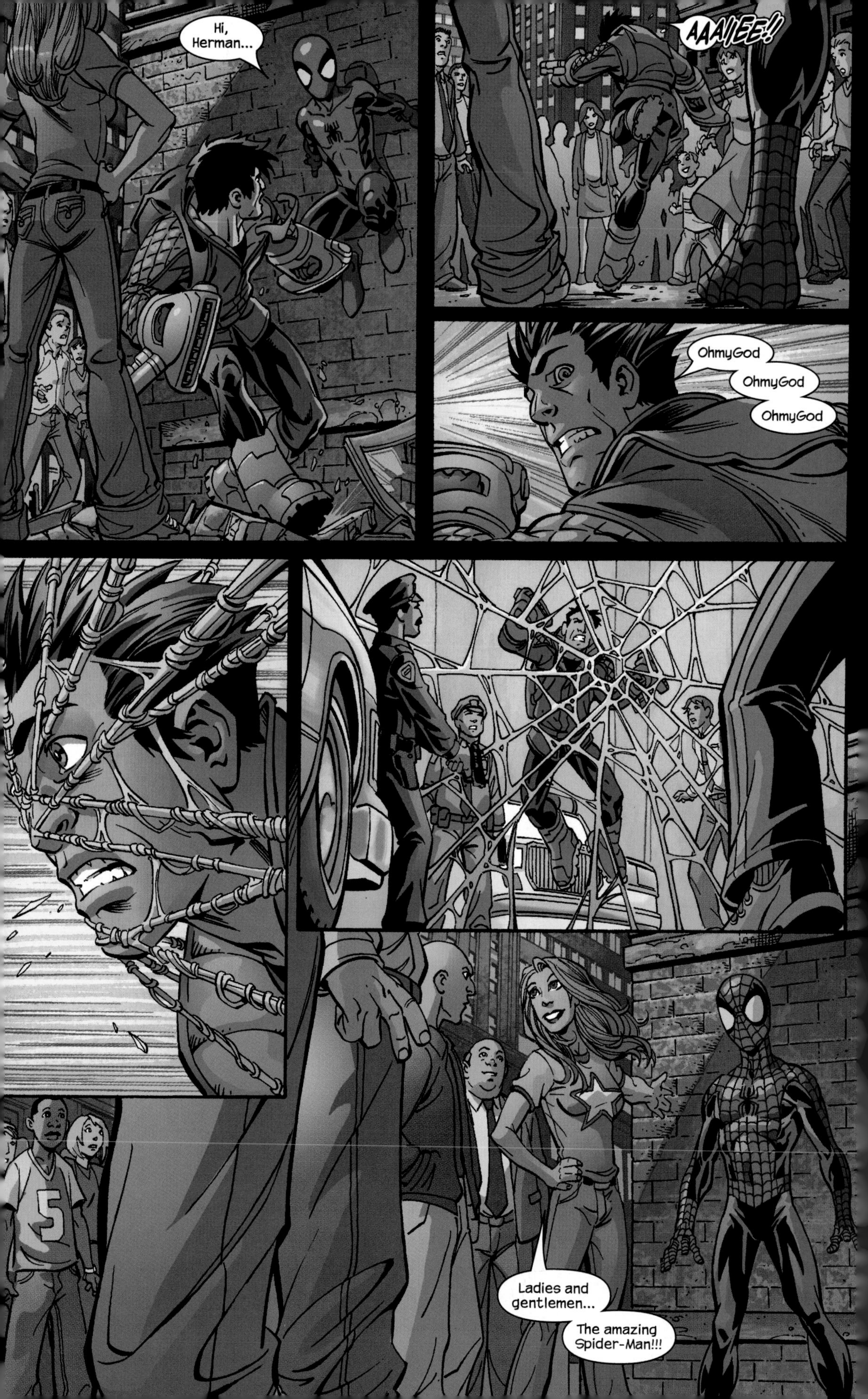
Hi, Herman...
AAAIIEE!!
OhmyGod
OhmyGod
OhmyGod
Ladies and gentlemen...
The amazing Spider-Man!!!

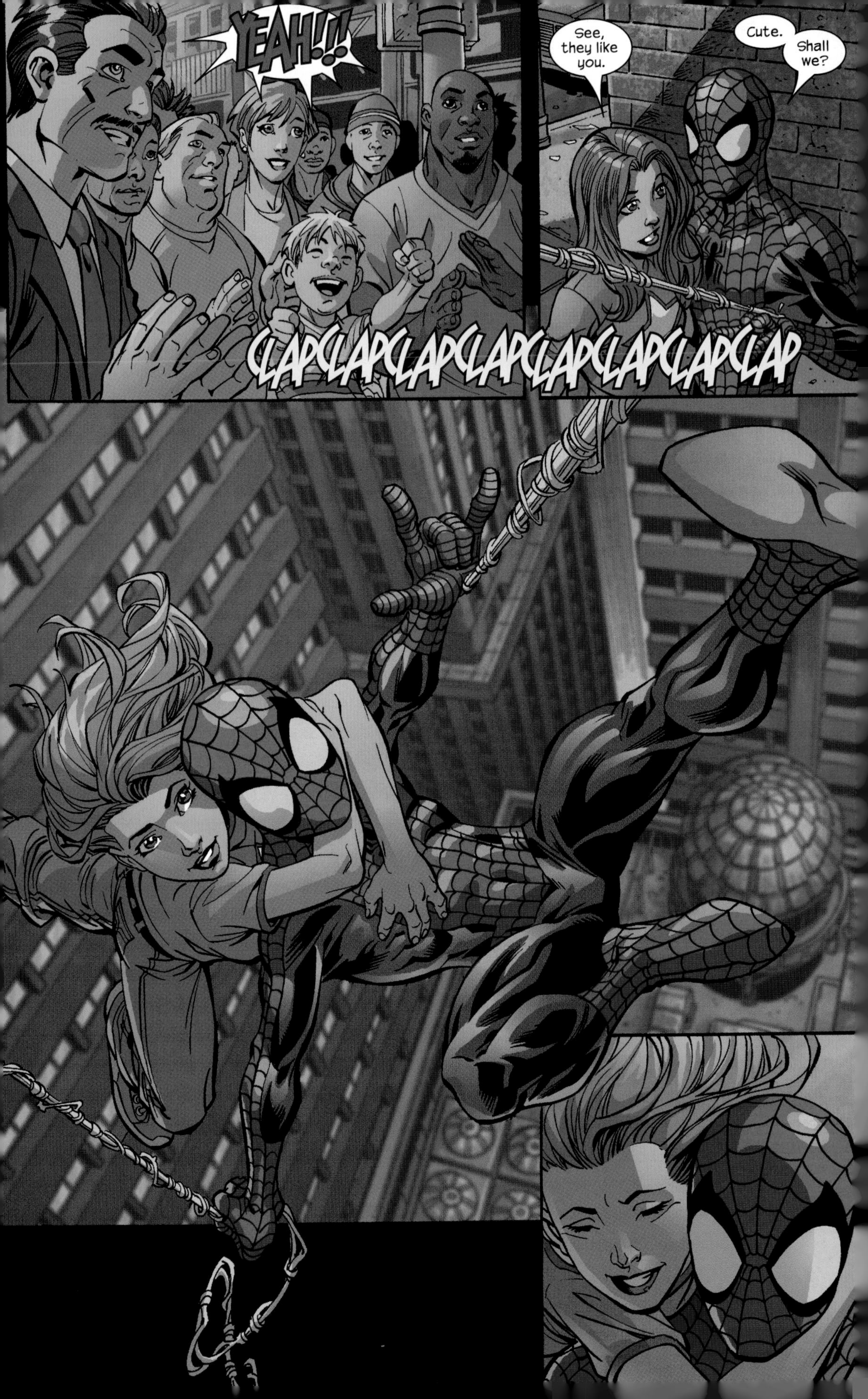
YEAH!!!
CLAPCLAPCLAPCLAPCLAPCLAPCLAPCLAP
See, they like you.
Cute.
Shall we?

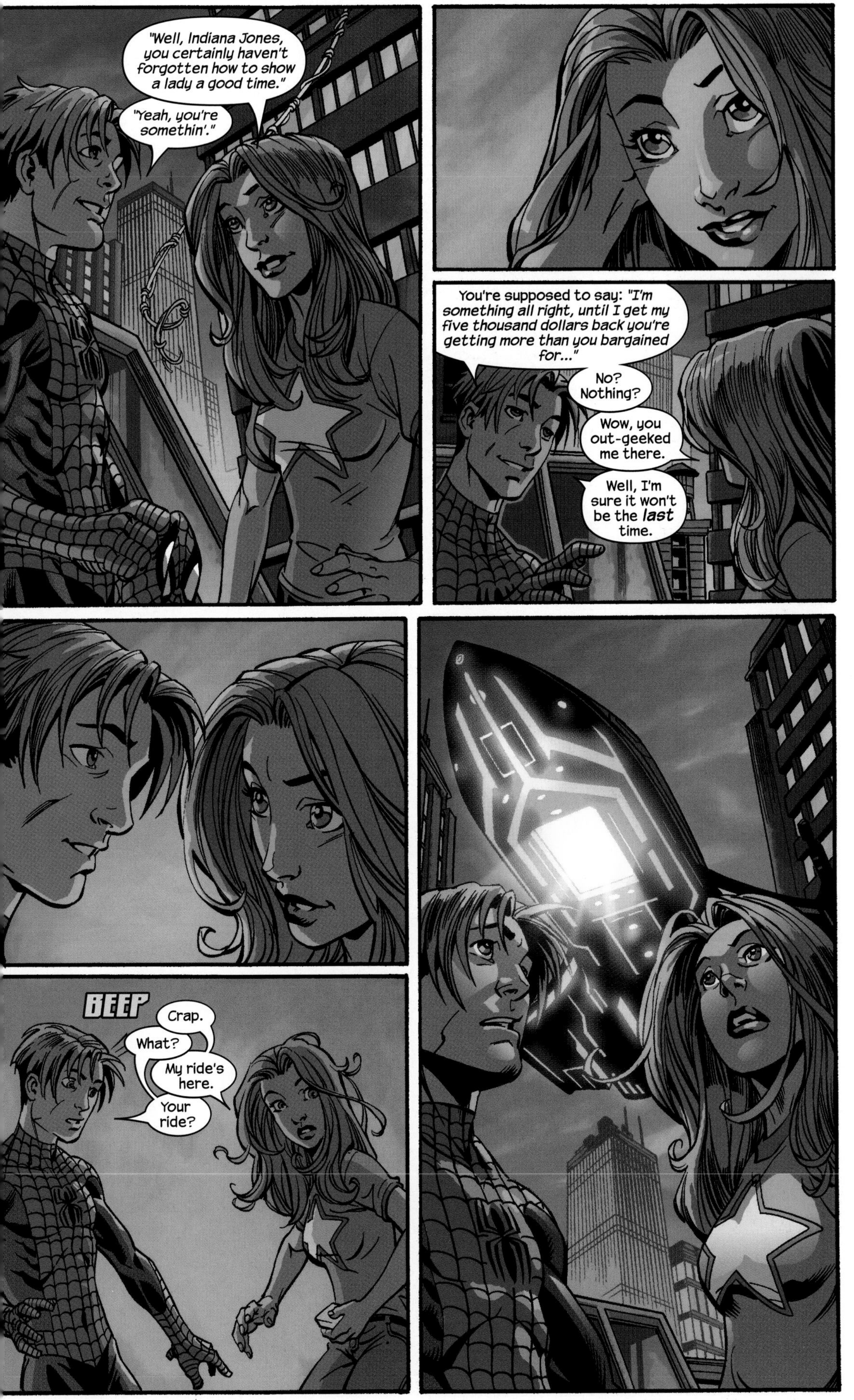
"Well, Indiana Jones, you certainly haven't forgotten how to show a lady a good time."
"Yeah, you're somethin'."
You're supposed to say: "I'm something all right, until I get my five thousand dollars back you're getting more than you bargained for..."
No? Nothing?
Wow, you out-geeked me there.
Well, I'm sure it won't be the last time.
BEEP
Crap.
What?
My ride's here.
Your ride?

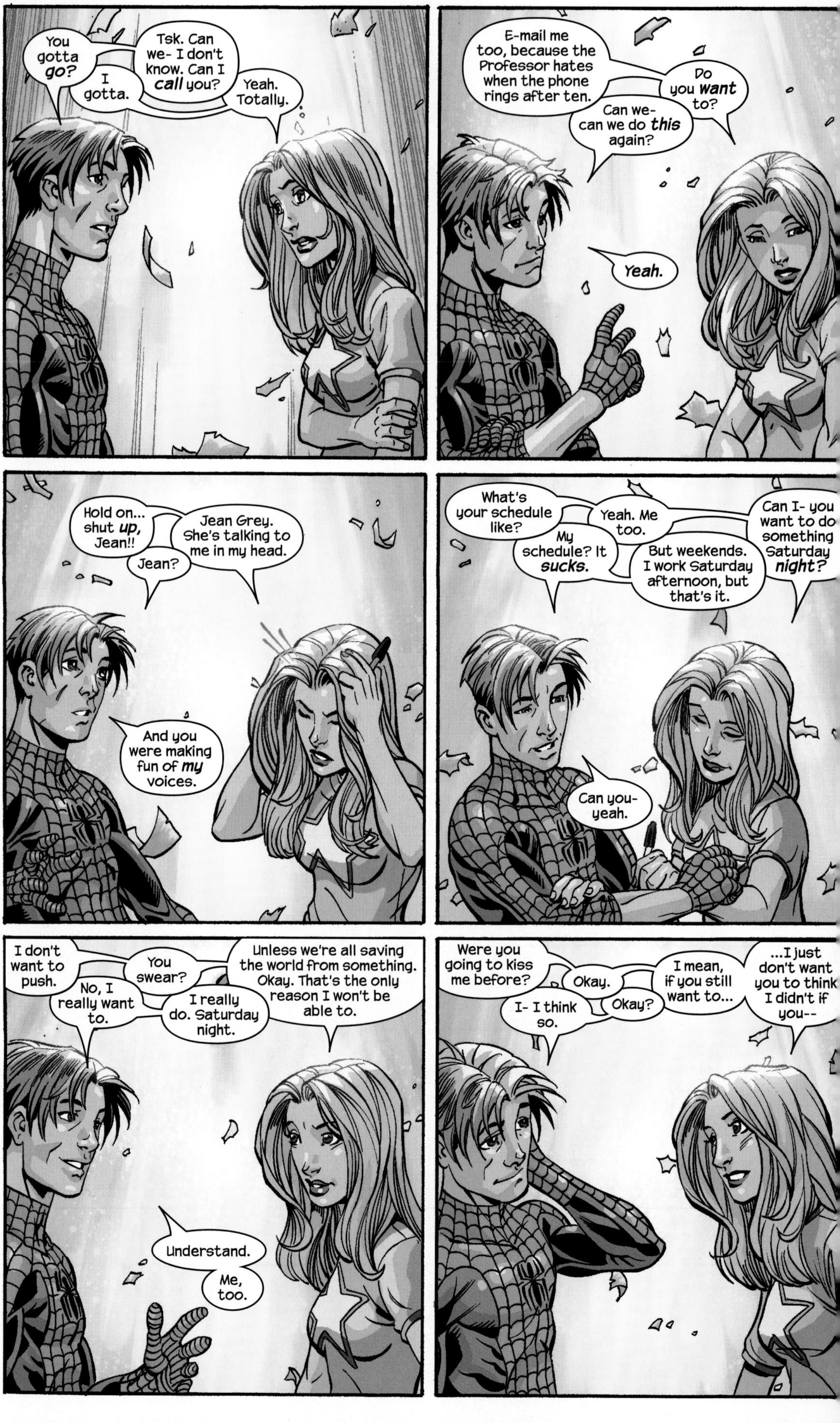
You gotta go?
I gotta.
Tsk. Can we- I don't know. Can I call you?
Yeah. Totally.
E-mail me too, because the Professor hates when the phone rings after ten.
Do you want to?
Can we- can we do this again?
Yeah.
Hold on... shut up, Jean!!
Jean?
Jean Grey. She's talking to me in my head.
And you were making fun of my voices.
What's your schedule like?
My schedule? It sucks.
Yeah. Me too.
But weekends. I work Saturday afternoon, but that's it.
Can I- you want to do something Saturday night?
Can you- yeah.
I don't want to push.
No, I really want to.
You swear?
I really do. Saturday night.
Unless we're all saving the world from something. Okay. That's the only reason I won't be able to.
Understand.
Me, too.
Were you going to kiss me before?
I- I think so.
Okay.
Okay?
I mean, if you still want to...
...I just don't want you to think I didn't if you--

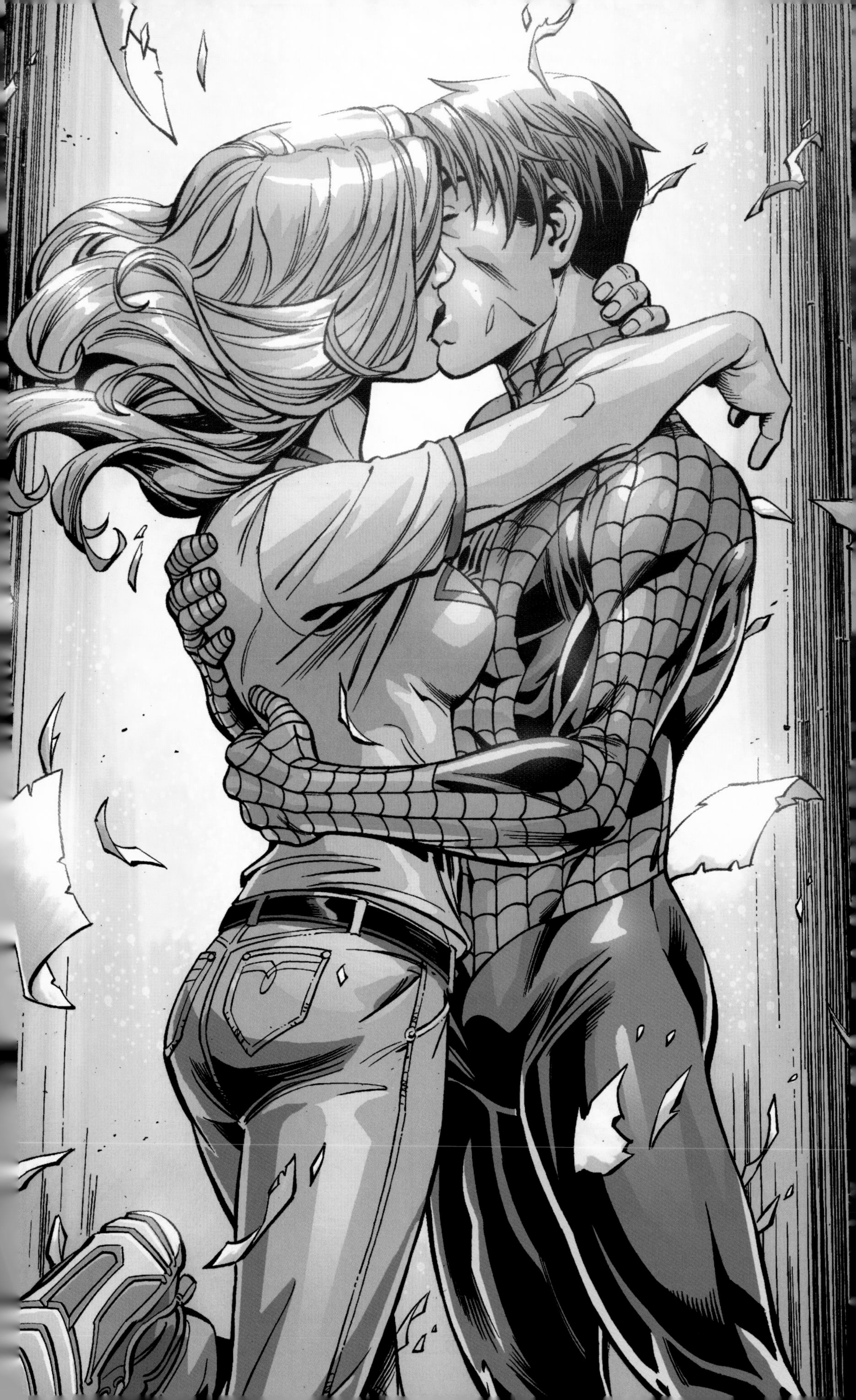

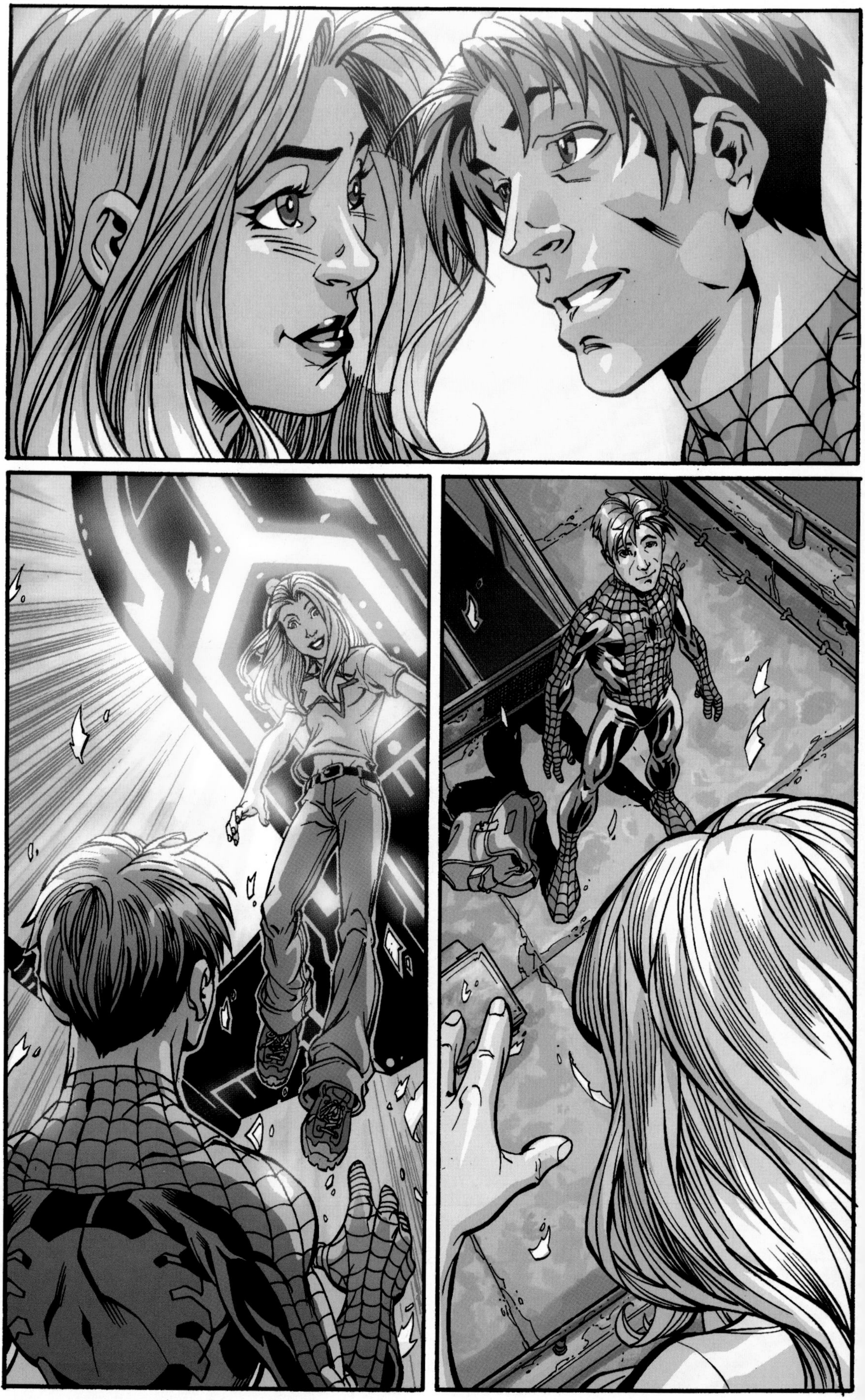

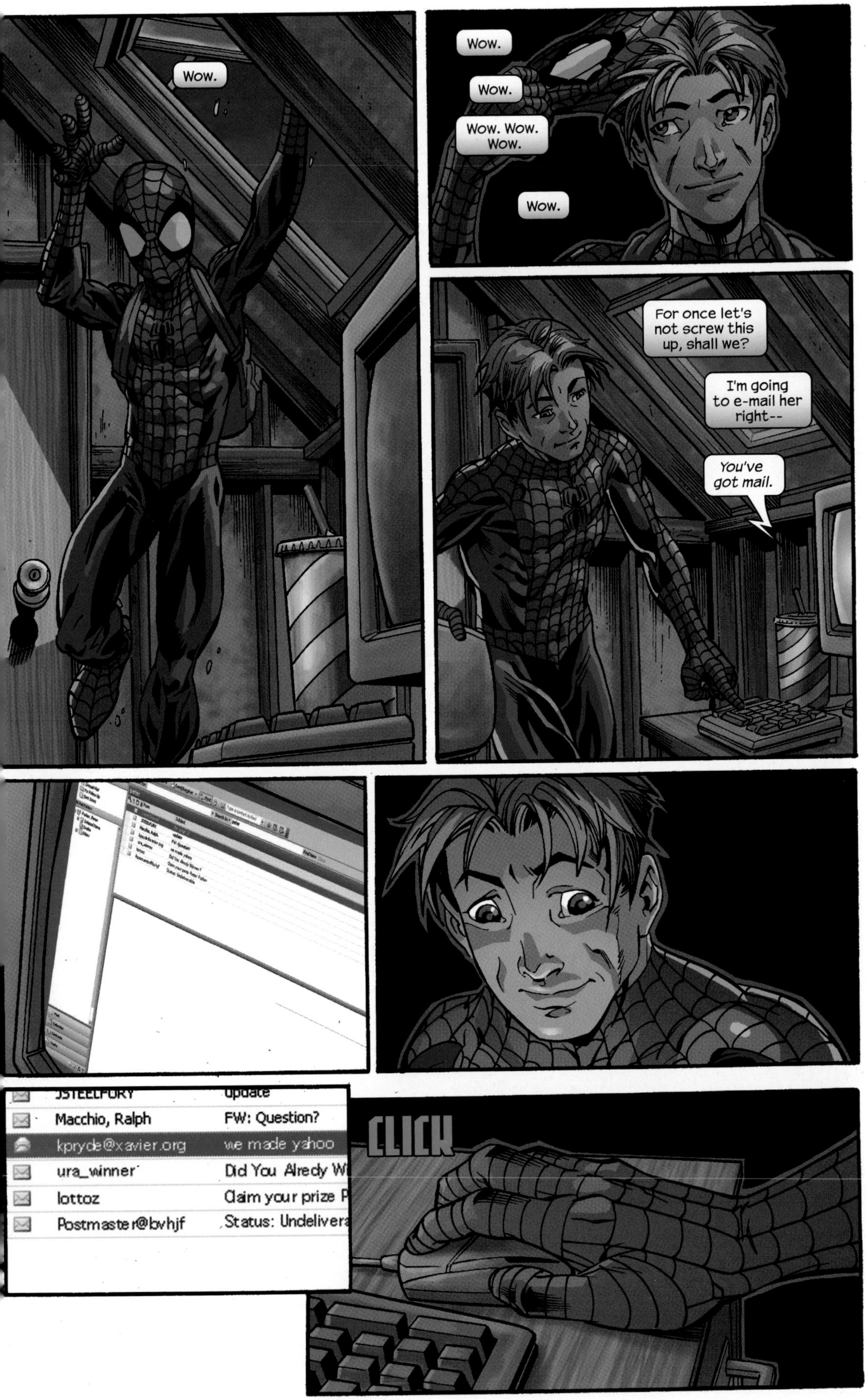
Wow.
Wow.
Wow.
Wow. Wow. Wow.
Wow.
For once let's not screw this up, shall we?
I'm going to e-mail her right--
You've got mail.
Macchio, Ralph FW: Question?
kpryde@xavier.org we made yahoo
ura_winner Did You Alredy Wi
lottoz Claim your prize P
Postmaster@bvhjf Status: Undelivera
CLICK

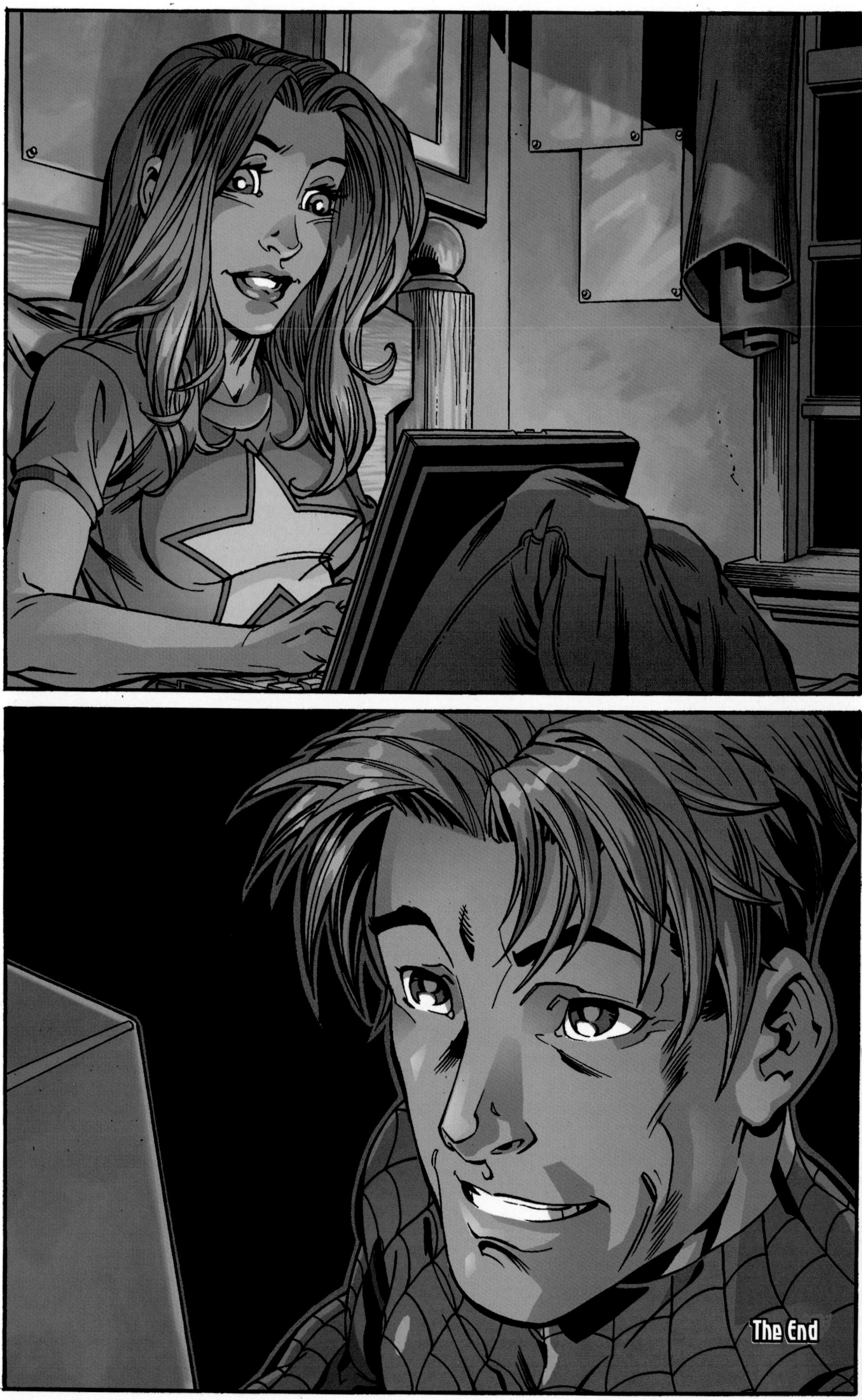
The End

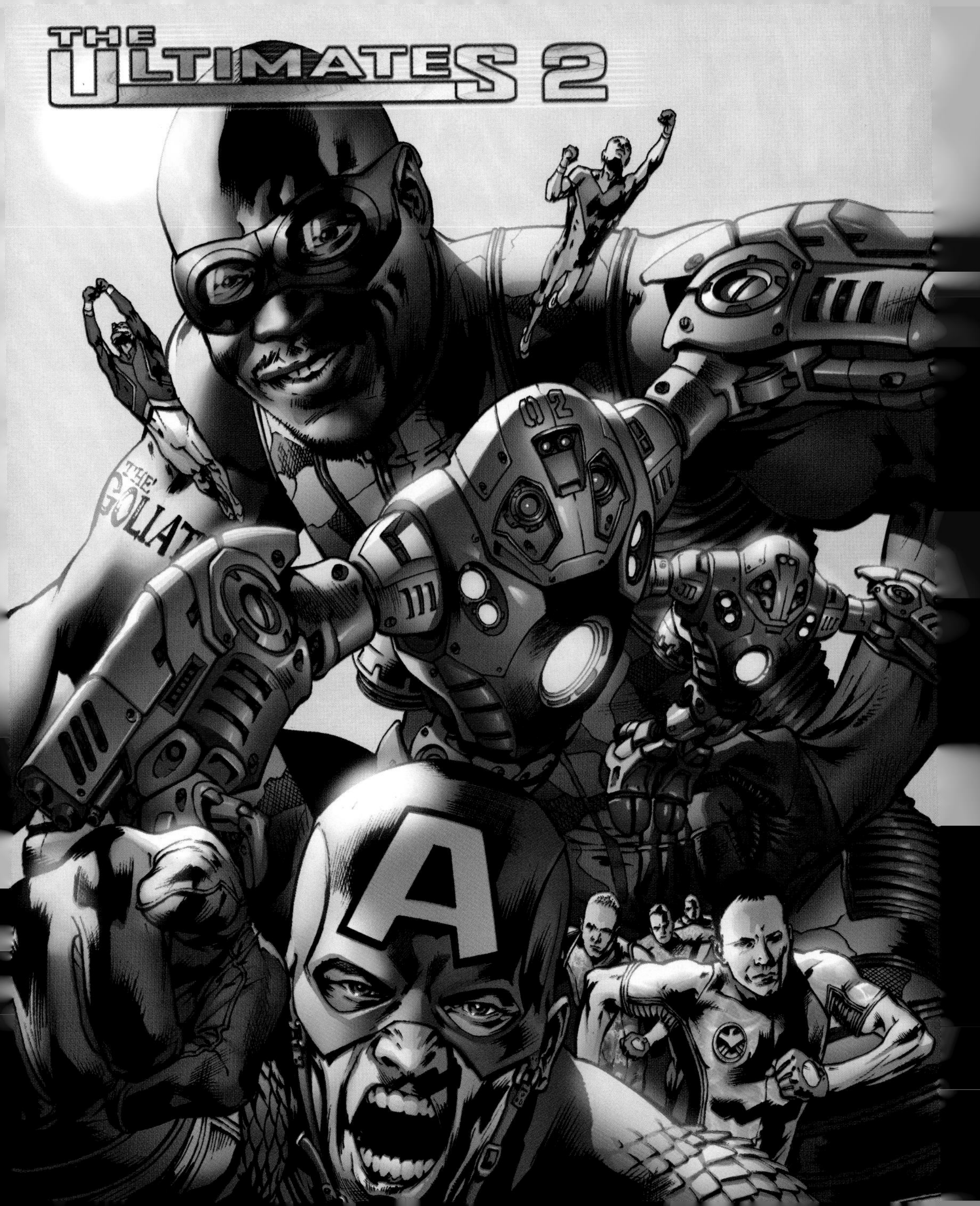
THE ULTIMATES 2
THE
GOLIAT

With this in mind, Steve Rogers volunteered for a covert military experiment that turned him into Captain America. After a few years of exemplary service, Captain America fell in battle-- his body wasn't recovered. Years passed and Captain America was found frozen in suspended animation. When he awoke, he was convinced to join Iron Man, The Wasp, Giant Man, Black Widow, Hawkeye, and Thor in forming the superhuman defense initiative run by Nick Fury, called The Ultimates.

THE RESERVES

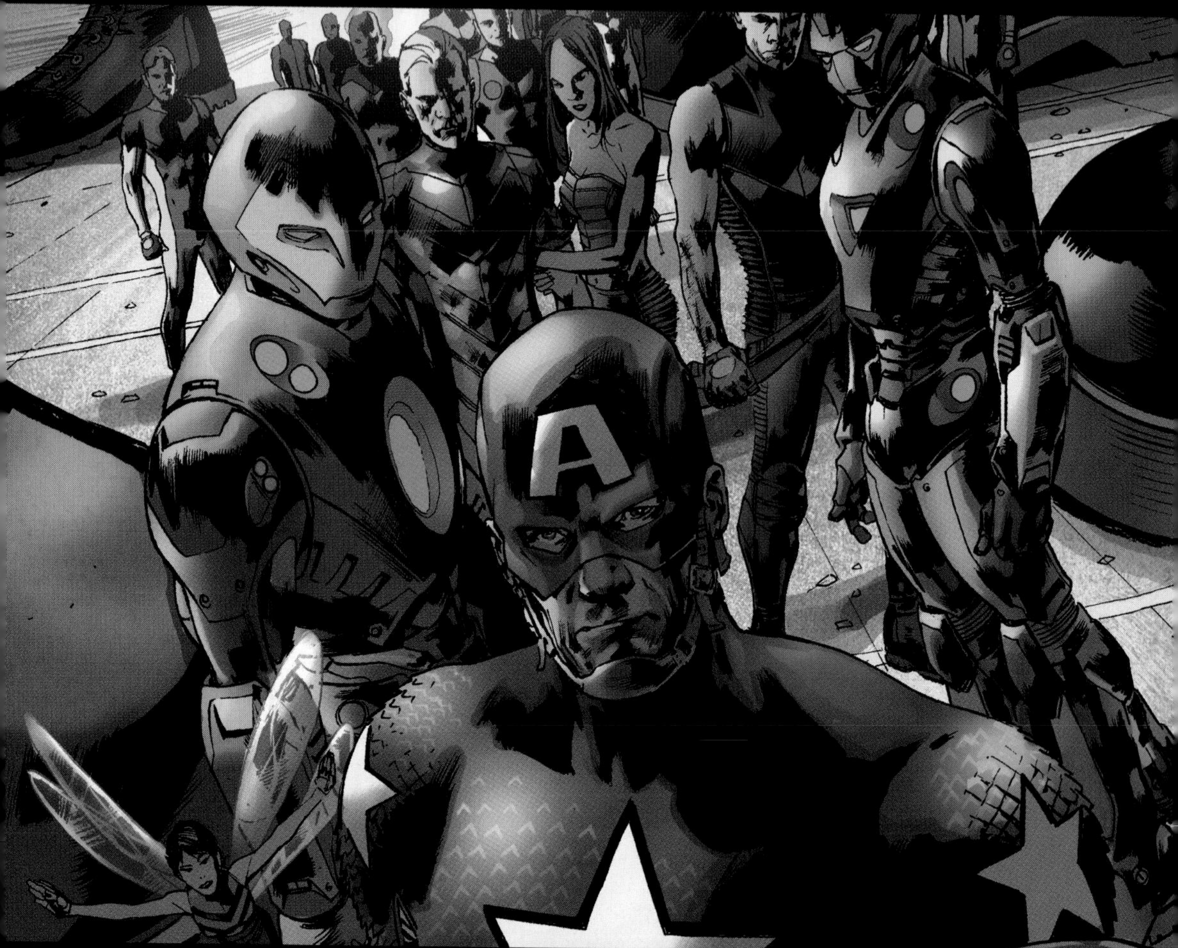

STAN LEE PRESENTS:

THE ULTIMATES

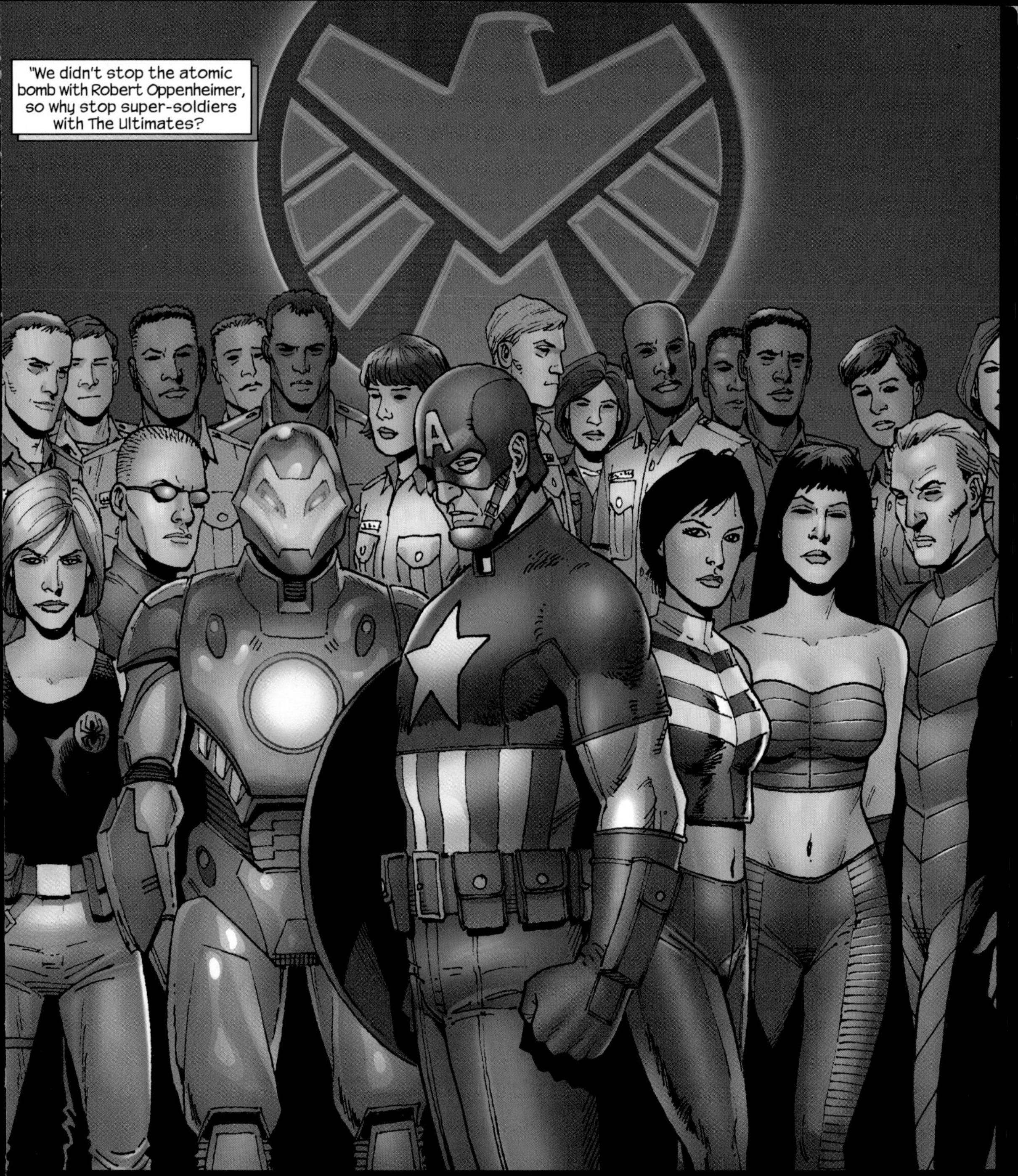
"We didn't stop the atomic bomb with Robert Oppenheimer, so why stop super-soldiers with The Ultimates?

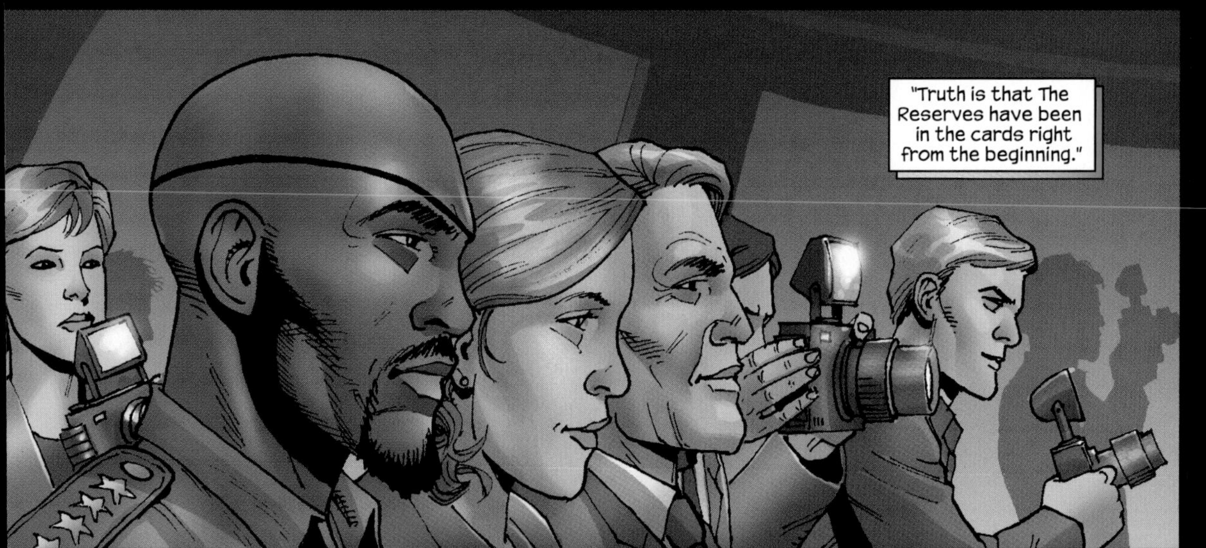
"Truth is that The Reserves have been in the cards right from the beginning."

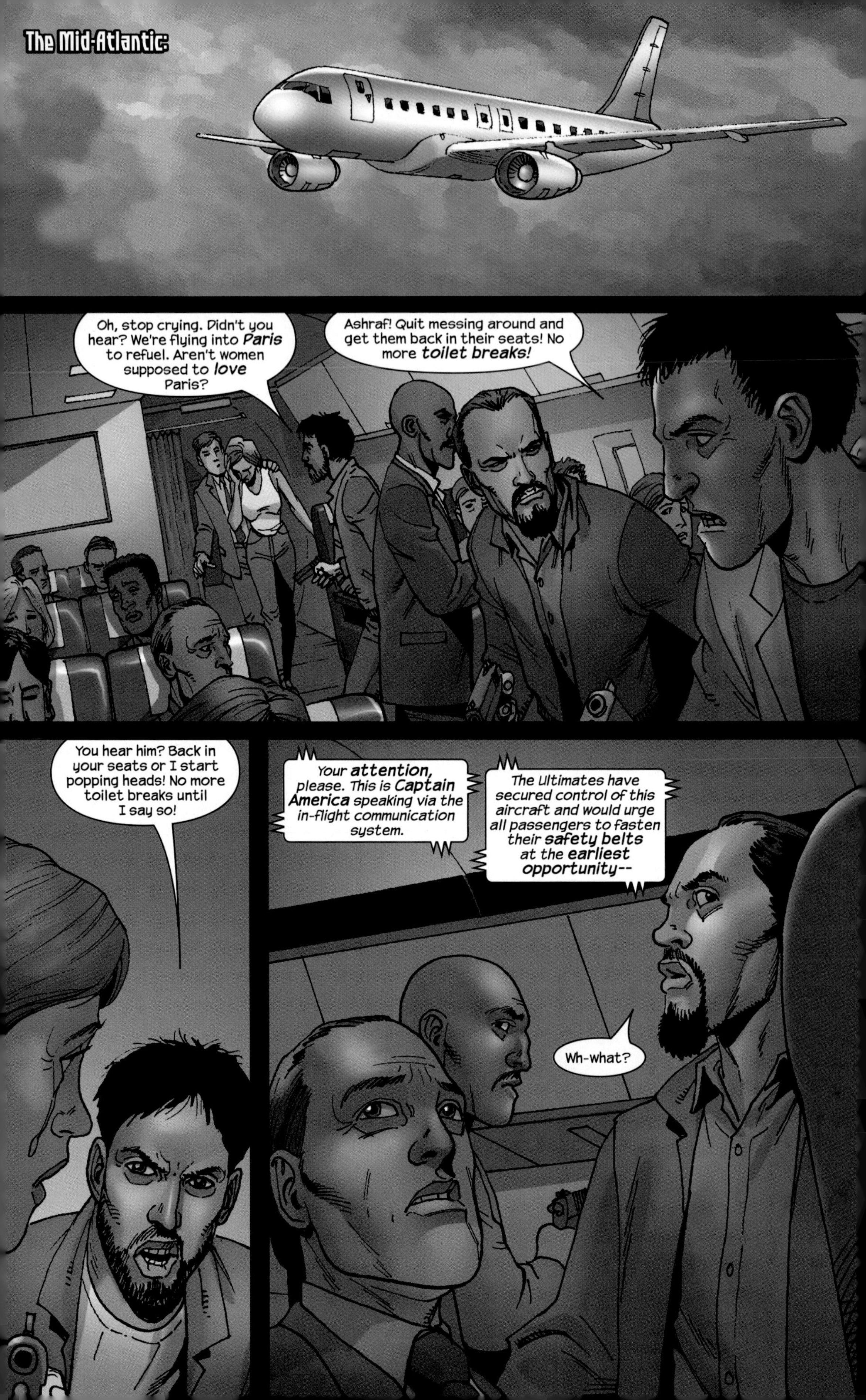
The Mid-Atlantic:
Oh, stop crying. Didn't you hear? We're flying into *Paris* to refuel. Aren't women supposed to *love* Paris?
Ashraf! Quit messing around and get them back in their seats! No more *toilet breaks!*
You hear him? Back in your seats or I start popping heads! No more toilet breaks until I say so!
Your **attention,** *please. This is* **Captain America** *speaking via the in-flight communication system.*
The Ultimates have secured control of this aircraft and would urge all passengers to fasten their **safety belts** *at the* **earliest opportunity--**
Wh-what?

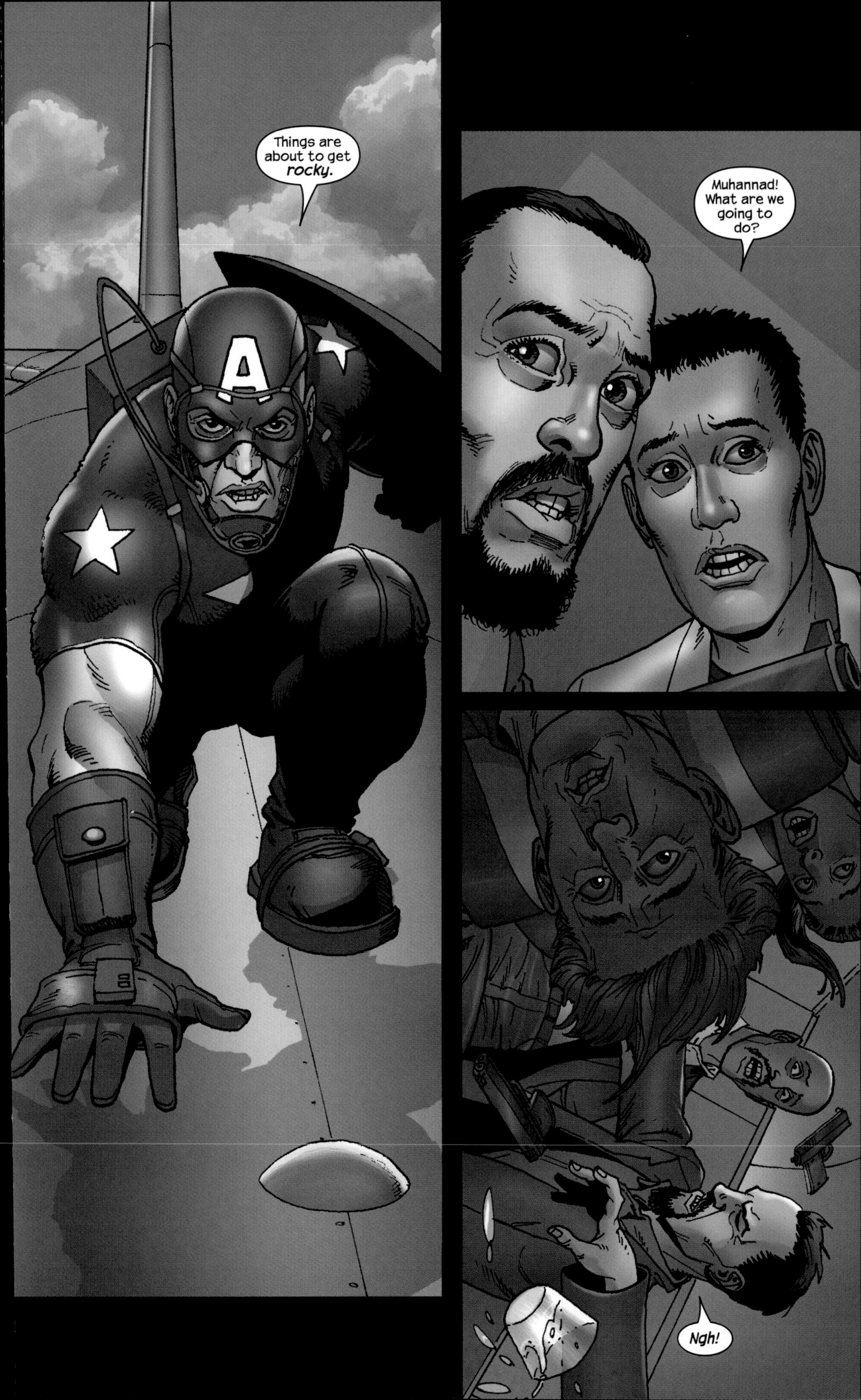
Things are about to get rocky.
Muhannad! What are we going to do?
Ngh!

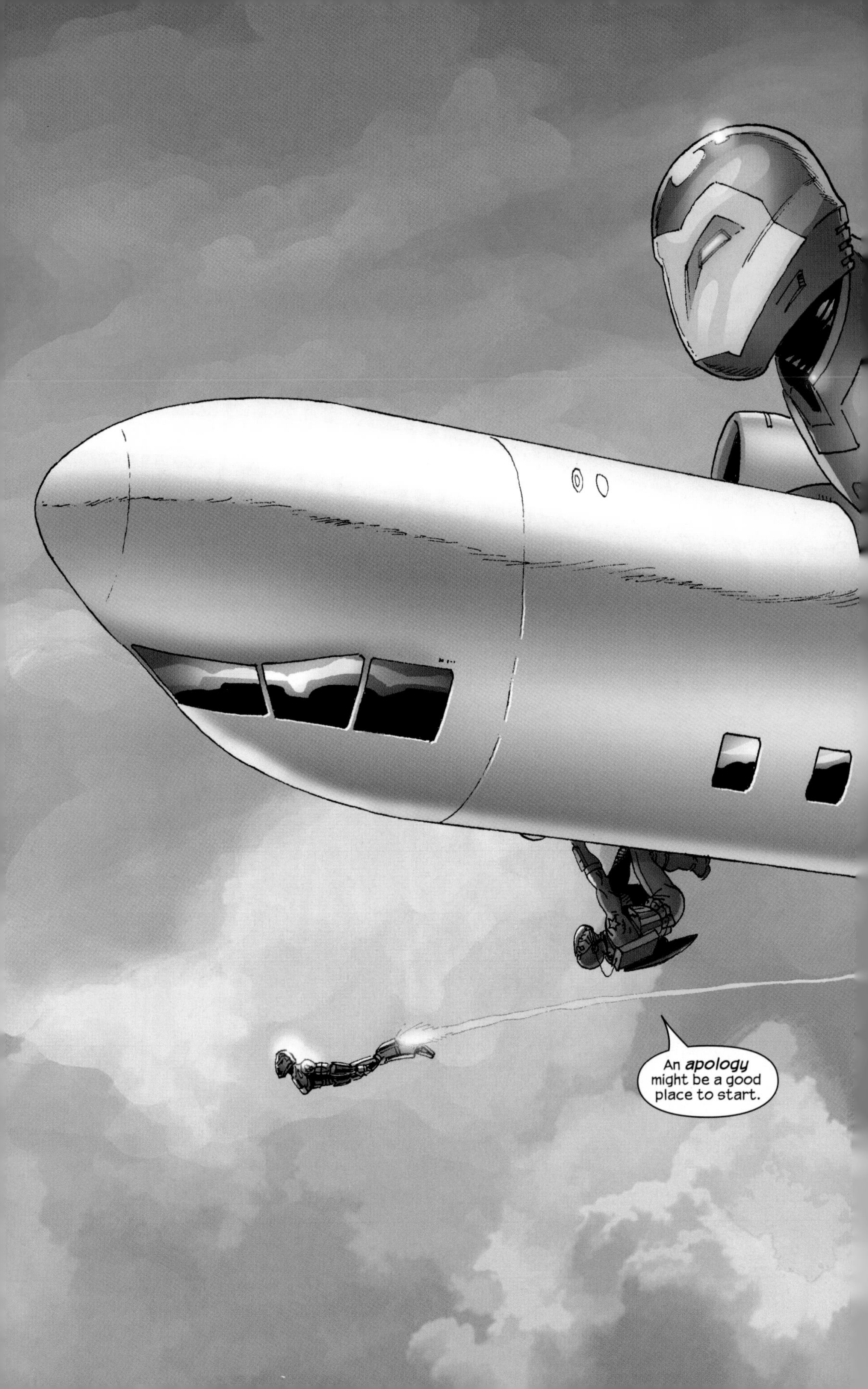
An *apology* might be a good place to start.

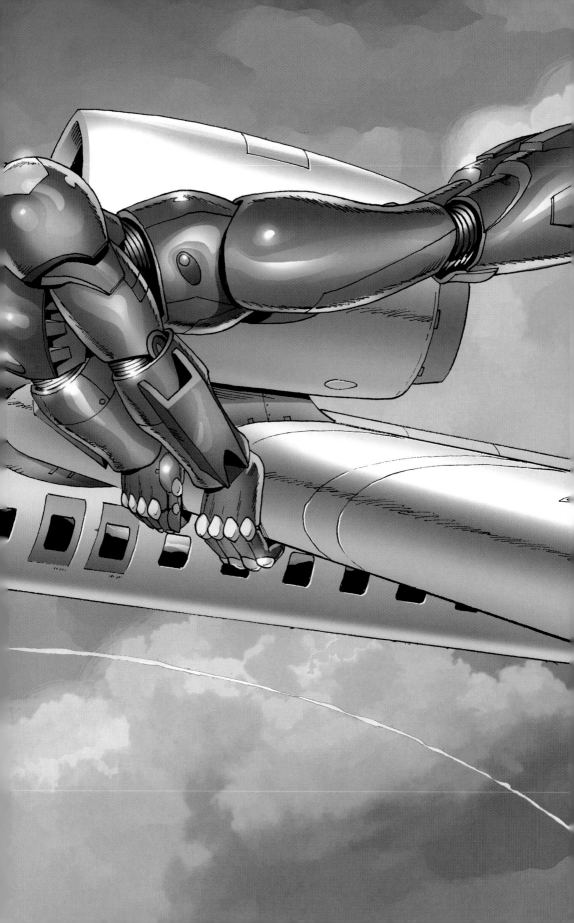

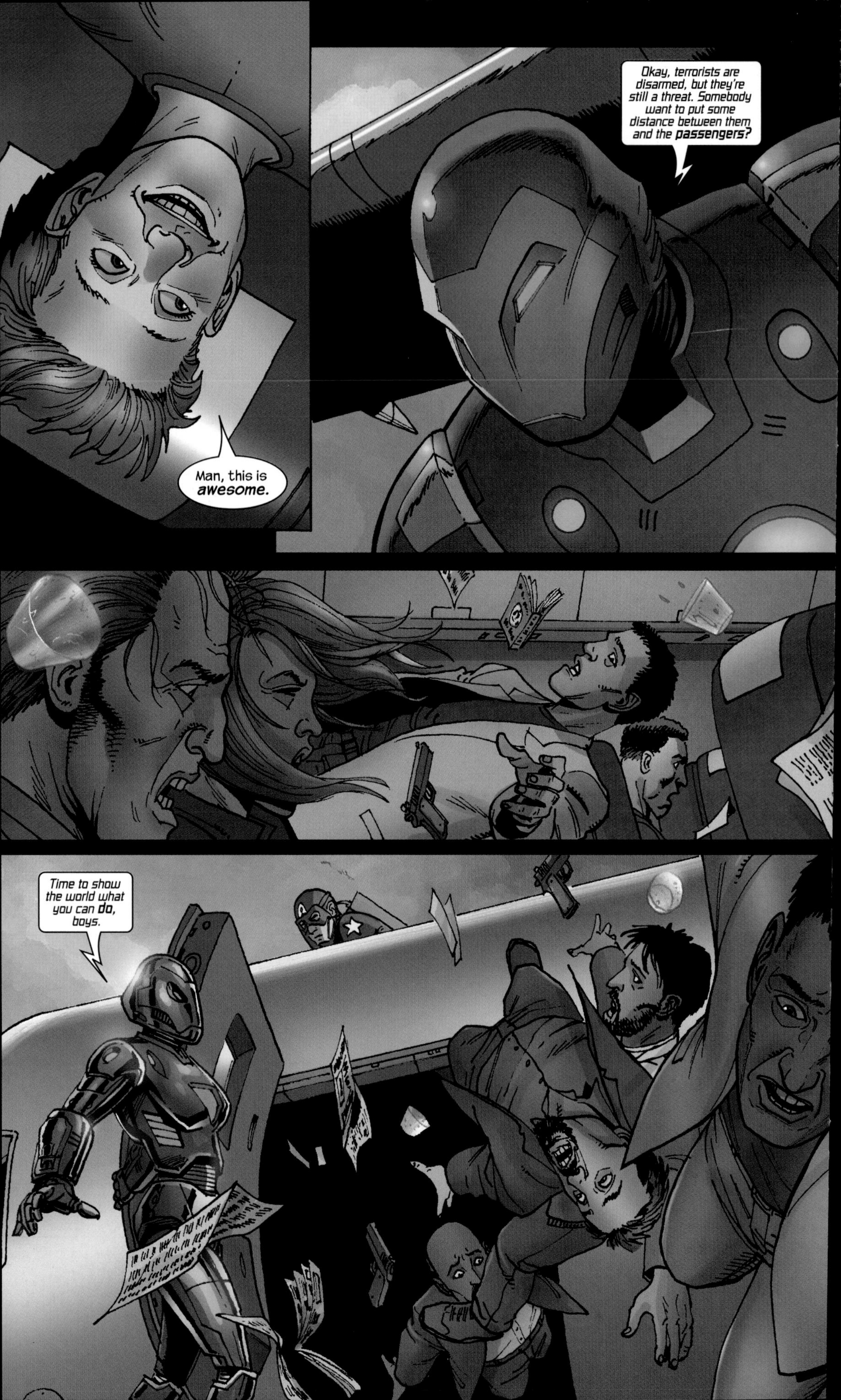
Man, this is *awesome.*
Okay, terrorists are disarmed, but they're still a threat. Somebody want to put some distance between them and the **passengers?**
Time to show the world what you can **do,** boys.

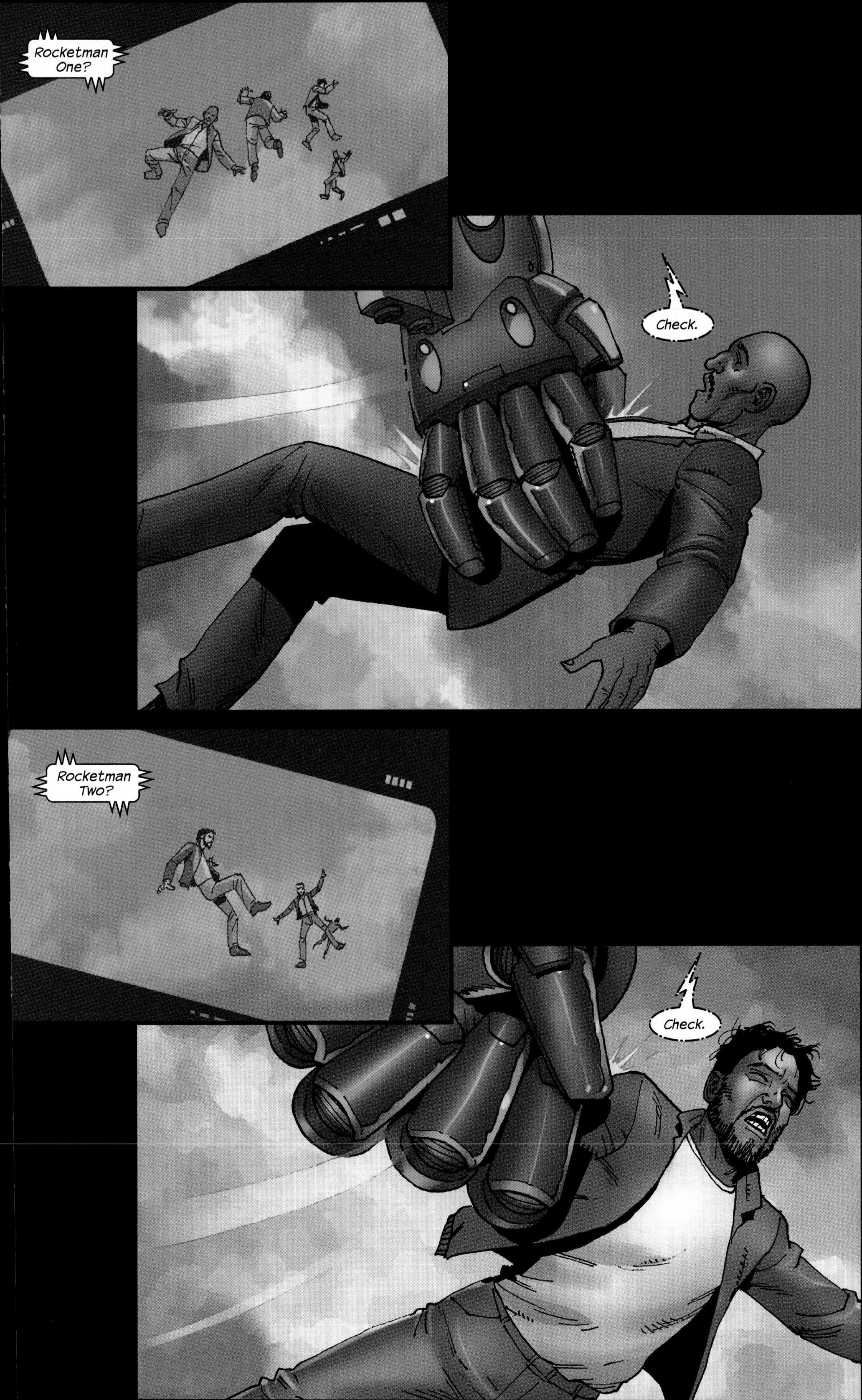
Rocketman One?
Check.
Rocketman Two?
Check.

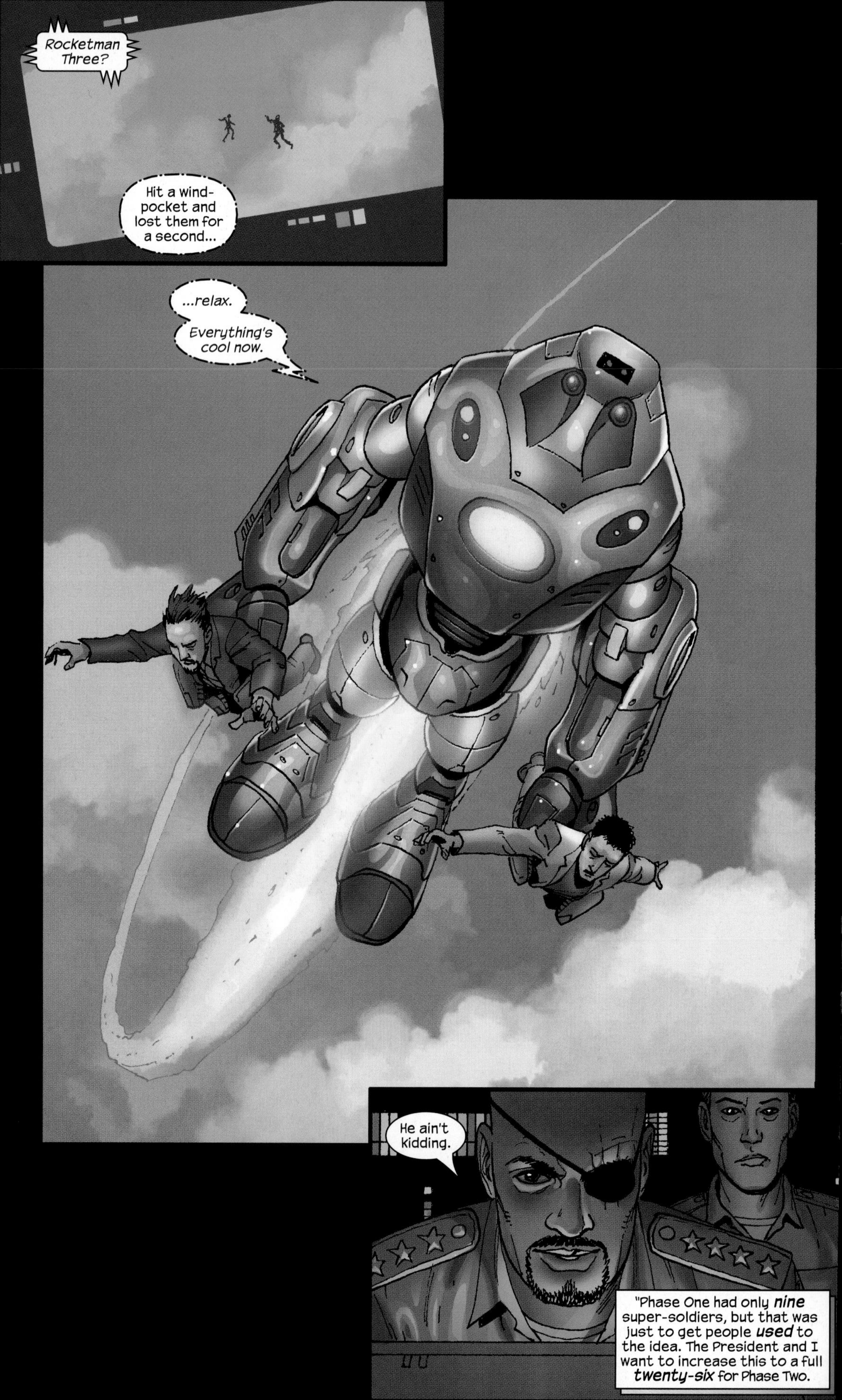

Rocketman Three?
Hit a wind-pocket and lost them for a second...
...relax.
Everything's cool now.
He ain't kidding.
"Phase One had only *nine* super-soldiers, but that was just to get people *used* to the idea. The President and I want to increase this to a full *twenty-six* for Phase Two.

"The Five Goliaths already saw action in The Gulf a few weeks back and there's seven or eight *others* ready to go public as soon as Dr. Brankin signs off on them.

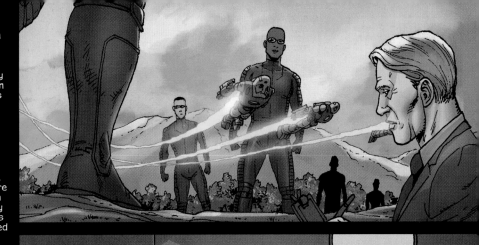

"Rocketmen One, Two and Three were customized from some of the early *Iron Man* designs we finally convinced Tony Stark to part with.

"The Four Seasons are just about ready; four marines from Wisconsin who all signed up on the same day and couldn't believe their *luck* when I handpicked them for The Reserves.

"Thunderbolt still needs a few tweaks, Intangi-Girl's still a month away from being ready and we haven't even finalized what we're doing with Owen, Rusk and O'Donohue.

"But the one that *really* has us psyched is *Lieberman*.

"Outside of the Giant Men, he's the only one whose powers aren't completely dependent on the *uniforms* we've put together.

"Enhanced *speed*, enhanced *strength*, skin close to *indescructible* and his brain hard-wired to the S.H.I.E.L.D. super-computer...

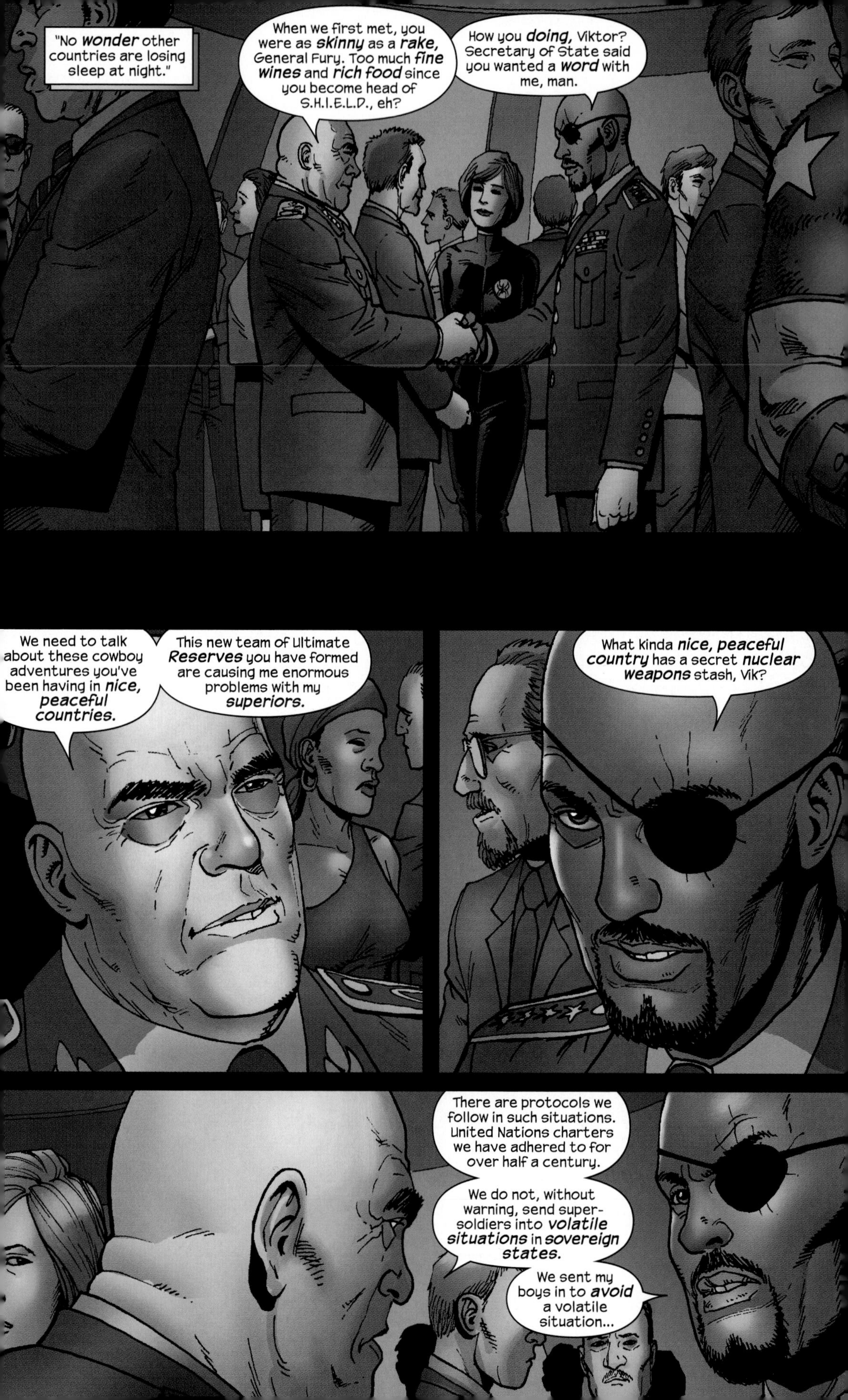
"No *wonder* other countries are losing sleep at night."
When we first met, you were as *skinny* as a *rake,* General Fury. Too much *fine wines* and *rich food* since you become head of S.H.I.E.L.D., eh?
How you *doing,* Viktor? Secretary of State said you wanted a *word* with me, man.
We need to talk about these cowboy adventures you've been having in *nice, peaceful countries.*
This new team of Ultimate *Reserves* you have formed are causing me enormous problems with my *superiors.*
What kinda *nice, peaceful country* has a secret *nuclear weapons* stash, Vik?
There are protocols we follow in such situations. United Nations charters we have adhered to for over half a century.
We do not, without warning, send super-soldiers into *volatile situations* in *sovereign states.*
We sent my boys in to *avoid* a volatile situation...

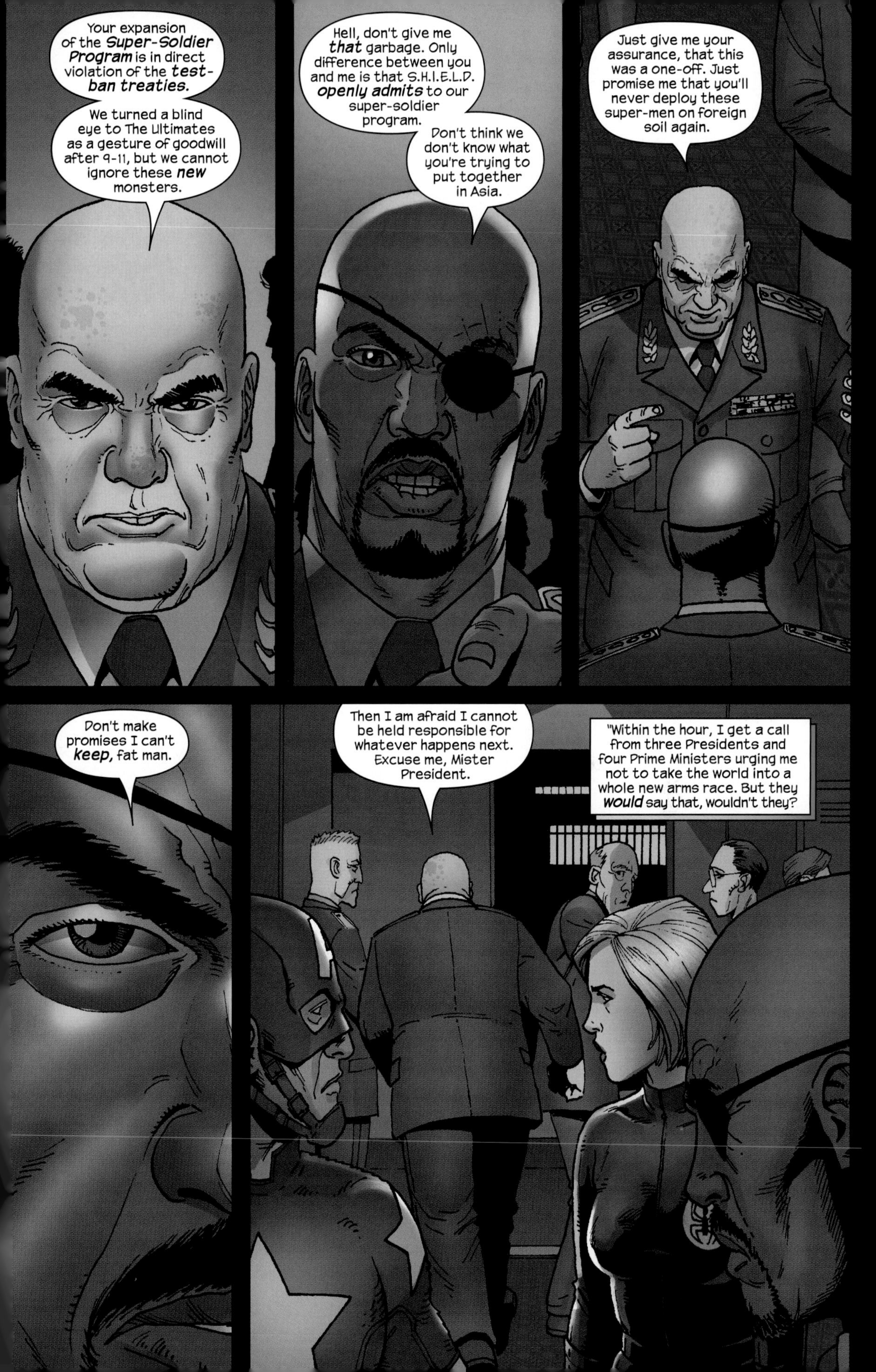
Your expansion of the Super-Soldier Program is in direct violation of the test-ban treaties.
We turned a blind eye to The Ultimates as a gesture of goodwill after 9-11, but we cannot ignore these new monsters.
Hell, don't give me that garbage. Only difference between you and me is that S.H.I.E.L.D. openly admits to our super-soldier program.
Don't think we don't know what you're trying to put together in Asia.
Just give me your assurance, that this was a one-off. Just promise me that you'll never deploy these super-men on foreign soil again.
Don't make promises I can't keep, fat man.
Then I am afraid I cannot be held responsible for whatever happens next. Excuse me, Mister President.
"Within the hour, I get a call from three Presidents and four Prime Ministers urging me not to take the world into a whole new arms race. But they would say that, wouldn't they?

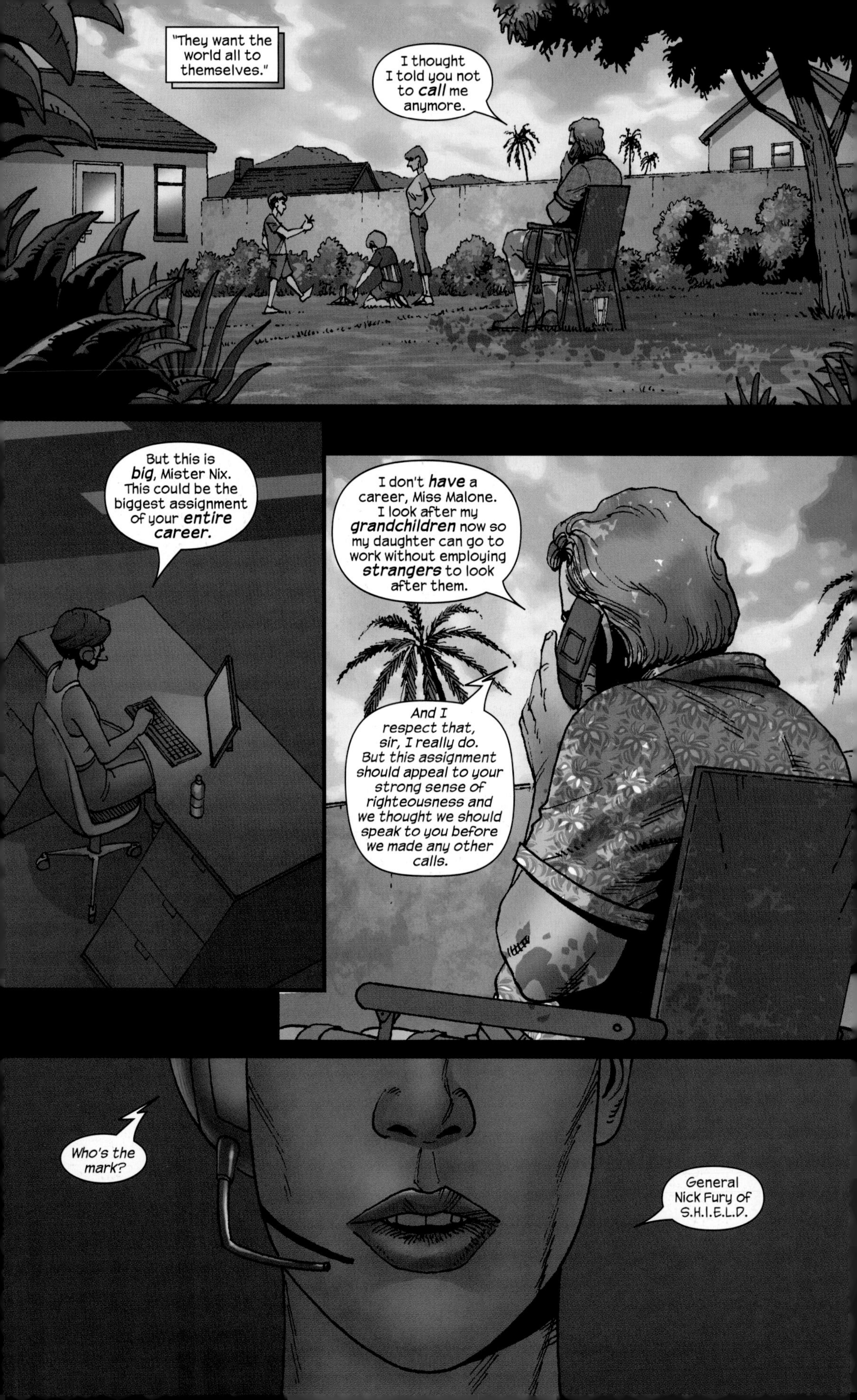
"They want the world all to themselves."
I thought I told you not to call me anymore.
But this is big, Mister Nix. This could be the biggest assignment of your entire career.
I don't have a career, Miss Malone. I look after my grandchildren now so my daughter can go to work without employing strangers to look after them.
And I respect that, sir, I really do. But this assignment should appeal to your strong sense of righteousness and we thought we should speak to you before we made any other calls.
Who's the mark?
General Nick Fury of S.H.I.E.L.D.

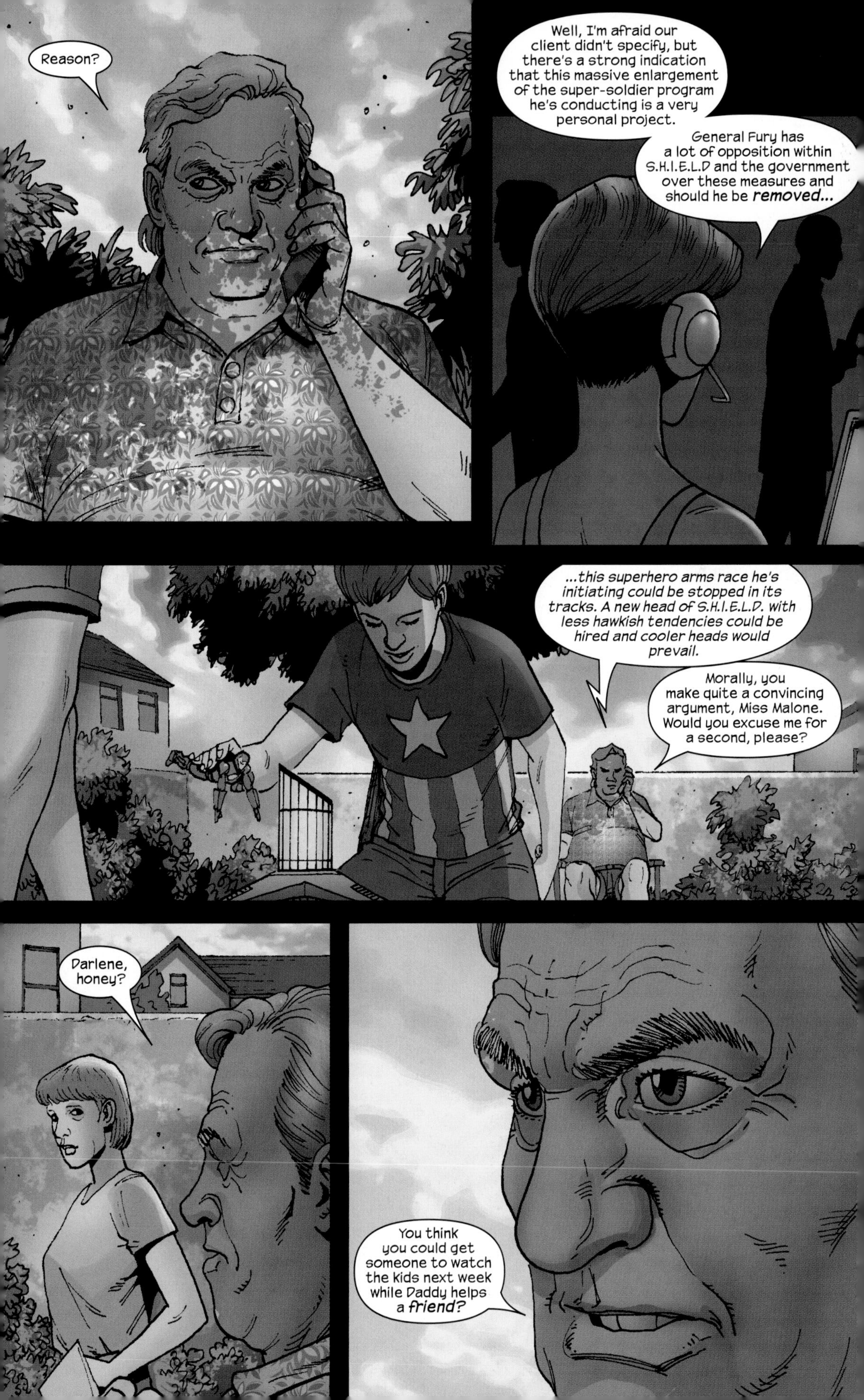
Reason?
Well, I'm afraid our client didn't specify, but there's a strong indication that this massive enlargement of the super-soldier program he's conducting is a very personal project.
General Fury has a lot of opposition within S.H.I.E.L.D and the government over these measures and should he be *removed...*
...this superhero arms race he's initiating could be stopped in its tracks. A new head of S.H.I.E.L.D. with less hawkish tendencies could be hired and cooler heads would prevail.
Morally, you make quite a convincing argument, Miss Malone. Would you excuse me for a second, please?
Darlene, honey?
You think you could get someone to watch the kids next week while Daddy helps a *friend?*

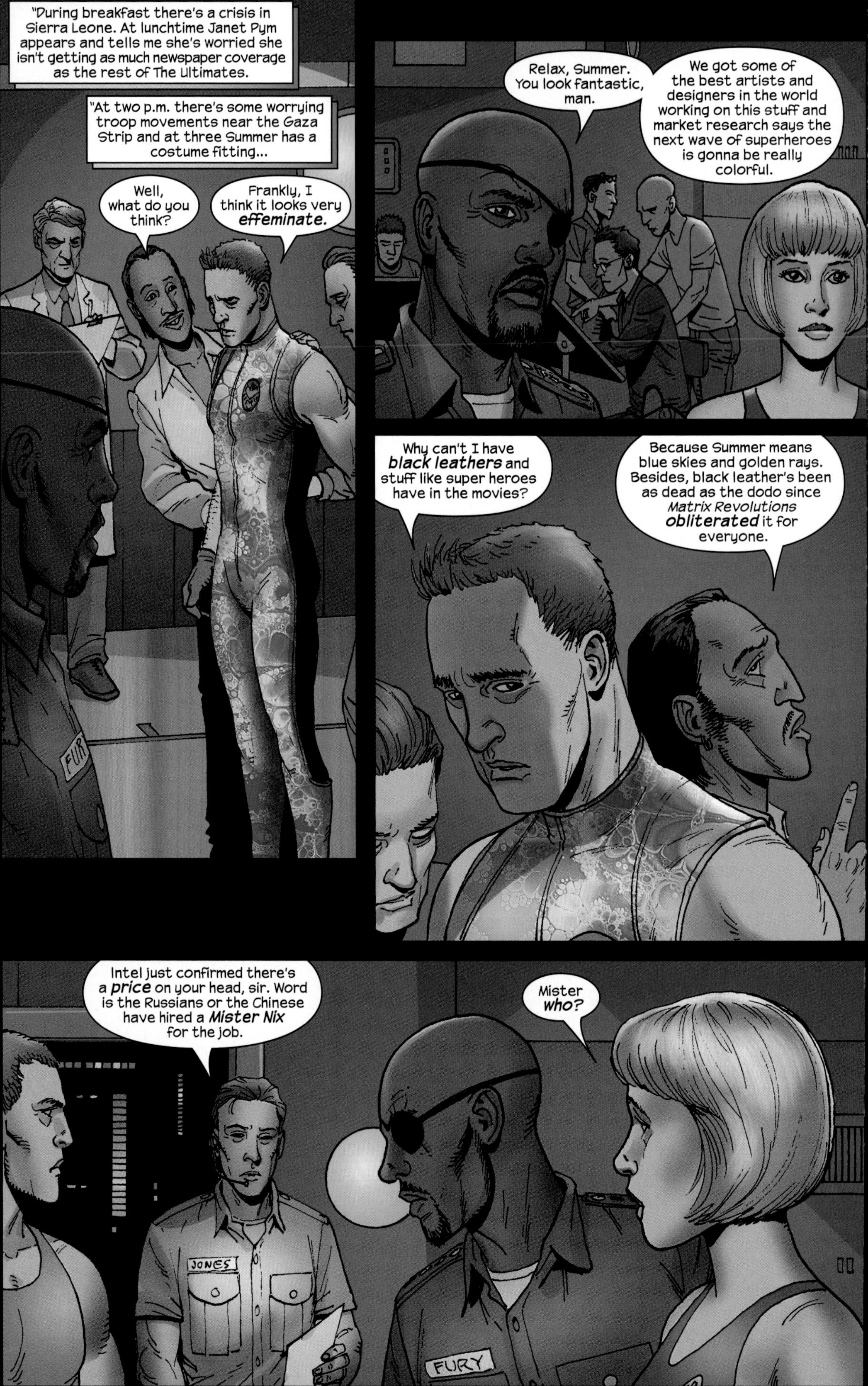
"During breakfast there's a crisis in Sierra Leone. At lunchtime Janet Pym appears and tells me she's worried she isn't getting as much newspaper coverage as the rest of The Ultimates.
"At two p.m. there's some worrying troop movements near the Gaza Strip and at three Summer has a costume fitting...
Well, what do you think?
Frankly, I think it looks very *effeminate.*
FUR
Relax, Summer. You look fantastic, man.
We got some of the best artists and designers in the world working on this stuff and market research says the next wave of superheroes is gonna be really colorful.
Why can't I have *black leathers* and stuff like super heroes have in the movies?
Because Summer means blue skies and golden rays. Besides, black leather's been as dead as the dodo since *Matrix Revolutions* ***obliterated*** it for everyone.
Intel just confirmed there's a *price* on your head, sir. Word is the Russians or the Chinese have hired a *Mister Nix* for the job.
Mister *who?*
JONES
FURY

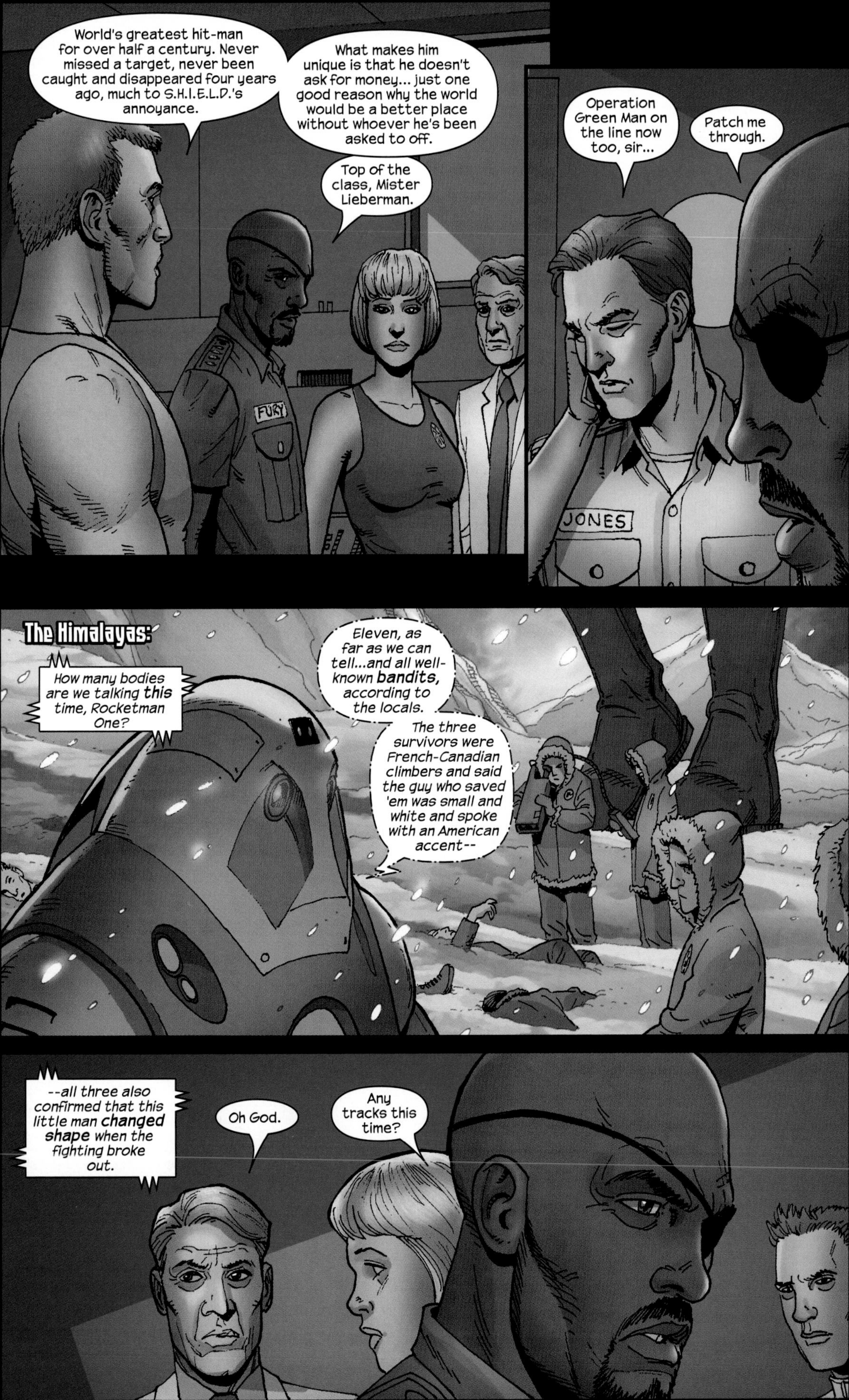
World's greatest hit-man for over half a century. Never missed a target, never been caught and disappeared four years ago, much to S.H.I.E.L.D.'s annoyance.
What makes him unique is that he doesn't ask for money... just one good reason why the world would be a better place without whoever he's been asked to off.
Top of the class, Mister Lieberman.
FURY
Operation Green Man on the line now too, sir...
Patch me through.
JONES
The Himalayas:
How many bodies are we talking this time, Rocketman One?
Eleven, as far as we can tell...and all well-known bandits, according to the locals.
The three survivors were French-Canadian climbers and said the guy who saved 'em was small and white and spoke with an American accent--
--all three also confirmed that this little man changed shape when the fighting broke out.
Oh God.
Any tracks this time?

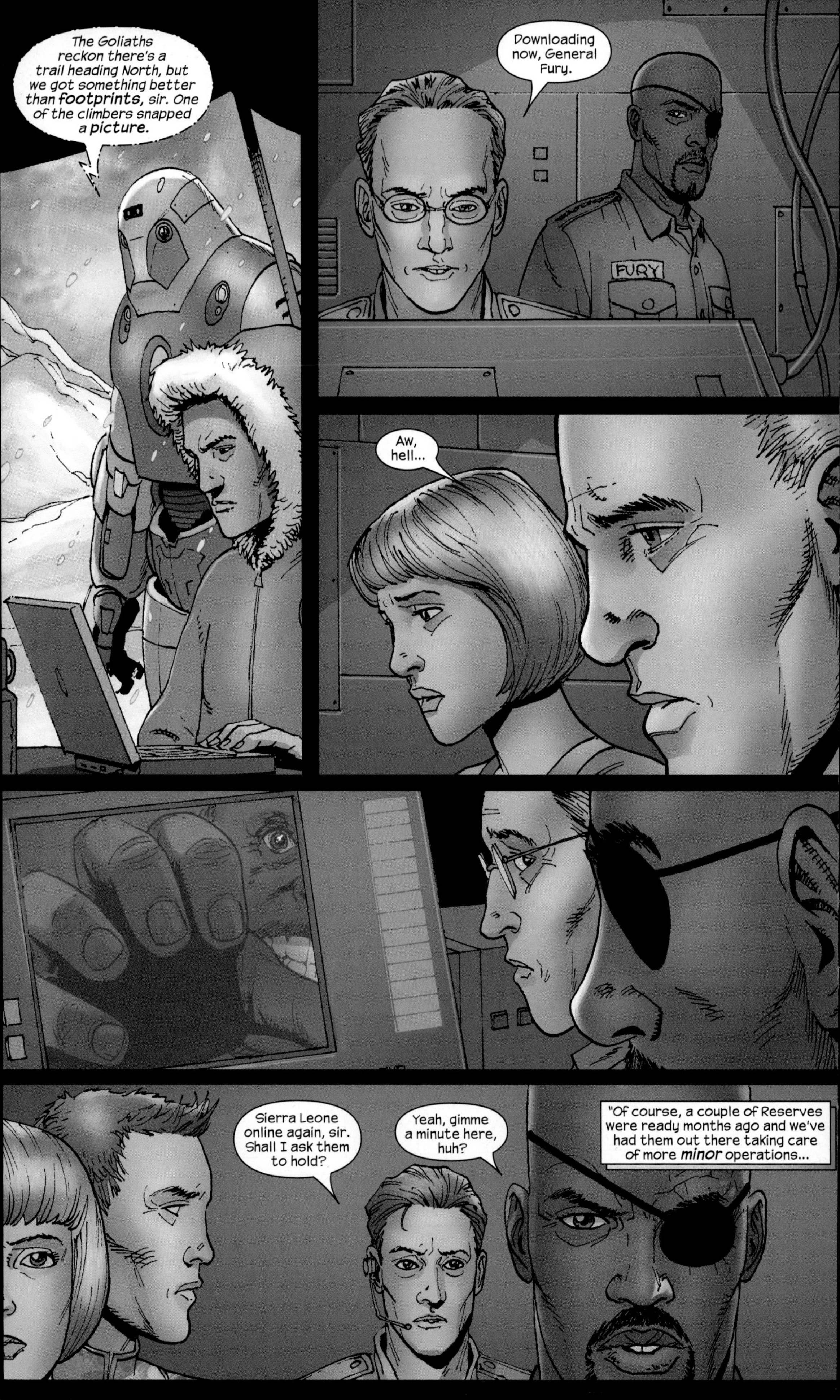

The Goliaths reckon there's a trail heading North, but we got something better than *footprints*, sir. One of the climbers snapped a *picture*.
Downloading now, General Fury.
FURY
Aw, hell...
Sierra Leone online again, sir. Shall I ask them to hold?
Yeah, gimme a minute here, huh?
"Of course, a couple of Reserves were ready months ago and we've had them out there taking care of more *minor* operations...

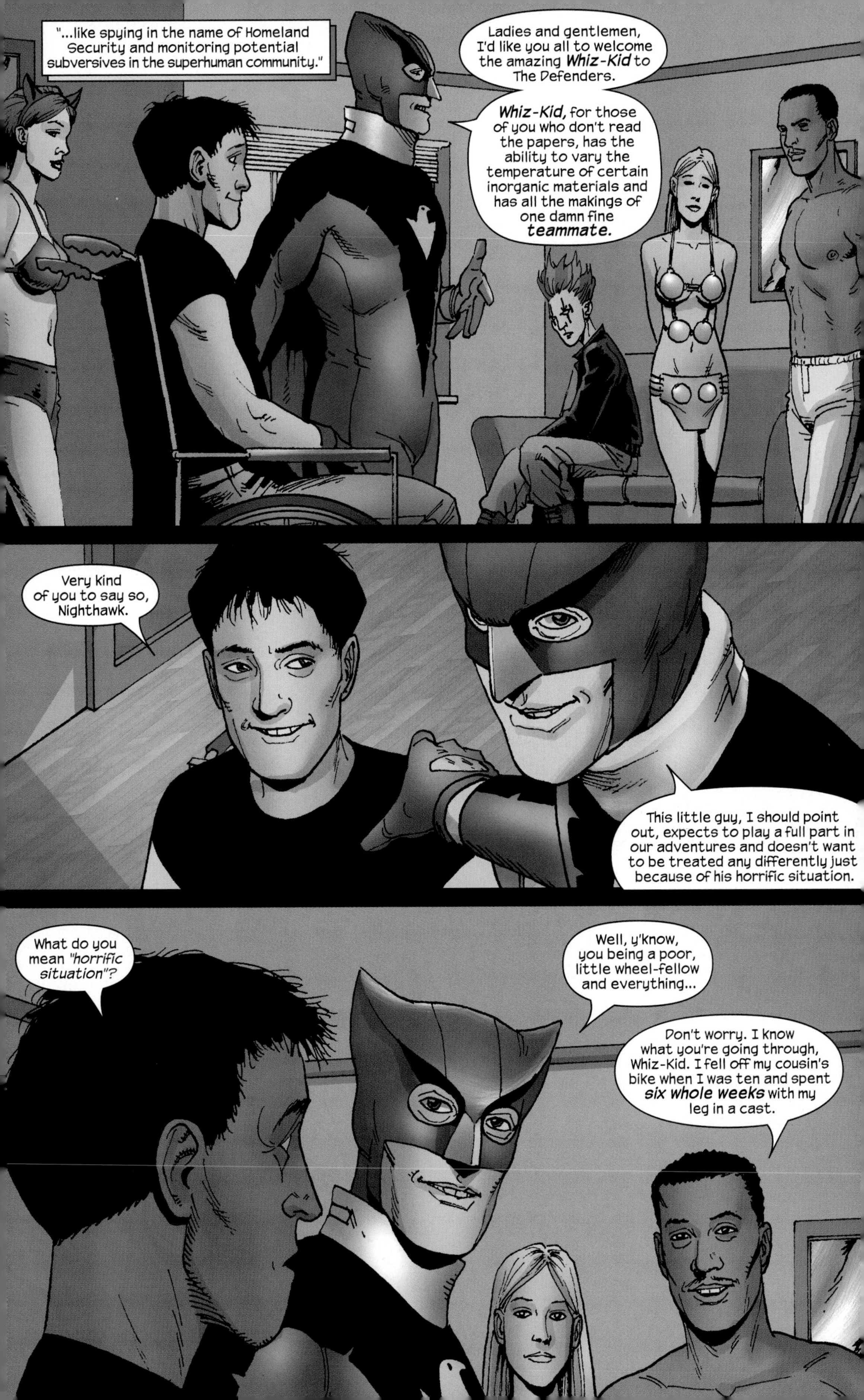

"...like spying in the name of Homeland Security and monitoring potential subversives in the superhuman community."
Ladies and gentlemen, I'd like you all to welcome the amazing *Whiz-Kid* to The Defenders.
Whiz-Kid, for those of you who don't read the papers, has the ability to vary the temperature of certain inorganic materials and has all the makings of one damn fine *teammate.*
Very kind of you to say so, Nighthawk.
This little guy, I should point out, expects to play a full part in our adventures and doesn't want to be treated any differently just because of his horrific situation.
What do you mean *"horrific situation"*?
Well, y'know, you being a poor, little wheel-fellow and everything...
Don't worry. I know what you're going through, Whiz-Kid. I fell off my cousin's bike when I was ten and spent *six whole weeks* with my leg in a cast.

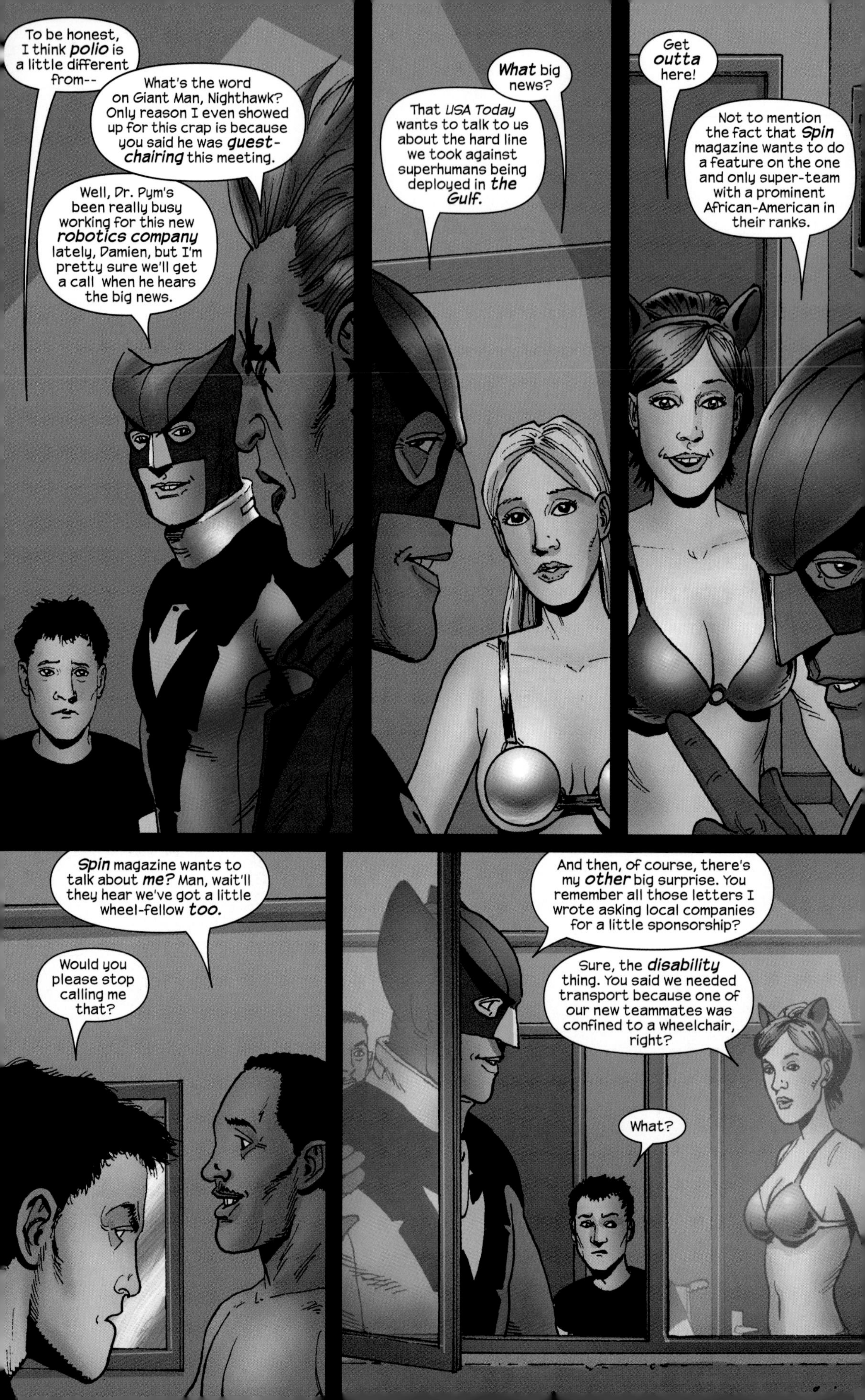
To be honest, I think *polio* is a little different from--
What's the word on Giant Man, Nighthawk? Only reason I even showed up for this crap is because you said he was *guest-chairing* this meeting.
Well, Dr. Pym's been really busy working for this new *robotics company* lately, Damien, but I'm pretty sure we'll get a call when he hears the big news.
What big news?
That *USA Today* wants to talk to us about the hard line we took against superhumans being deployed in *the Gulf.*
Get *outta* here!
Not to mention the fact that *Spin* magazine wants to do a feature on the one and only super-team with a prominent African-American in their ranks.
Spin magazine wants to talk about *me?* Man, wait'll they hear we've got a little wheel-fellow *too.*
Would you please stop calling me that?
And then, of course, there's my *other* big surprise. You remember all those letters I wrote asking local companies for a little sponsorship?
Sure, the *disability* thing. You said we needed transport because one of our new teammates was confined to a wheelchair, right?
What?

Well, guys, it looks like corporate America just delivered to the tune of *four thousand dollars.*

Dude, that is *awesome.*

The Defenders are officially *mobile,* folks.

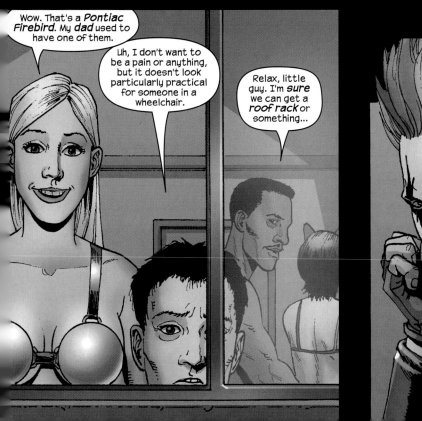

Wow. That's a *Pontiac Firebird.* My *dad* used to have one of them.

Uh, I don't want to be a pain or anything, but it doesn't look particularly practical for someone in a wheelchair.

Relax, little guy. I'm *sure* we can get a *roof rack* or something...

Somebody's going to *die* for putting me on this assignment.

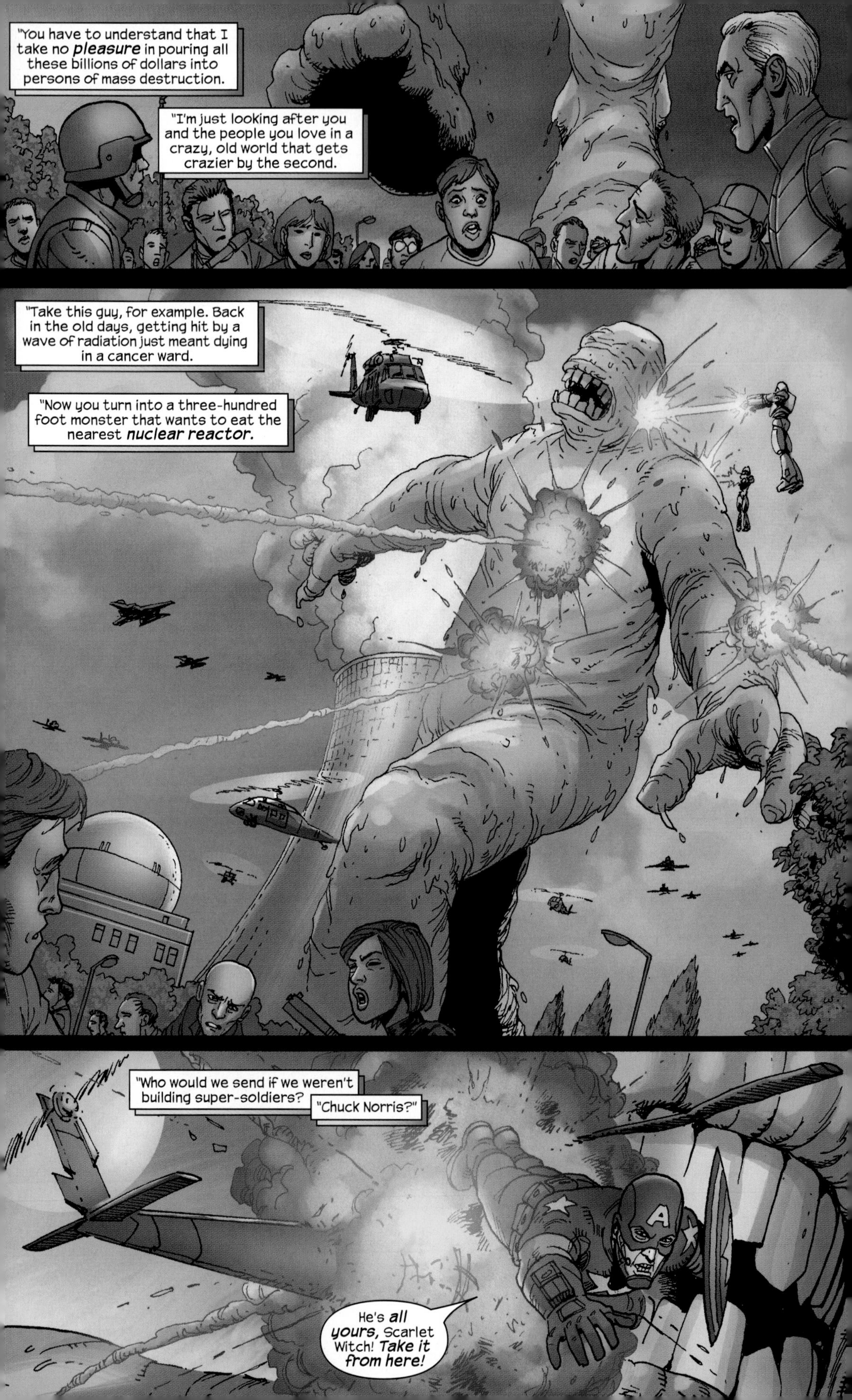
"You have to understand that I take no *pleasure* in pouring all these billions of dollars into persons of mass destruction.
"I'm just looking after you and the people you love in a crazy, old world that gets crazier by the second.
"Take this guy, for example. Back in the old days, getting hit by a wave of radiation just meant dying in a cancer ward.
"Now you turn into a three-hundred foot monster that wants to eat the nearest *nuclear reactor.*
"Who would we send if we weren't building super-soldiers?
"Chuck Norris?"
He's *all yours,* Scarlet Witch! *Take it from here!*

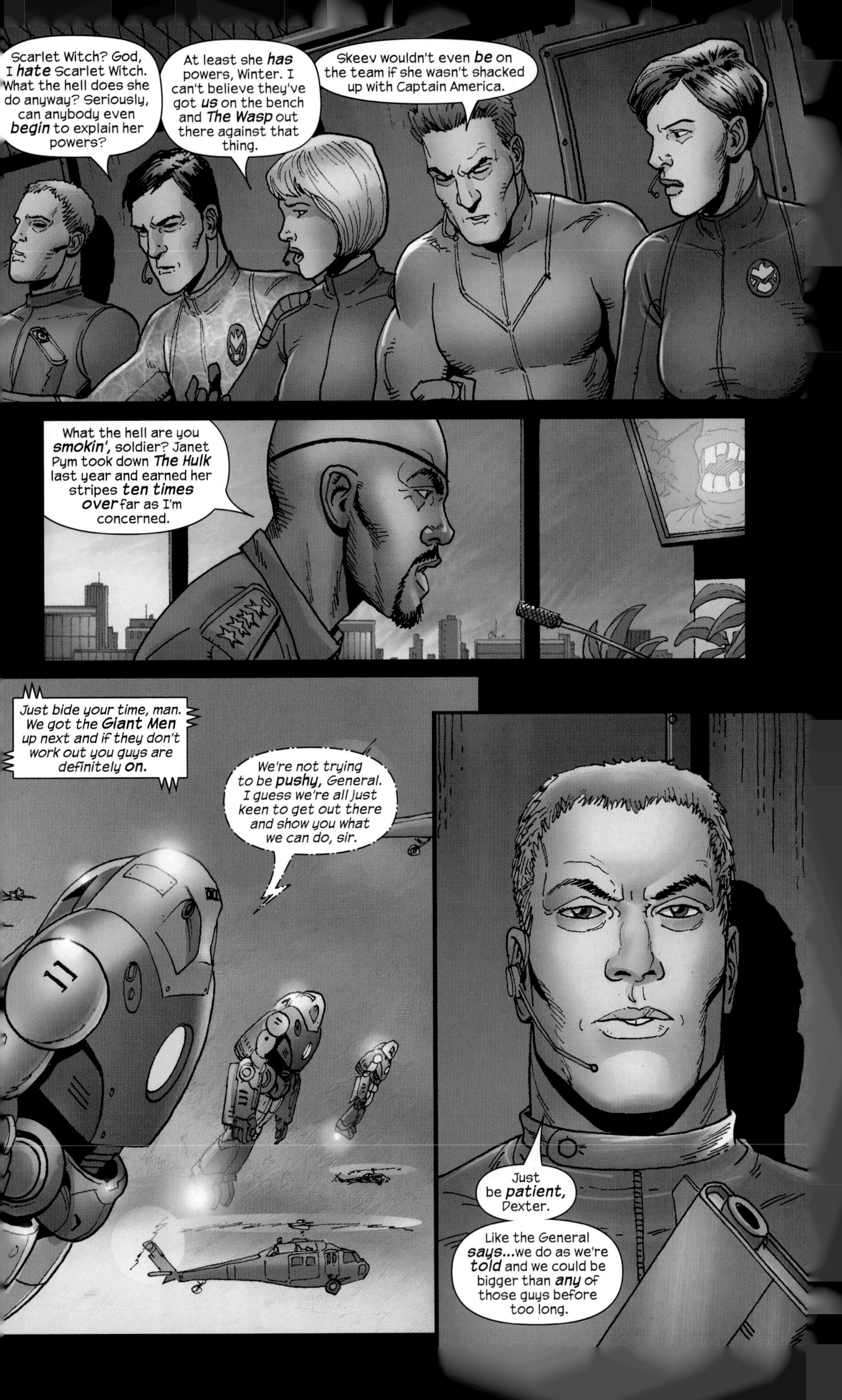
Scarlet Witch? God, I hate Scarlet Witch. What the hell does she do anyway? Seriously, can anybody even begin to explain her powers?
At least she has powers, Winter. I can't believe they've got us on the bench and The Wasp out there against that thing.
Skeev wouldn't even be on the team if she wasn't shacked up with Captain America.
What the hell are you smokin', soldier? Janet Pym took down The Hulk last year and earned her stripes ten times over far as I'm concerned.
Just bide your time, man. We got the Giant Men up next and if they don't work out you guys are definitely on.
We're not trying to be pushy, General. I guess we're all just keen to get out there and show you what we can do, sir.
Just be patient, Dexter.
Like the General says...we do as we're told and we could be bigger than any of those guys before too long.

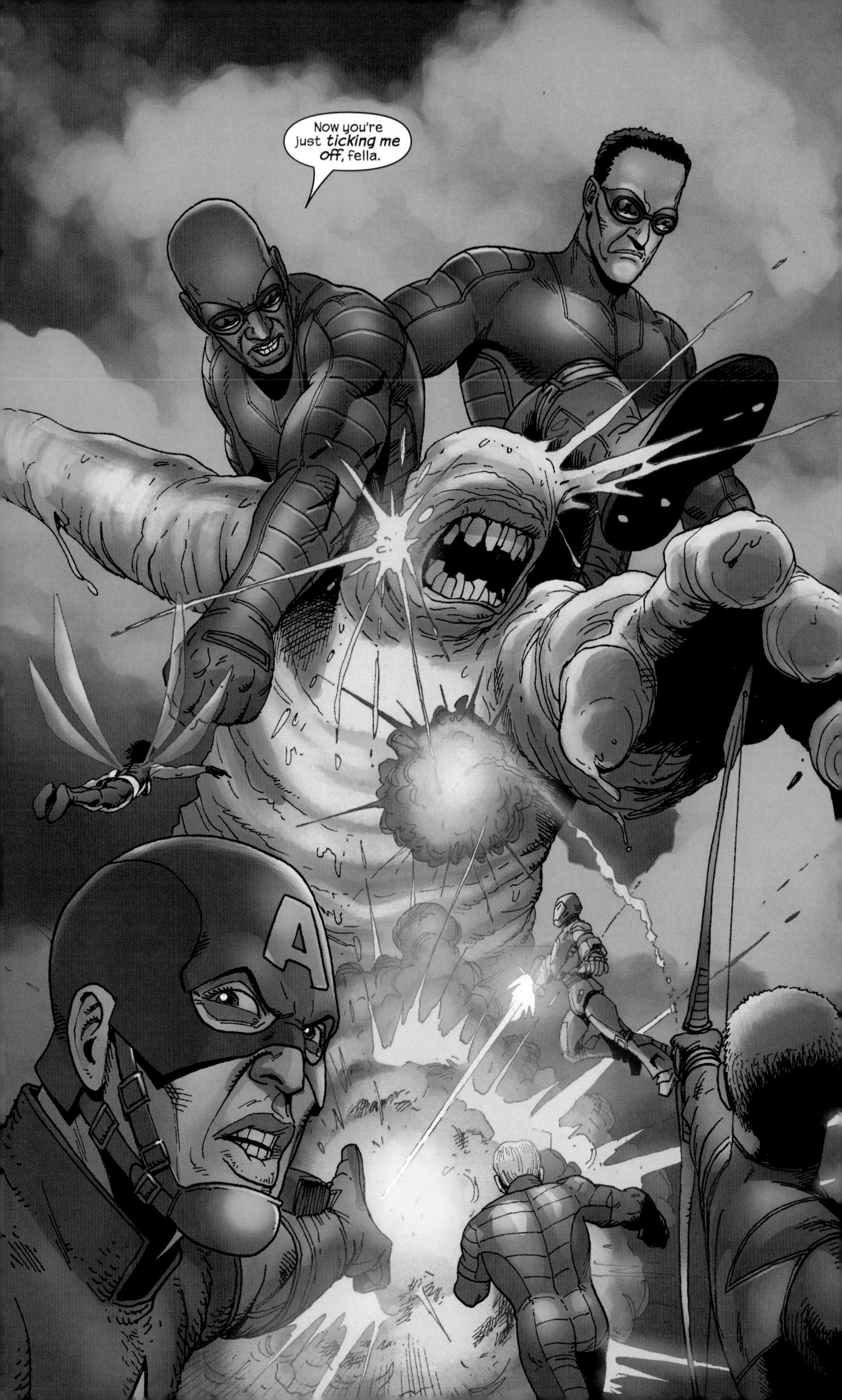
Now you're just *ticking me off*, fella.

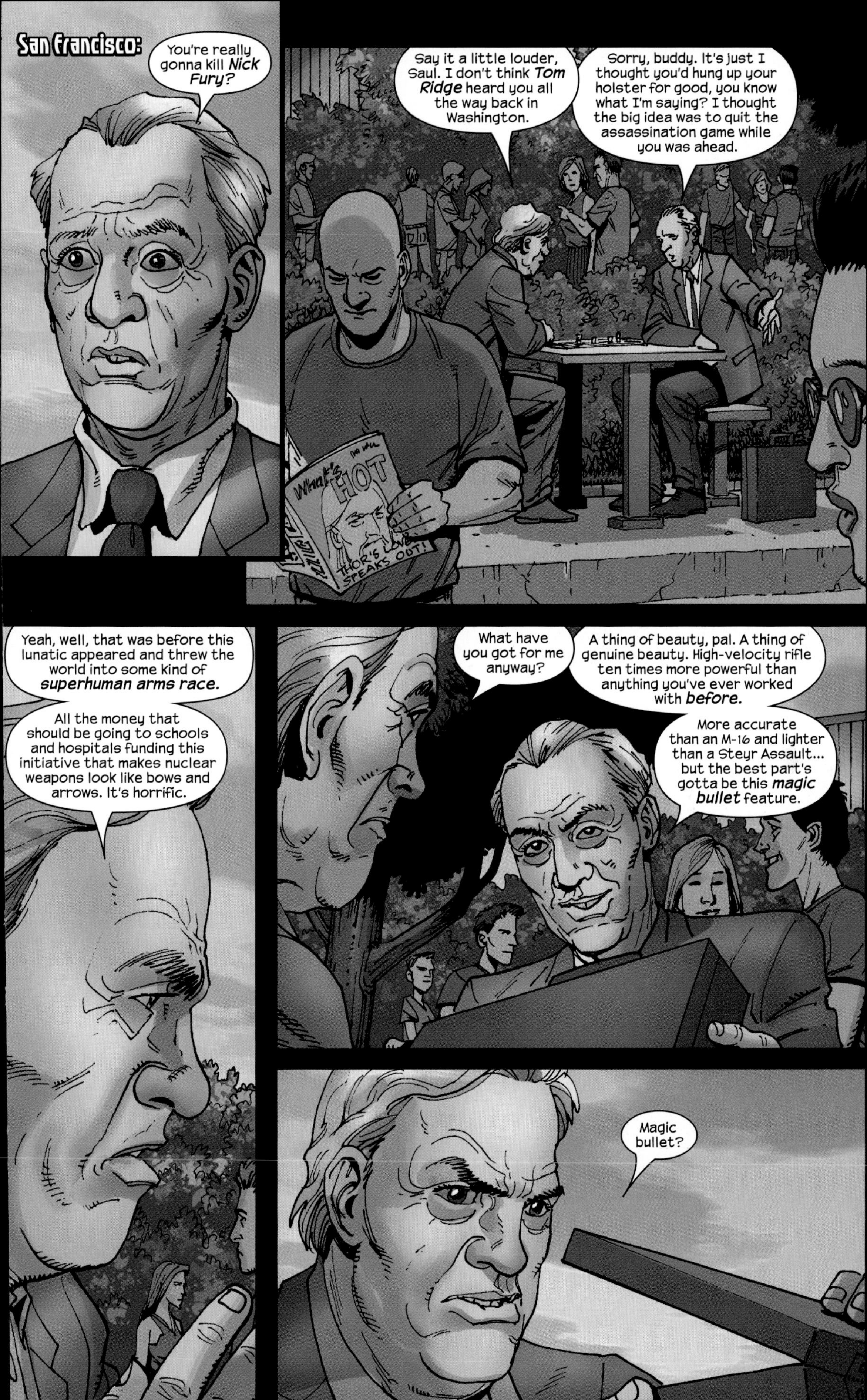
San Francisco:
You're really gonna kill *Nick Fury?*
Say it a little louder, Saul. I don't think *Tom Ridge* heard you all the way back in Washington.
Sorry, buddy. It's just I thought you'd hung up your holster for good, you know what I'm saying? I thought the big idea was to quit the assassination game while you was ahead.
What's HOT
Yeah, well, that was before this lunatic appeared and threw the world into some kind of *superhuman arms race.*
All the money that should be going to schools and hospitals funding this initiative that makes nuclear weapons look like bows and arrows. It's horrific.
What have you got for me anyway?
A thing of beauty, pal. A thing of genuine beauty. High-velocity rifle ten times more powerful than anything you've ever worked with *before.*
More accurate than an M-16 and lighter than a Steyr Assault... but the best part's gotta be this *magic bullet* feature.
Magic bullet?

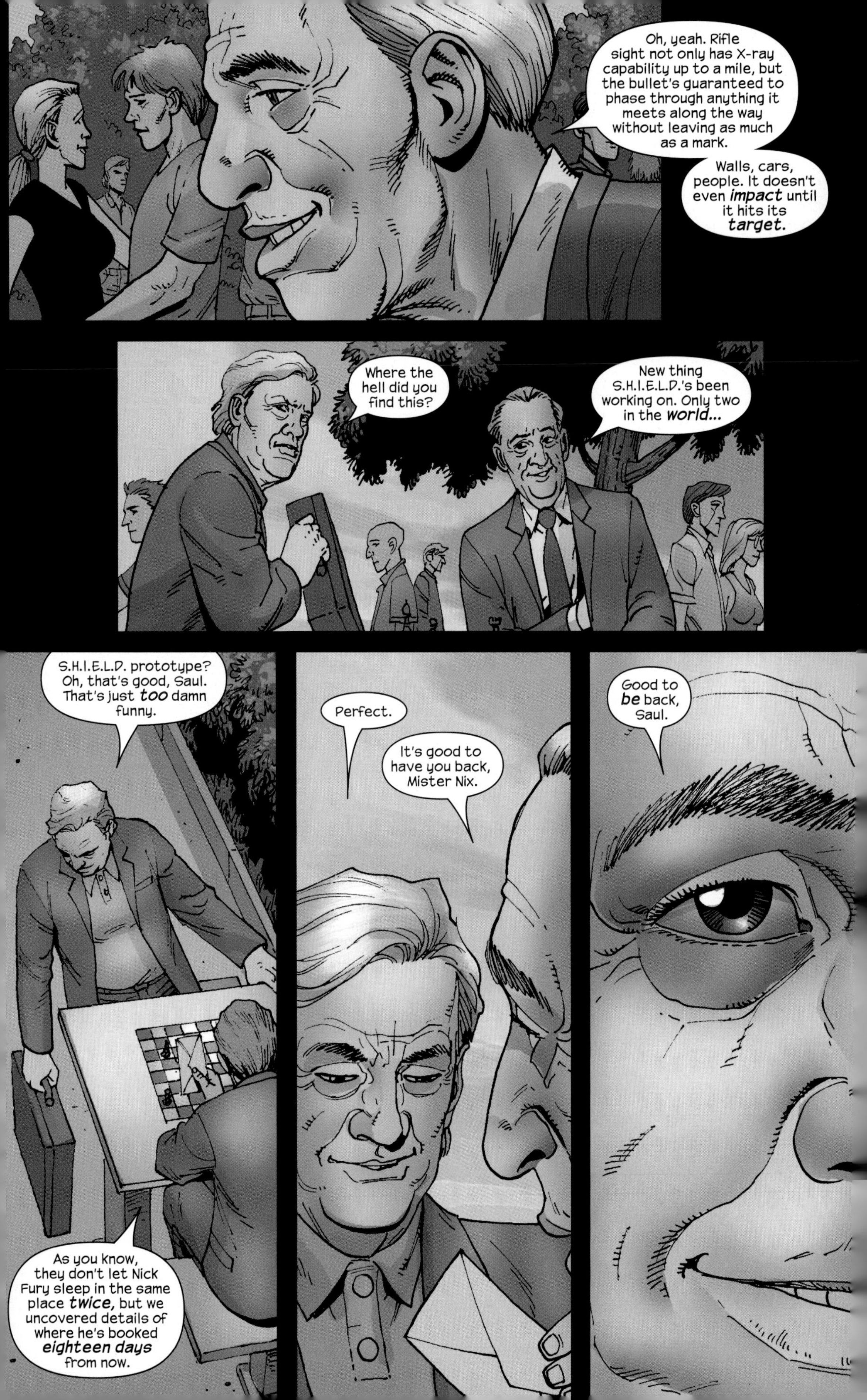

Oh, yeah. Rifle sight not only has X-ray capability up to a mile, but the bullet's guaranteed to phase through anything it meets along the way without leaving as much as a mark.
Walls, cars, people. It doesn't even *impact* until it hits its *target.*
Where the hell did you find this?
New thing S.H.I.E.L.D.'s been working on. Only two in the *world...*
S.H.I.E.L.D. prototype? Oh, that's good, Saul. That's just *too* damn funny.
As you know, they don't let Nick Fury sleep in the same place *twice,* but we uncovered details of where he's booked *eighteen days* from now.
Perfect.
It's good to have you back, Mister Nix.
Good to *be* back, Saul.

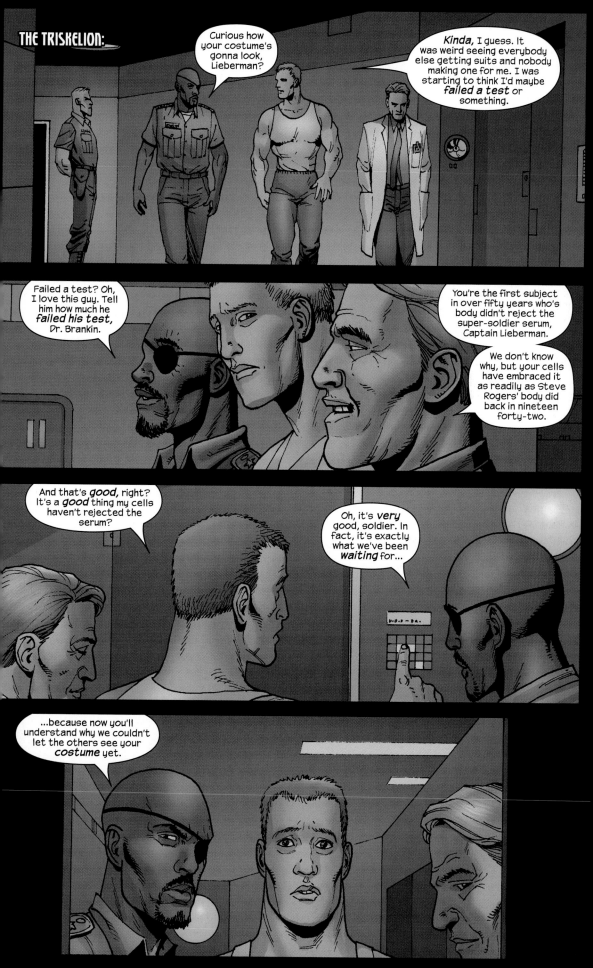

Curious how your costume's gonna look, Lieberman?

Kinda, I guess. It was weird seeing everybody else getting suits and nobody making one for me. I was starting to think I'd maybe *failed a test* or something.

Failed a test? Oh, I love this guy. Tell him how much he *failed his test*, Dr. Brankin.

You're the first subject in over fifty years who's body didn't reject the super-soldier serum, Captain Lieberman.

We don't know why, but your cells have embraced it as readily as Steve Rogers' body did back in nineteen forty-two.

And that's *good*, right? It's a *good* thing my cells haven't rejected the serum?

Oh, it's *very* good, soldier. In fact, it's exactly what we've been *waiting* for...

...because now you'll understand why we couldn't let the others see your *costume* yet.

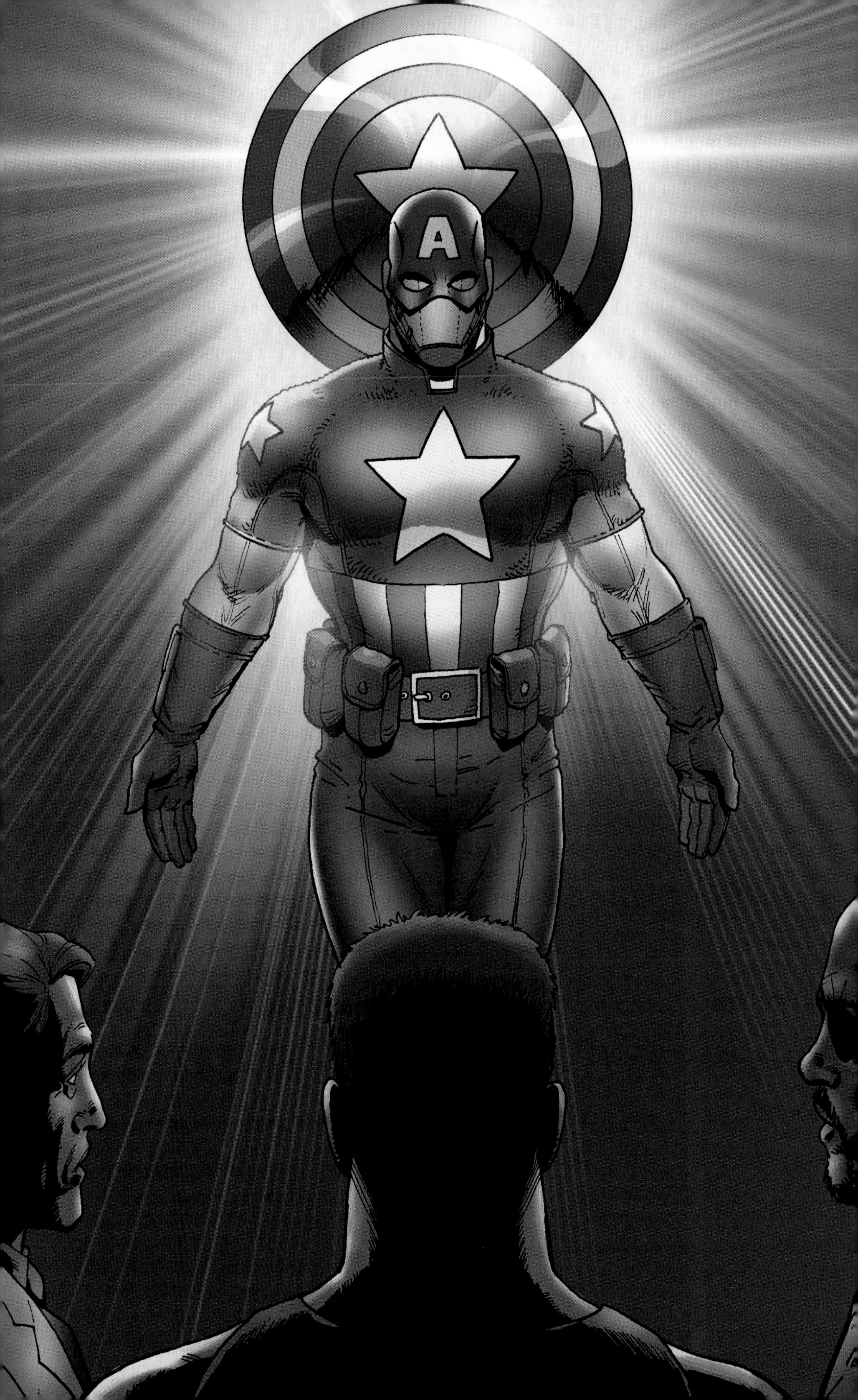

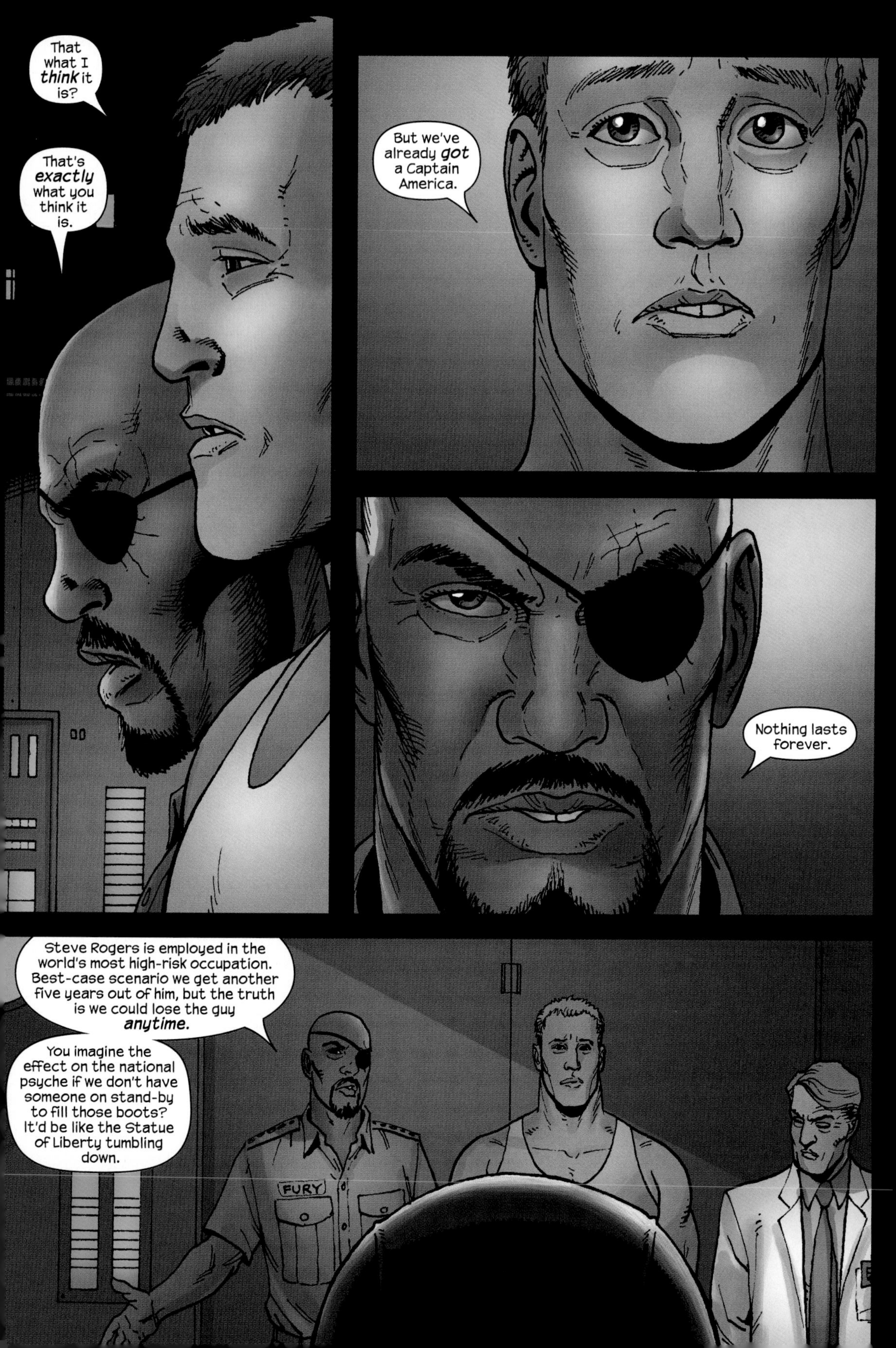

That what I *think* it is?
That's *exactly* what you think it is.
But we've already *got* a Captain America.
Nothing lasts forever.
Steve Rogers is employed in the world's most high-risk occupation. Best-case scenario we get another five years out of him, but the truth is we could lose the guy *anytime.*
You imagine the effect on the national psyche if we don't have someone on stand-by to fill those boots? It'd be like the Statue of Liberty tumbling down.
FURY

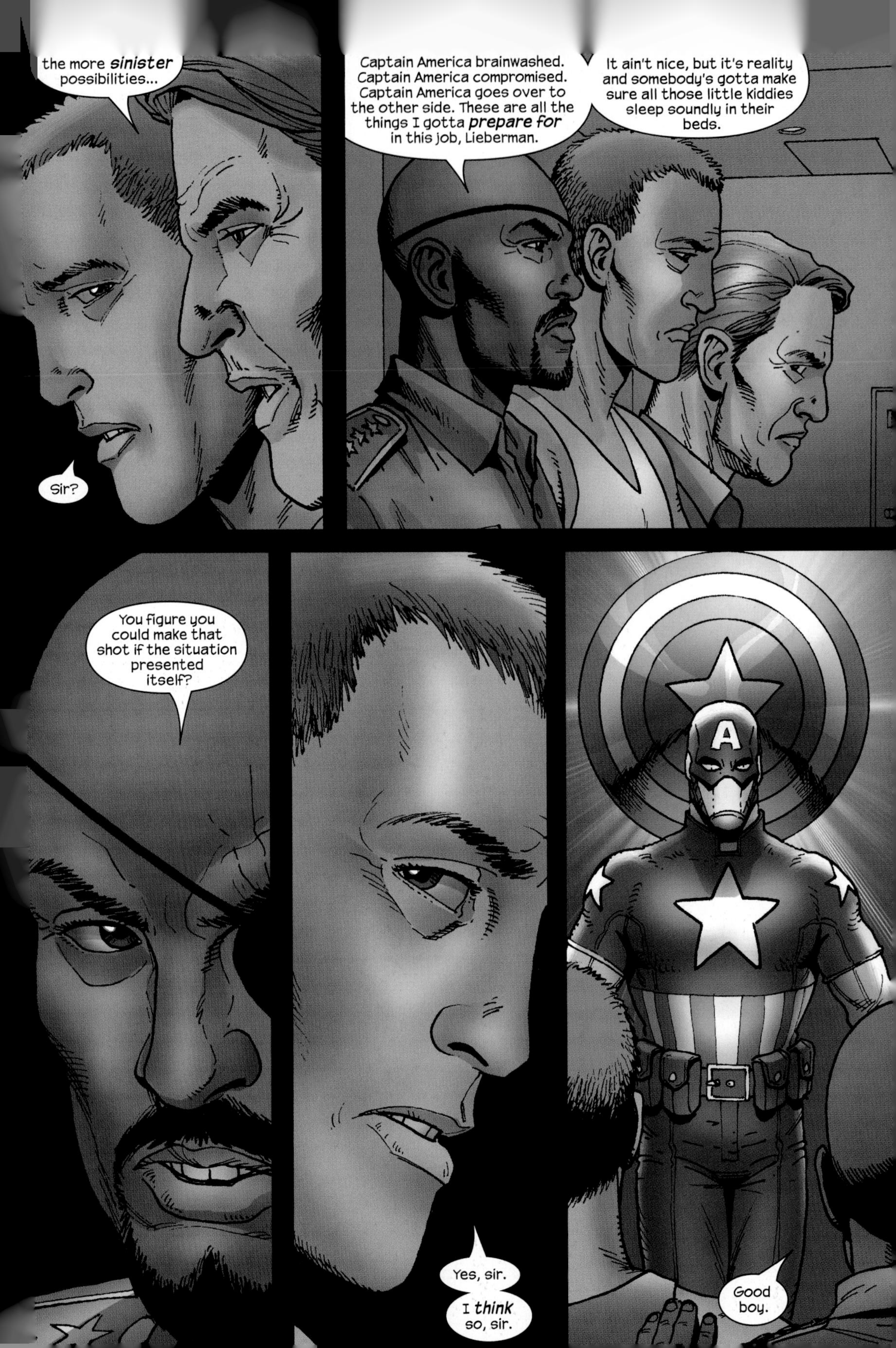
the more *sinister* possibilities...
Sir?
Captain America brainwashed. Captain America compromised. Captain America goes over to the other side. These are all the things I gotta *prepare for* in this job, Lieberman.
It ain't nice, but it's reality and somebody's gotta make sure all those little kiddies sleep soundly in their beds.
You figure you could make that shot if the situation presented itself?
Yes, sir.
I *think* so, sir.
Good boy.

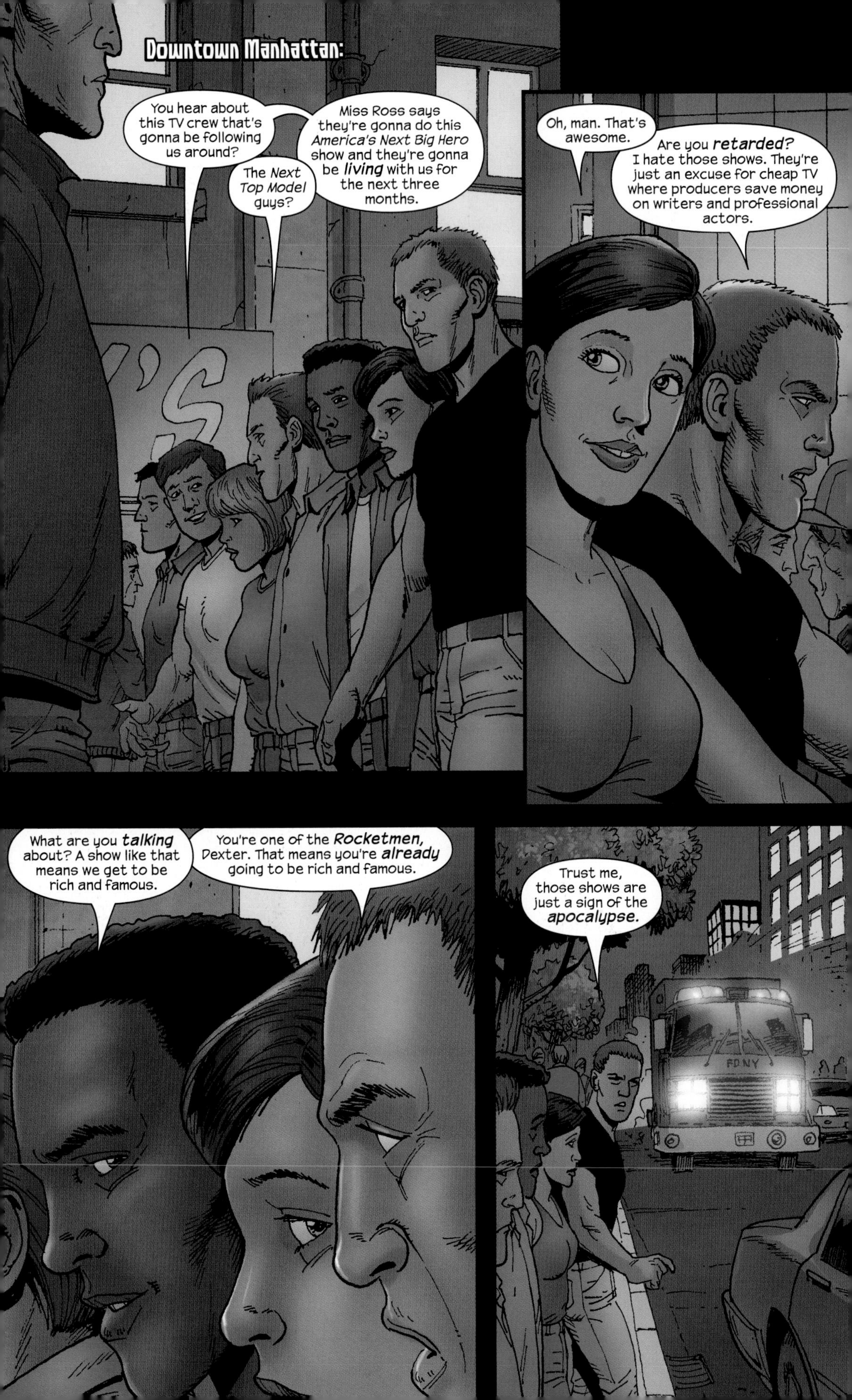
Downtown Manhattan:
You hear about this TV crew that's gonna be following us around?
The *Next Top Model* guys?
Miss Ross says they're gonna do this *America's Next Big Hero* show and they're gonna be ***living*** with us for the next three months.
Oh, man. That's awesome.
Are you ***retarded?*** I hate those shows. They're just an excuse for cheap TV where producers save money on writers and professional actors.
What are you ***talking*** about? A show like that means we get to be rich and famous.
You're one of the ***Rocketmen,*** Dexter. That means you're ***already*** going to be rich and famous.
Trust me, those shows are just a sign of the ***apocalypse.***
FDNY

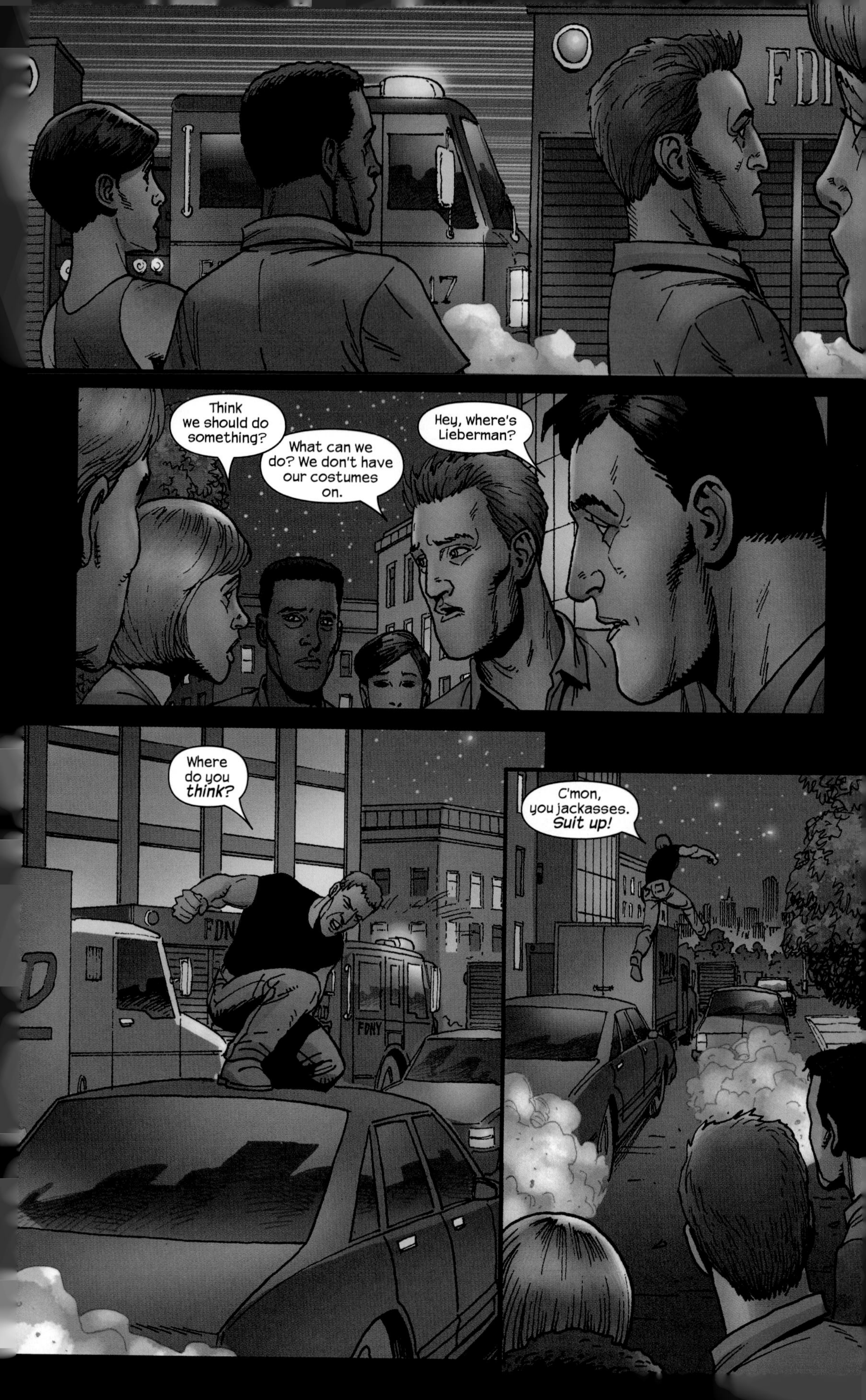
Think we should do something?
What can we do? We don't have our costumes on.
Hey, where's Lieberman?
Where do you *think?*
C'mon, you jackasses. *Suit up!*

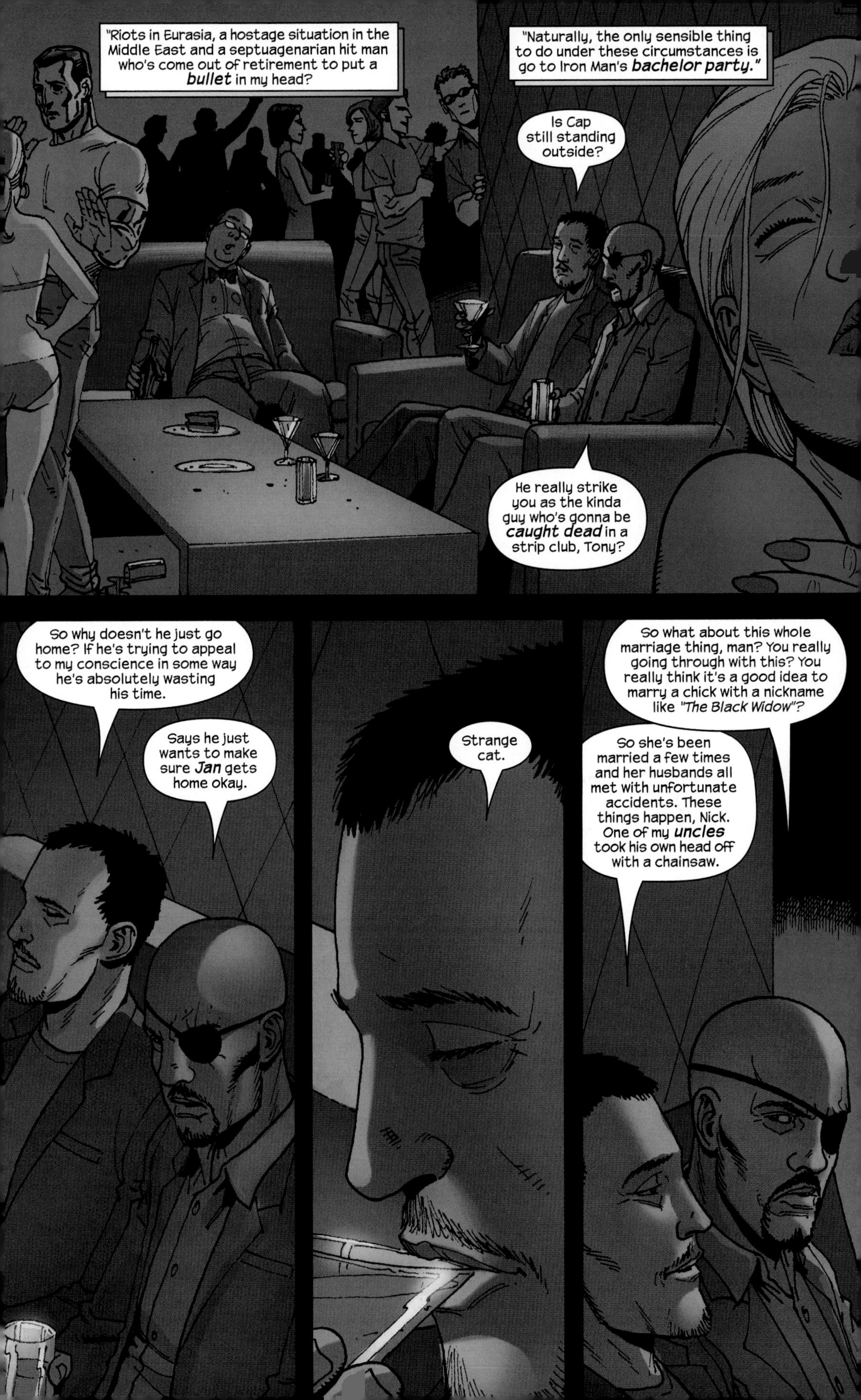
"Riots in Eurasia, a hostage situation in the Middle East and a septuagenarian hit man who's come out of retirement to put a bullet in my head?
"Naturally, the only sensible thing to do under these circumstances is go to Iron Man's bachelor party."
Is Cap still standing outside?
He really strike you as the kinda guy who's gonna be caught dead in a strip club, Tony?
So why doesn't he just go home? If he's trying to appeal to my conscience in some way he's absolutely wasting his time.
Says he just wants to make sure Jan gets home okay.
Strange cat.
So what about this whole marriage thing, man? You really going through with this? You really think it's a good idea to marry a chick with a nickname like "The Black Widow"?
So she's been married a few times and her husbands all met with unfortunate accidents. These things happen, Nick. One of my uncles took his own head off with a chainsaw.

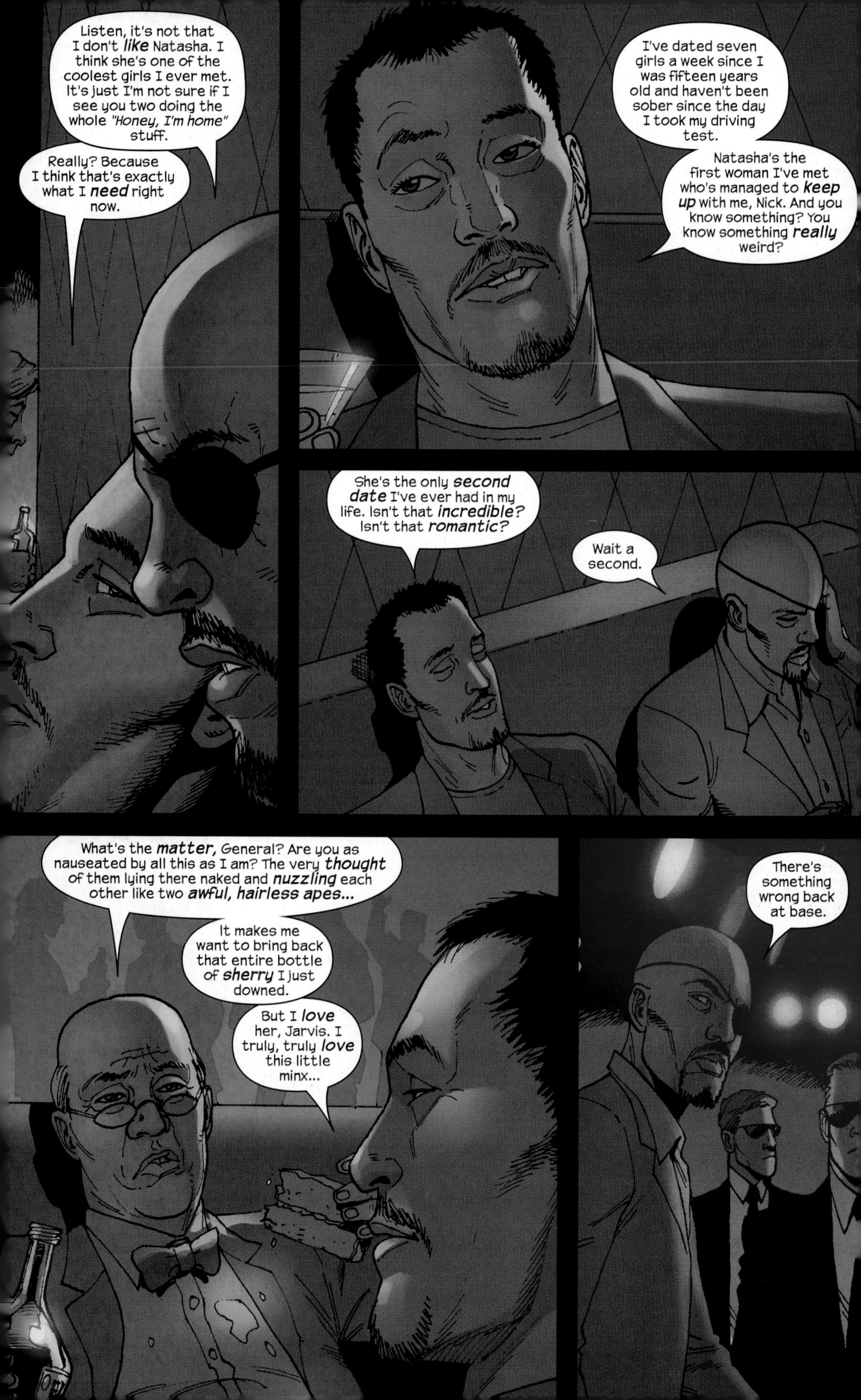
Listen, it's not that I don't like Natasha. I think she's one of the coolest girls I ever met. It's just I'm not sure if I see you two doing the whole "Honey, I'm home" stuff.
Really? Because I think that's exactly what I need right now.
I've dated seven girls a week since I was fifteen years old and haven't been sober since the day I took my driving test.
Natasha's the first woman I've met who's managed to keep up with me, Nick. And you know something? You know something really weird?
She's the only second date I've ever had in my life. Isn't that incredible? Isn't that romantic?
Wait a second.
What's the matter, General? Are you as nauseated by all this as I am? The very thought of them lying there naked and nuzzling each other like two awful, hairless apes...
It makes me want to bring back that entire bottle of sherry I just downed.
But I love her, Jarvis. I truly, truly love this little minx...
There's something wrong back at base.

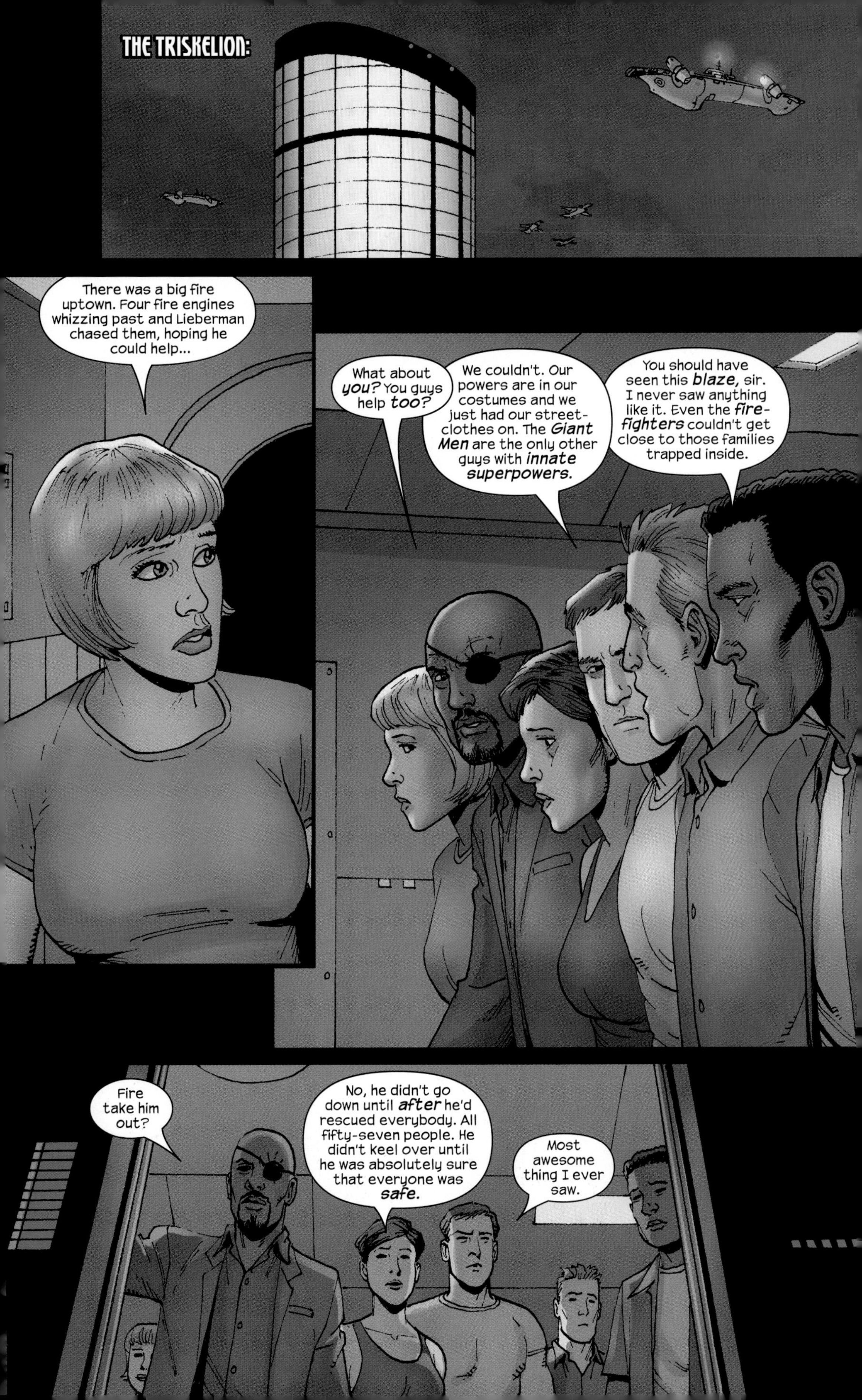
THE TRISKELION:
There was a big fire uptown. Four fire engines whizzing past and Lieberman chased them, hoping he could help...
What about you? You guys help too?
We couldn't. Our powers are in our costumes and we just had our street-clothes on. The Giant Men are the only other guys with innate superpowers.
You should have seen this blaze, sir. I never saw anything like it. Even the fire-fighters couldn't get close to those families trapped inside.
Fire take him out?
No, he didn't go down until after he'd rescued everybody. All fifty-seven people. He didn't keel over until he was absolutely sure that everyone was safe.
Most awesome thing I ever saw.

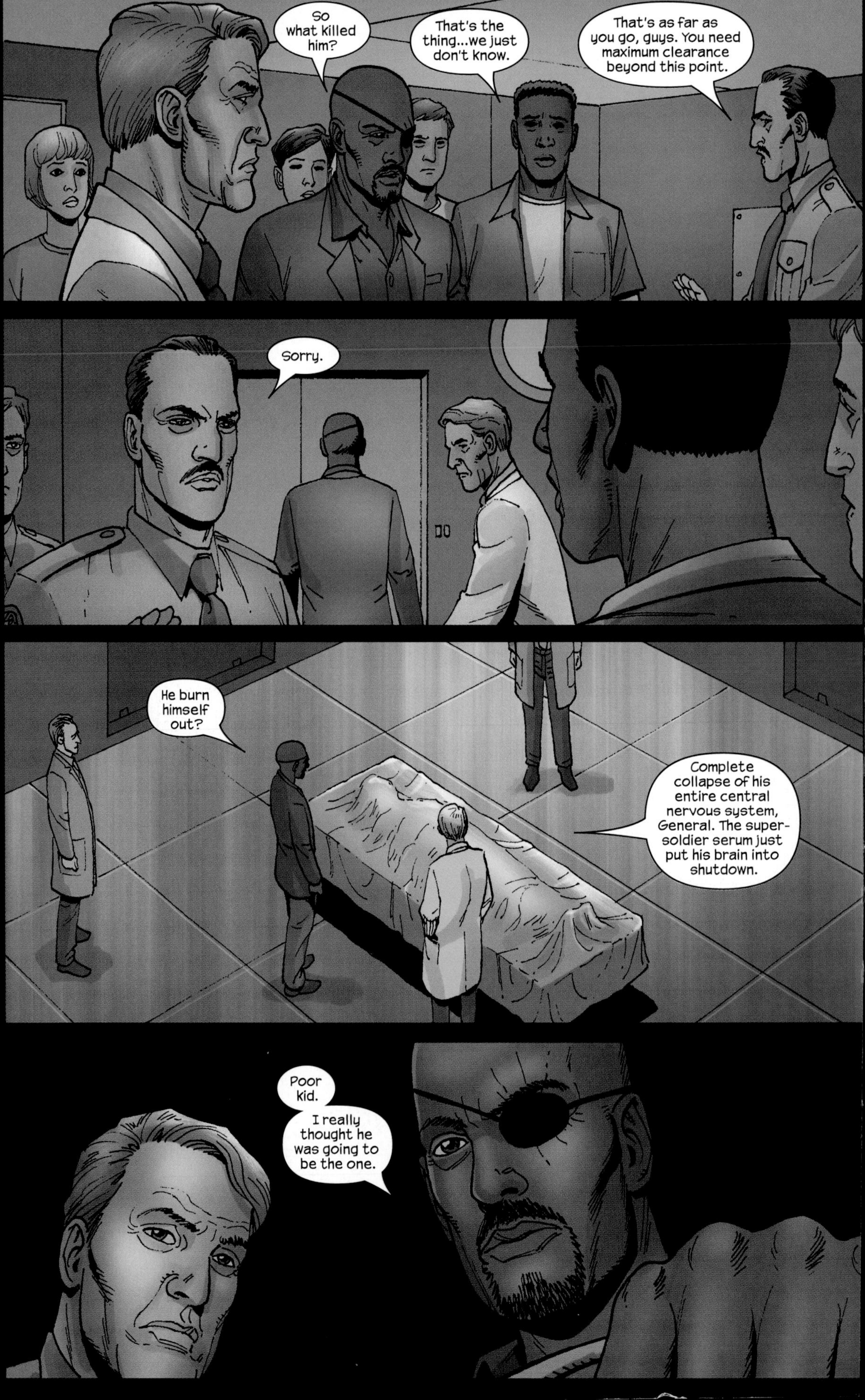
So what killed him?
That's the thing...we just don't know.
That's as far as you go, guys. You need maximum clearance beyond this point.
Sorry.
He burn himself out?
Complete collapse of his entire central nervous system, General. The super-soldier serum just put his brain into shutdown.
Poor kid.
I really thought he was going to be the one.

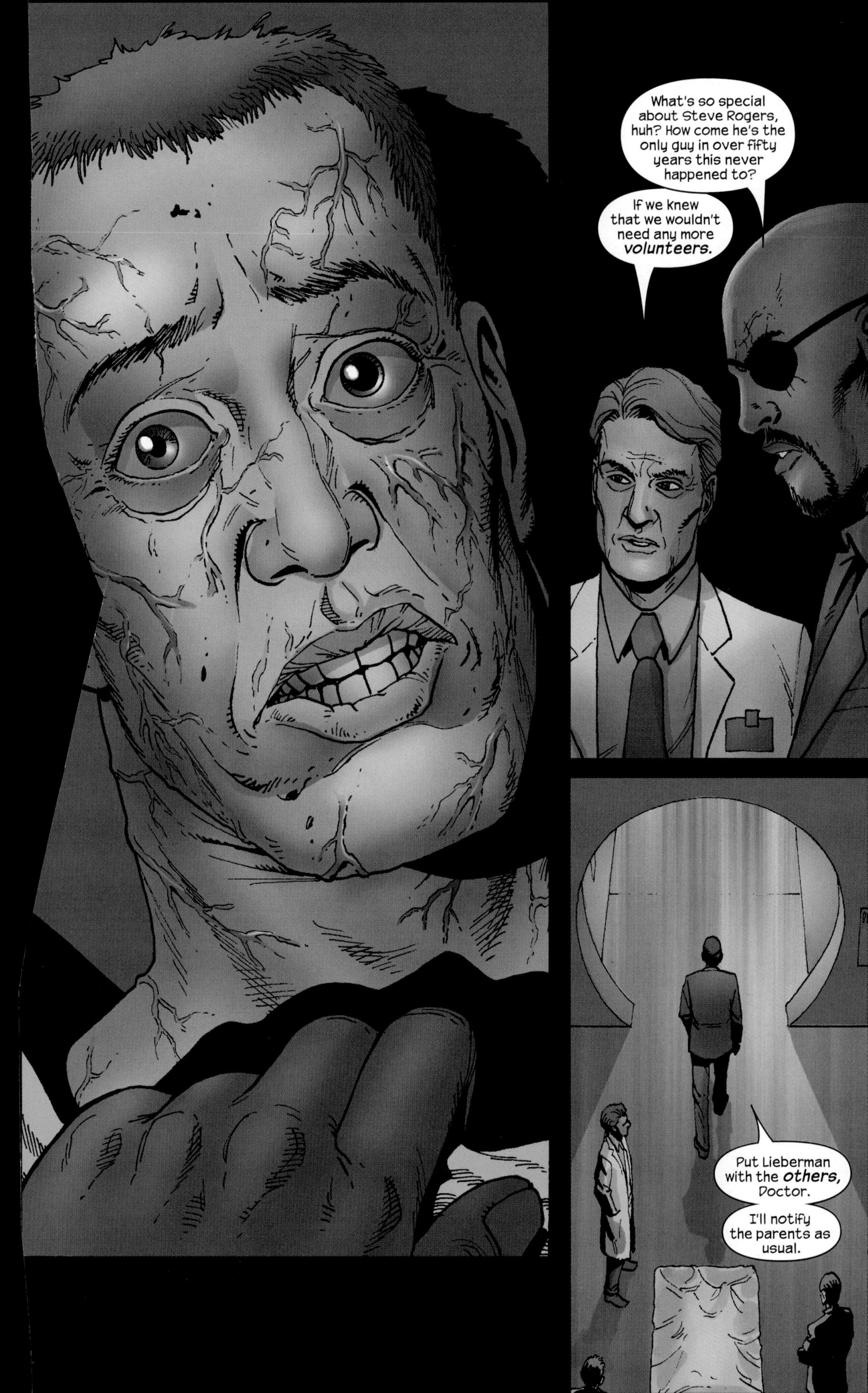
What's so special about Steve Rogers, huh? How come he's the only guy in over fifty years this never happened to?
If we knew that we wouldn't need any more *volunteers.*
Put Lieberman with the *others,* Doctor.
I'll notify the parents as usual.

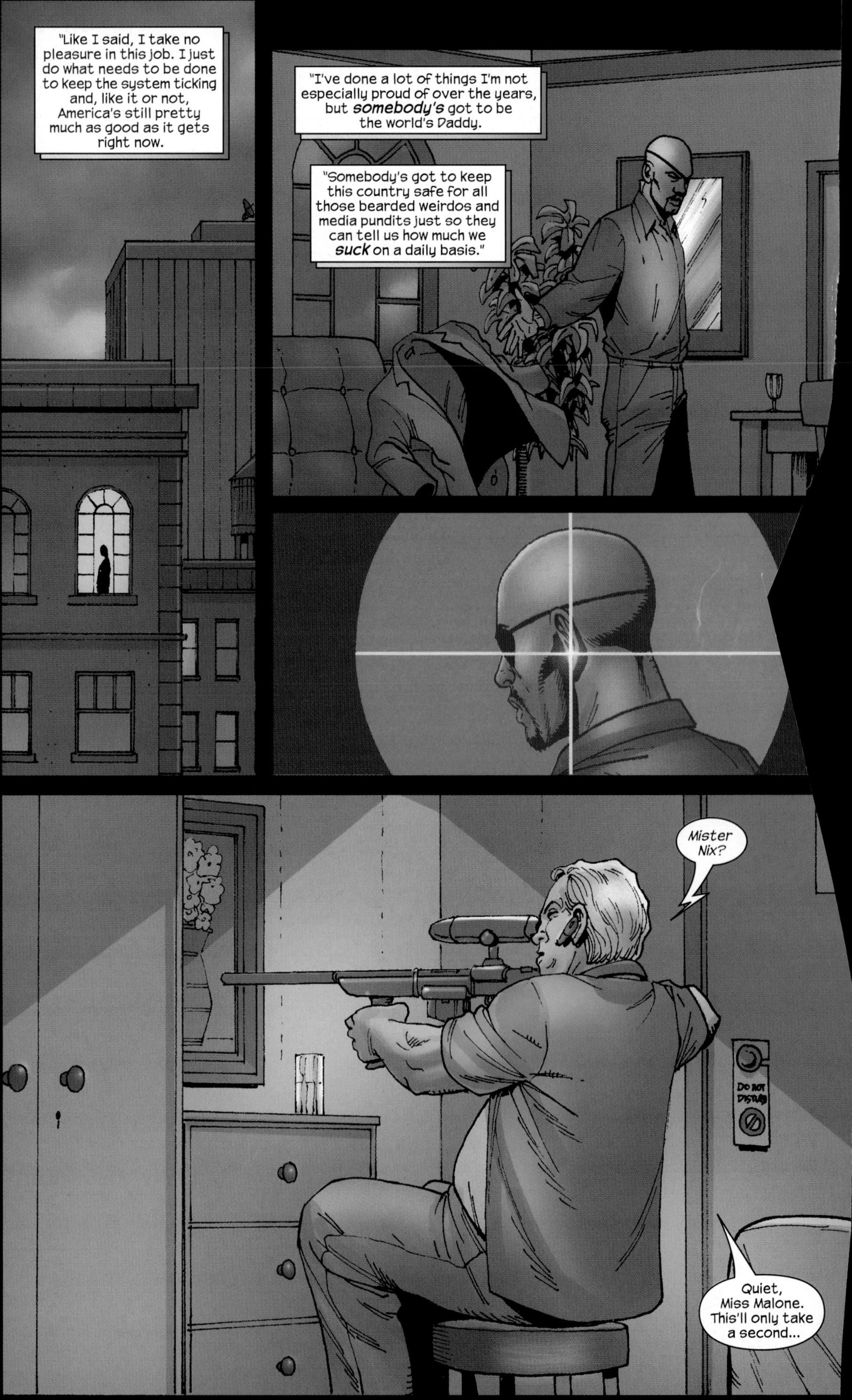
"Like I said, I take no pleasure in this job. I just do what needs to be done to keep the system ticking and, like it or not, America's still pretty much as good as it gets right now.
"I've done a lot of things I'm not especially proud of over the years, but *somebody's* got to be the world's Daddy.
"Somebody's got to keep this country safe for all those bearded weirdos and media pundits just so they can tell us how much we *suck* on a daily basis."
Mister Nix?
Quiet, Miss Malone. This'll only take a second...
DO NOT DISTURB

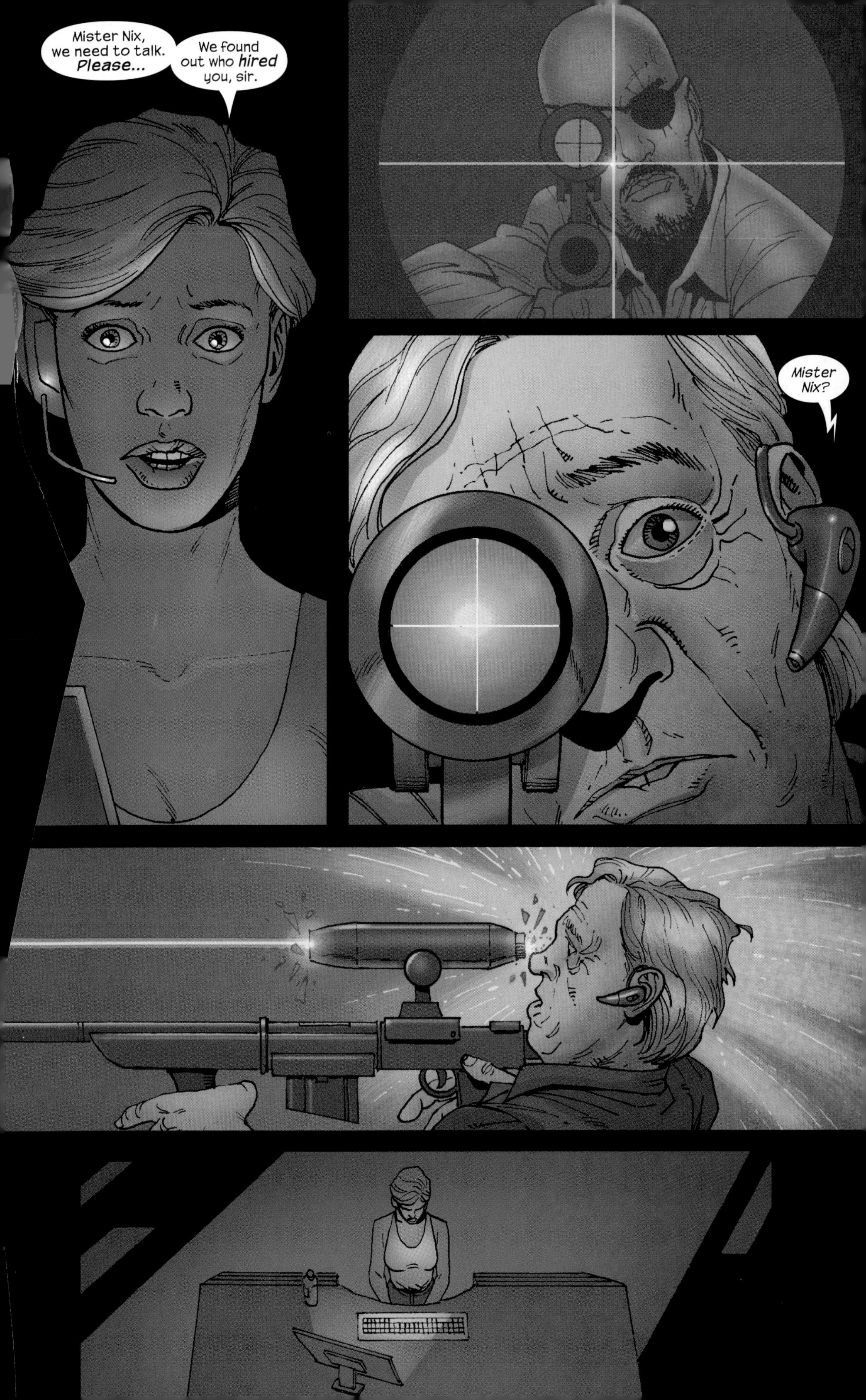
Mister Nix, we need to talk. *Please...*
We found out who *hired* you, sir.
Mister Nix?

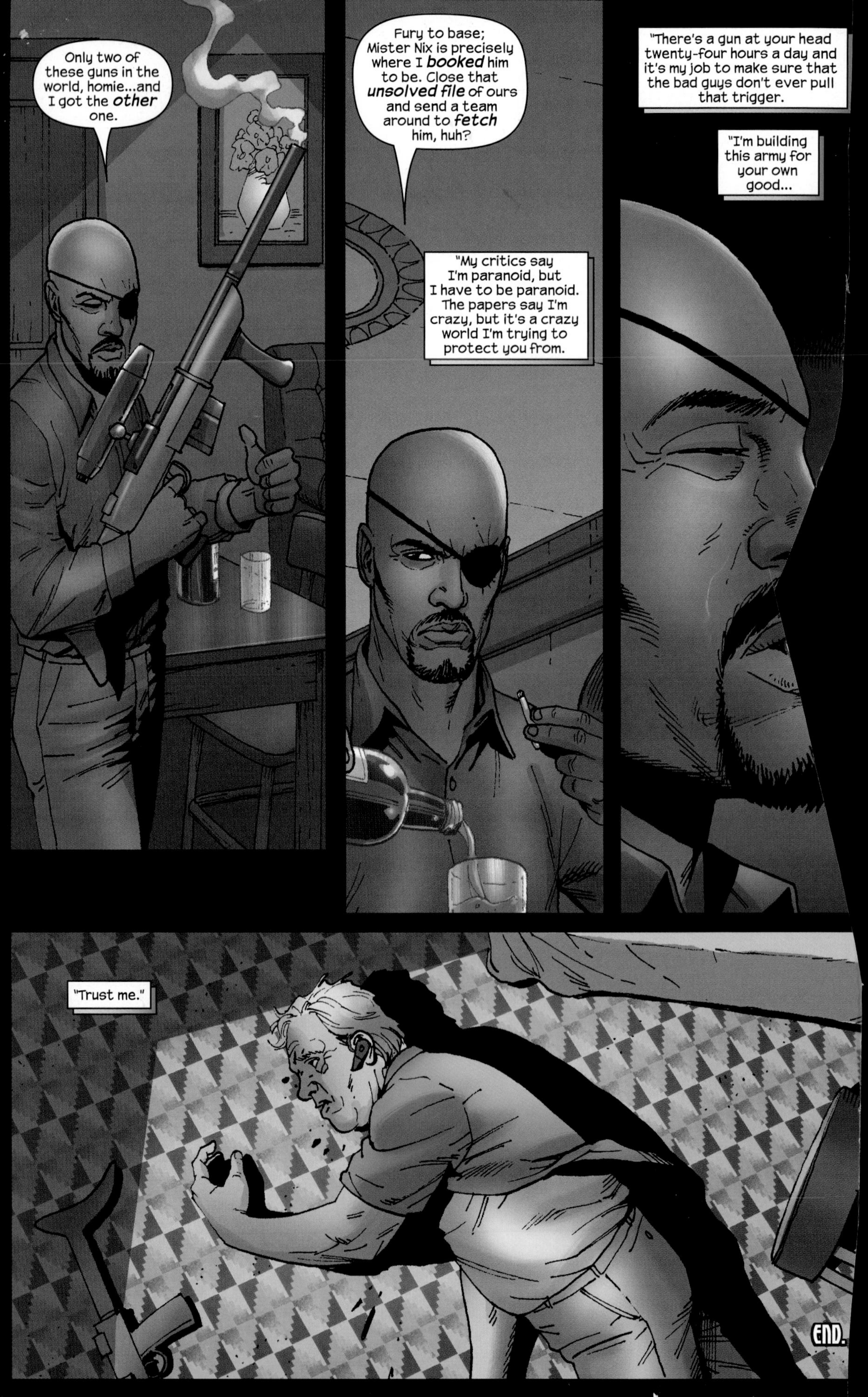
Only two of these guns in the world, homie...and I got the *other* one.
Fury to base; Mister Nix is precisely where I *booked* him to be. Close that *unsolved file* of ours and send a team around to *fetch* him, huh?
"My critics say I'm paranoid, but I have to be paranoid. The papers say I'm crazy, but it's a crazy world I'm trying to protect you from.
"There's a gun at your head twenty-four hours a day and it's my job to make sure that the bad guys don't ever pull that trigger.
"I'm building this army for your own good...
"Trust me."
END.